Rick Steves'

PRAGUE
& THE CZECH REPUBLIC

Rick Steves & Jan (Honza) Vihan

PRAGUE

1. Archbishop's Palace
2. Basilica of St. George and Convent
3. Bethlehem Chapel
4. Black Light Theater (3)
5. Castle Square
6. Ceremonial Hall
7. Changing of the Guard
8. Charles Bridge
9. Charles University
10. Church of St. Mary the Victorious
11. Church of St. Nicholas (in Little Quarter)
12. Church of St. Nicholas (in Old Town)
13. Convent of St. Agnes of Bohemia
14. To Dancing House
15. Estates Theatre
16. Golden Lane

17. Havelská Market
18. Jewish Quarter
19. Kampa Island
20. Karlova Street
21. Klaus Synagogue
22. Klementinum
23. Lennon Wall
24. To Loreta Church
25. Lucerna Gallery
26. Maisel Synagogue
27. Monument to Victims of Communism Who Survived
28. Mucha Museum
29. Municipal House
30. Mus. of Applied Arts
31. Mus. of Communism
32. Museum of Czech Cubism (in Black Madonna House)

33. Na Příkopě Street
34. Náprstek Museum of Asian, African & American Cultures
35. National Gallery in Sternberg Palace
36. National Museum
37. National Theatre
38. Nerudova Street
39. Old Jewish Cemetery
40. Old Royal Palace
41. Old Town Hall, Astronomical Clock, Tower & Chapel
42. Old Town Square & Jan Hus Memorial
43. Old-New Synagogue
44. Petřín Tower & Mus. of Jára Cimrman
45. Pinkas Synagogue
46. Powder Tower
47. Prague Castle

48. Royal Gardens
49. Royal Summer Pa
50. Schwarzenberg Pa
51. Spanish Synagogue
52. St. Martin in the V
53. St. Vitus Cathedra
54. St. Wenceslas Sta
55. To Strahov Mona- stery & Library
56. Terraced Gardens
57. Torture Museum
58. Toy and Barbie Museum
59. Týn Church
60. Ungelt Courtyard House at the Gol Ring Gallery
61. Vrtba Garden
62. Wallenstein Palace Garden
63. Wenceslas Square

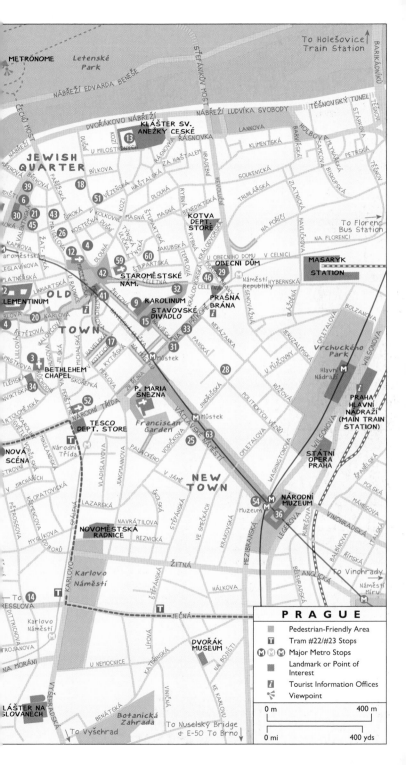

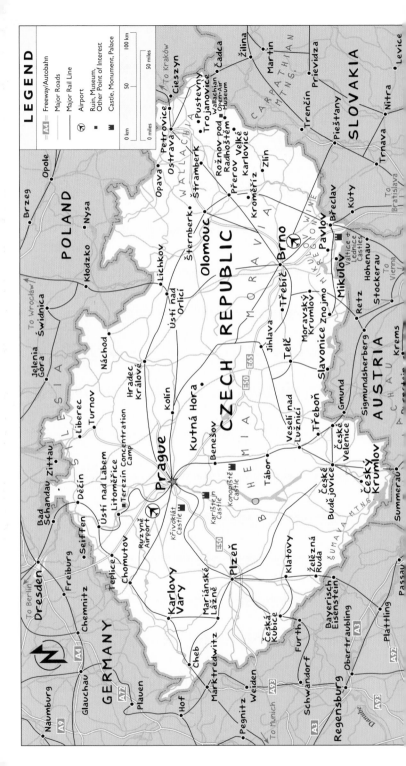

Rick Steves'
PRAGUE
& THE CZECH REPUBLIC

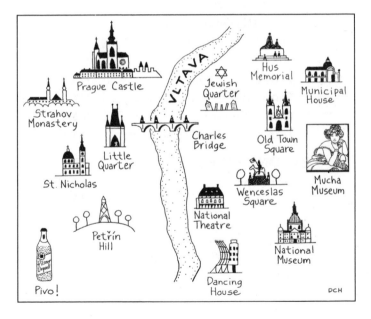

Prague Castle · VLTAVA · Jewish Quarter · Hus Memorial · Municipal House · Strahov Monastery · Charles Bridge · Old Town Square · Little Quarter · St. Nicholas · Wenceslas Square · Mucha Museum · Petřín Hill · National Theatre · National Museum · Pivo! · Dancing House

DCH

AVALON
TRAVEL

CONTENTS

TOP DESTINATIONS IN THE CZECH REPUBLIC

DAY TRIPS:
Kutná Hora,
Terezín &
Castles

Prague.

WALLACHIA

CZECH REPUBLIC

.Olomouc

Třebíč

Moravský
Krumlov

Télč

Třeboň.

MIKULOV WINE
REGION

Český.
Krumlov

Slavonice

50 Kilometers

50 Miles

INTRODUCTION

Wedged between Germany and Austria, the Czech Republic is one of the most comfortable and easy-to-explore countries of the former Warsaw Pact. Since the fall of communism in 1989, the Czech capital, Prague, has quickly become one of Europe's most popular destinations. Come see what all the fuss is about...but don't overlook the rest of the country. Even in a quick visit, you can enjoy a fine introduction to the entire Czech Republic.

This book focuses on Prague, but also includes the best small-town and back-to-nature destinations in the countryside. If you want to experience the best two weeks that the Czech Republic has to offer, this book is all you need.

Experiencing Czech culture, people, and natural wonders economically and hassle-free has been my goal for three decades of traveling, tour guiding, and writing. With this new edition, I pass on to you the lessons I've learned.

This book is selective, including only the top destinations and sights. For example, the Czech Republic has dozens of charming medieval towns, but I take you to only the most pleasant: Třeboň and Slavonice.

The best is, of course, only my opinion. But after spending a third of my adult life exploring and researching Europe, I've developed a sixth sense for what travelers enjoy.

About This Book

Rick Steves' Prague & the Czech Republic is a personal tour guide in your pocket. Better yet, it's actually two tour guides in your pocket: The co-author and researcher of this guidebook is Honza Vihan, a Prague native who leads Prague and Eastern Europe tours for my company, Rick Steves' Europe Through the Back Door. Together, Honza and I keep this book up-to-date and accurate. For simplicity we've shed our respective egos to become "I" in this book, though at times, you'll know from the intimacy of some of the comments that Honza is sharing his perspective as a Czech citizen.

The first half of this book focuses on Prague, following this format:

Planning Your Time, a suggested schedule with thoughts on how best to use your limited time.

Orientation includes tourist information, tips on public transportation, local tour options, helpful hints, and an easy-to-read map designed to make the text clear and your arrival smooth.

The **Town** and **Quarter** chapters provide a succinct overview of Prague's most important sights, arranged by neighborhood, with ratings:

▲▲▲—Don't miss;

▲▲—Try hard to see;

▲—Worthwhile if you can make it;

No rating—Worth knowing about.

Sleeping describes my favorite hotels, from budget deals to splurges.

Eating serves up good-value restaurants, ranging from fun, inexpensive eateries to classy splurges.

Shopping gives you tips for shopping painlessly and enjoyably, without letting it overwhelm your vacation or ruin your budget.

Entertainment is your guide to fun, including a wide array of concerts and nightclubs—as well as other Czech entertainment options, from the unique Black Light Theater to hockey and soccer matches.

Transportation Connections covers how to get to nearby destinations by train, bus, and private car.

The second half of the book, **Beyond Prague,** is devoted to the rest of the Czech Republic. It includes day trips from Prague, as well as farther-flung destinations elsewhere in the country. Each one is covered as a mini-vacation of its own.

At the end of the book, you'll find:

Czech History and Language explains the complicated, tumultuous, and ultimately uplifting background of this country. You'll also learn some tips and essential Czech phrases to help you communicate with the locals.

The **appendix** is a traveler's tool kit, with a handy packing checklist, recommended books and films, instructions on how to use the telephone, useful phone numbers, and the procedure for dealing with lost credit cards. You'll also find detailed information on driving and public transportation, as well as a climate chart, a festival list, and a hotel reservation form.

Study this book and put together the plan of your travel dreams. Then have a great trip! Traveling like a temporary local,

Map Legend

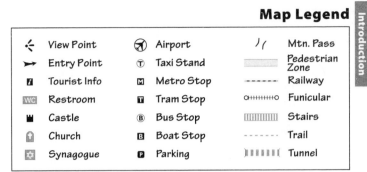

⚲ View Point	✈ Airport	)(Mtn. Pass
➤ Entry Point	Ⓣ Taxi Stand	Pedestrian Zone
🅙 Tourist Info	Ⓜ Metro Stop	------ Railway
WC Restroom	Ⓣ Tram Stop	O++++++O Funicular
🏰 Castle	Ⓑ Bus Stop	‖‖‖‖‖ Stairs
⛪ Church	Ⓑ Boat Stop	------ Trail
✡ Synagogue	Ⓟ Parking	)‖‖‖‖‖(Tunnel

Use this legend to help you navigate the maps in this book.

and taking advantage of the information here, you'll enjoy the absolute most of every mile, minute, and dollar. As you travel the route I know and love, I'm happy that you'll be meeting some of my favorite Czech people.

PLANNING

Trip Costs

There are two price tiers in the Czech Republic: Prague and everywhere else. Outside of Prague, you'll be amazed at the low prices for accommodations, food, transportation, and sightseeing. In Prague, you'll find prices closer to the Western European range. Prague hotels are particularly expensive, often surpassing Western prices. But even in Prague, things that natives pay for—such as transportation and food (in local-style, rather than in tourist-oriented, restaurants)—are very affordable. Despite the expense of Prague, if you avoid overpriced restaurants on the main tourist drag, and if you use my listings to stay only at the best-value hotels, a trip to the Czech Republic can still be substantially less expensive than a trip to Western European destinations.

Five components make up your trip cost: airfare, surface transportation, room and board, sightseeing and entertainment, and shopping and miscellany.

Airfare: A basic, round-trip flight from the US to Prague costs $600–1,200 (even cheaper in winter), depending on what city you fly from and when. If your travels take you beyond the Czech Republic, consider saving time and money in Europe by flying "open jaw" (into one city and out of another; for instance, into Prague and out of Vienna).

Surface Transportation: Point-to-point train and bus tickets within the Czech Republic are inexpensive—a second-class train ticket from Prague to the farthest reaches of the country won't run you more than about $25. Renting a car is convenient for

The Czech Republic's Best Two-Week Trip by Car

Day	Plan	Sleep in
1	Arrive in Prague	Prague
2	Prague	Prague
3	Prague	Prague
4	Day-trip to Terezín Concentration Camp	Prague
5	To Český Krumlov	Český Krumlov
6	Český Krumlov	Český Krumlov
7	To Telč via Třeboň	Telč
8	Telč and Slavonice	Telč
9	To Pavlov via Třebíč and Moravský Krumlov	Pavlov
10	Mikulov Wine Region and Lednice	Pavlov
11	To Olomouc	Olomouc
12	Olomouc	Olomouc
13	Return to Prague	Prague
14	Prague	Prague

exploring the Czech countryside, but doing so is much more expensive than public transportation (figure about $500 per week, including gas and insurance). And those with more money than time could consider hiring a car with a private driver (a full-day, round-trip excursion from Prague to Český Krumlov runs about $170; see page 151).

Room and Board: Plan on spending an average of $100 a day per person for room and board in Prague. A $100-a-day budget per person allows $10 for lunch, $20 for dinner, and $70 for lodging (based on two people splitting the cost of a $140 double room that includes breakfast). That's doable. Outside of Prague, hotel rates plummet to $70 or less for a decent double, and food prices also drop—making $50 a day per person a reasonable budget in the Czech countryside. Even in Prague, students and tightwads can eat and sleep for $30 a day ($15 per hostel bed, $15 for meals and snacks).

Sightseeing and Entertainment: Sightseeing is inexpensive here. Most sights generally cost about $3–6. A few biggies cost much more (such as Prague Castle—up to $17, or the Jewish Quarter—$25), but that's rare. Figure $25–30 for concerts, Black Light Theater performances, and other splurge experiences. You can hire a private guide for as little as $80 for four hours. An overall average of $20 a day works for most travelers. Don't skimp here. After all, this category is the driving force behind your trip—you

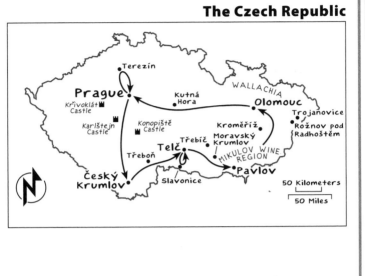

The Czech Republic

came to sightsee, enjoy, and experience the Czech Republic.

Shopping and Miscellany: Figure $1 per stamped postcard, coffee, beer, or ice-cream cone. Shopping can vary in cost from nearly nothing to a small fortune. Good budget travelers find that this category has little to do with assembling a trip full of lifelong and wonderful memories.

When to Go

The "tourist season" runs roughly from Easter through October. July and August have their advantages, with the best weather, very long days (daylight until after 21:00), fewer tourists in Prague than in the peak months of May and September, and busy festivals held in small towns around the country. In spring and fall (May, June, September, and early October), the weather is milder, and the colors and scents are powerful.

Winter travelers find the concert season in full swing, with remarkably fewer tourists, but some accommodations and sights are either closed or open on a limited schedule. Seeing Charles Bridge blanketed by fresh snow easily makes the hours spent out in the cold worthwhile. But the weather can be too cold and dreary, and night will draw the shades on your sightseeing before dinnertime. Use the climate chart in the appendix as a guide.

The Czech Republic's Best 12-Day Trip by Bus and Train

Day	Plan	Sleep in
1	Arrive in Prague	Prague
2	Prague	Prague
3	Prague	Prague
4	Day-trip to Terezín Concentration Camp	Prague
5	To Český Krumlov	Český Krumlov
6	Český Krumlov	Český Krumlov
7	To Telč via Třeboň	Telč
8	Telč and Slavonice	Telč
9	To Olomouc via Třebíč	Olomouc
10	Olomouc	Olomouc
11	Return to Prague	Prague
12	Prague	Prague

With more time in the Czech Republic, consider a pair of other destinations that are a little more difficult—but still possible—to reach by public transportation: Hikers enjoy Wallachia, which fits easily into the above schedule after Olomouc (make your home base in Trojanovice). Wine-lovers head for the Mikulov Wine Region, easiest to visit between Telč and Olomouc (make your home base in Pavlov).

Beyond the Czech borders, consider adding Budapest, Hungary, and Kraków, Poland—each an easy, direct night-train trip away from Prague (or an even quicker connection from Olomouc). For more on these destinations beyond the Czech Republic, see the current edition of *Rick Steves' Eastern Europe*.

Sightseeing Priorities

Depending on the length of your trip, here are my recommended priorities. Presuming you're traveling by public transportation, I've taken geographical proximity into account.

3 days:	Prague
4–5 days, add:	Your choice of nearby day trips (Kutná Hora, Terezín Concentration Camp, and the three castles: Konopiště, Karlštejn, or Křivoklát)
5 days, add:	Český Krumlov (and skip day trips)
7 days, add:	Olomouc
8–9 days, add:	Třeboň, Telč, and Třebíč
More:	Your choice among Moravský Krumlov, Šumava, Wallachia, Slavonice, or the Mikulov Wine Region with Lednice/Valtice.

Major Holidays and Weekends

Popular places are even busier on weekends...and can be inundated on three-day weekends. Plan ahead and reserve your accommodations and transportation well in advance. Reserve in advance for Prague for any weekend, the months of May and September, and major holidays such as Easter, Christmas, and New Year's. Also check the list of festivals and holidays on page 292 of the appendix.

This list assumes you're primarily interested in the Czech Republic. But note that Prague also splices neatly into a wider-ranging trip that can include such nearby destinations as Vienna (4–6 hrs by train), Budapest (7–8.5 hrs), Kraków (7.5–8 hrs), Munich (6 hrs), and Berlin (5 hrs).

Travel Smart

Your trip to the Czech Republic is like a complex play—easier to follow and really appreciate on a second viewing. While no one does the same trip twice to gain that advantage, reading this book in its entirety before your trip accomplishes much the same thing.

Design an itinerary that enables you to visit the various sights at the best possible times. As you read this book, make note of festivals, colorful market days, and when sights are closed.

If you have only a few days for Prague, remember that the impressive sights of the Jewish Quarter are closed every Saturday, and other museums (particularly in the Old Town) are closed on Monday. Monday is also a problem day outside of Prague, when many museums are closed. Saturday morning feels like any bustling weekday, but at lunchtime, many shops close down until Monday morning. Sundays have the same pros and cons as they do for travelers in the US—sights are generally open but may have limited hours, shops and banks are closed, city traffic is light, and public-transportation options are fewer.

Be sure to mix intense and relaxed periods in your itinerary. Every trip (and every traveler) needs at least a few slack days. Pace yourself. Assume you will return.

Reread this book as you travel, and visit local tourist information offices. Upon arrival in a new town, lay the groundwork for a smooth departure; write down the schedule for the train or bus you'll take when you depart.

Plan ahead for laundry, picnics, and Internet stops. Get online at Internet cafés or your hotel to research transportation connections, confirm events, check the weather, and get directions to your next hotel. Buy a phone card (or carry a mobile phone) and use it

Know Before You Go

Your trip is more likely to go smoothly if you plan ahead.

Since **airline carry-on restrictions** are always changing, visit the Transportation Security Administration's website (www.tsa.gov/travelers) for an up-to-date list of what you can bring on the plane with you...and what you have to check. Remember to arrive with plenty of time to get through security.

Call your **debit and credit card companies** to let them know the countries you'll be visiting, so that they'll accept (and not deny) your international charges. Confirm your daily withdrawal limit; consider asking to have it raised so you can take out more cash at each ATM stop.

Be sure that your **passport** is valid at least six months after your ticketed date of return to the US. If you need to get or renew a passport, it can take up to three months (for more on passports, see www.travel.state.gov).

Book your rooms in advance if you'll be traveling during any major **holidays** (see "Major Holidays and Weekends," page 7). It's smart to reserve rooms in peak season if you'd like to stay in my lead listings and definitely for your first night.

If you plan to hire a **local guide** in summer, reserve ahead by email. Popular guides can get booked up.

To see Alfons Mucha's *Slav Epic* in 2009, confirm that the artwork will still be in the town of Moravský Krumlov (see page 221 for details).

If you're planning on **renting a car** in the Czech Republic, you are required to carry an International Driver's Permit (available at your local AAA office for $15 plus two passport photos; www.aaa.com). Confirm pick-up hours—many car-rental offices close Saturday afternoon and all day Sunday.

In this book I've listed many helpful **websites** for sights and hotels in the Czech Republic. Be aware that some of these websites may only be accessible from within Europe. If you can't access a Czech website, try emailing or calling instead.

for reservations, reconfirmations, and double-checking hours.

Connect with the culture. Set up your own quest to find the most characteristically Czech pub you can. (Anything with an English menu doesn't count.) Once inside, get recommendations from the locals on the best type of beer, and make it your goal to get the most interesting story you possibly can out of them.

Enjoy the friendliness of the Czech people. Slow down and ask questions—most locals are eager to point you toward their idea of the right direction. Keep a notepad in your pocket for organizing

Just the FAQs, Please

Whom do I call in case of emergency?
Dial 112 for medical or other emergencies and 158 for police.

What if my credit card is stolen?
Act immediately. See "Damage Control for Lost Cards," page 276, for instructions.

How do I make a phone call to, within, and from the Czech Republic?
For detailed dialing instructions, refer to page 279.

How can I get tourist information about my destination?
The Czech Republic has a national tourist information office in the US (see page 271) and offices in virtually every destination covered in this book. Note that Tourist Information is abbreviated **TI** in this book.

What's the best way to pack?
Light. For a recommended packing list, see page 297.

Does Rick have other resources that could help me?
For more on Rick's guidebooks, public television series, free audiotours, public radio show, website, guided tours, travel bags, accessories, and railpasses, see page 272.

Are there any updates to this guidebook?
Check www.ricksteves.com/update for changes to the most recent edition of this book.

Can you recommend any good books or movies for my trip?
For suggestions, see pages 275–276.

Do you have information on driving, train travel, and flights?
See pages 284–291 in the appendix.

How much do I tip?
Relatively little. For tips on tipping, see page 277.

Will I get a student or senior discount?
While discounts are not listed in this book, youths (under 18) and students (with International Student Identity Cards) often get discounts—but only by asking.

How can I get a VAT refund on major purchases?
See the details on page 278.

Does the Czech Republic use the metric system?
Yes. A liter is about a quart, four to a gallon. A kilometer is six-tenths of a mile. I figure kilometers to miles by cutting them in half and adding back 10 percent of the original (120 km: 60 + 12 = 72 miles, 300 km: 150 + 30 = 180 miles). For more metric conversions, see page 294.

your thoughts. Wear your money belt, and learn the local currency and how to estimate prices in dollars. Those who expect to travel smart, do.

PRACTICALITIES

Red Tape: You need a passport—but no visa or shots—to travel in the Czech Republic. Your passport must be valid for at least six months beyond the time you leave. Pack a photocopy of your passport in your luggage in case the original is lost or stolen.

Time: In Europe—and in this book—you'll use the 24-hour clock. It's the same through 12:00 noon, then keep going—13:00, 14:00, and so on. For anything after 12, subtract 12 and add P.M. (14:00 is 2:00 P.M.)

The Czech Republic is generally six/nine hours ahead of the East/West Coasts of the US. The exceptions are the beginning and end of Daylight Saving Time: Europe "springs forward" the last Sunday in March (two weeks after most of North America), and "falls back" the last Sunday in October (one week before North America). For a handy online time converter, try www.timeanddate .com/worldclock.

Watt's Up? Europe's electrical system is different from North America's in two ways: the shape of the plug (two round prongs) and the voltage of the current (220 volts instead of 110 volts). For your North American plug to work in Europe, you'll need an adapter, sold inexpensively at travel stores in the US. As for the voltage, most newer electronics or travel appliances (such as hair dryers, laptops, and battery chargers) automatically convert the voltage—if you see a range of voltages printed on the item or its plug (such as "110–220"), it'll work in Europe. Otherwise, you can buy a converter separately in the US (about $20).

News: Americans keep in touch in Europe with the *International Herald Tribune* (published almost daily via satellite throughout Europe). Every Tuesday, the European editions of *Time* and *Newsweek* hit the stands with articles of particular interest to travelers. Sports addicts can get their fix from *USA Today*. Good websites include www.prague.com and http://news.bbc.co.uk. For the local perspective, I pick up a copy of the English-language *Prague Post* (which also has a convenient events calendar). Many hotels have CNN or BBC television channels available.

MONEY

Banking

Throughout Europe, cash machines (ATMs) are the standard way for travelers to get local currency. Bring plastic—credit and/or

Exchange Rate

Though the Czech Republic joined the European Union in 2004, it'll be another few years before they officially begin using the euro. For now, the Czech Republic continues to use its traditional currency, the Czech crown (*koruna*, abbreviated Kč).

20 Czech crowns (Kč) = about $1.
This is the cost of one pint of beer.

Although the Czech Republic hasn't officially adopted the euro, many hotels, restaurants, and shops accept euro bills (but not coins or large bills). You may even see hotel rooms or souvenirs priced in euros (€). In this case, remember that €1 = 28 Kč = about $1.30. If you're using euros, expect bad rates and your change in the local currency. If you're just passing through the country, your euros will probably get you by— and they can actually be helpful in an emergency. But if you're staying awhile, get the local currency.

debit cards—along with several hundred dollars in hard cash as an emergency backup. It's smart to bring two cards, in case one gets demagnetized or eaten by a temperamental machine. Traveler's checks are a waste of time (long waits at slow banks) and a waste of money (in fees).

If you do need to exchange money, you can buy and sell easily at train stations (5 percent fee), banks, or hotels. Assume anyone trying to sell money on the streets is peddling obsolete (or Bulgarian) currency. Change bureaus advertise no commission and offer decent but deceptive rates. (These rates are for selling dollars—their rates for buying your dollars are worse.) Hidden fees abound; ask exactly how many crowns you'll walk away with before you agree to the transaction.

Cash from ATMs
To use a cash machine (called a *Bankomat* in the Czech Republic) to withdraw money from your account, you'll need a debit card (ideally with a Visa or MasterCard logo for maximum usability), plus a PIN code. Know your PIN code in numbers; there are only numbers—no letters—on European keypads.

Before you go, verify with your bank that your card will work overseas, and alert them that you'll be making withdrawals in Europe; otherwise, the bank may not approve transactions if it perceives unusual spending patterns.

Try to take out large sums of money to reduce your per-transaction bank fees. If the machine refuses your request, don't take it personally. Just try again and select a smaller amount.

Keep your cash safe. Thieves target tourists. Use a money belt—a pouch with a strap that you buckle around your waist like a belt, and wear under your clothes. A money belt provides peace of mind, allowing you to carry lots of cash safely. Don't waste time every few days tracking down a cash machine—withdraw a week's worth of money, stuff it in your money belt, and travel!

Credit and Debit Cards

For purchases, Visa and MasterCard are more commonly accepted than American Express. Just like at home, credit or debit cards work easily at larger hotels and shops, but smaller businesses prefer payment in local currency (in small bills—break large bills at a bank or larger store). Although larger restaurants take credit cards, it makes sense to pay in cash, particularly in Prague, where it's unwise to entrust your credit card to a potentially unscrupulous waiter (see page 123).

Credit and debit cards—whether used for purchases or ATM withdrawals—often come with additional, tacked-on "international transaction" fees of up to 3 percent plus $5 per transaction. To avoid unpleasant surprises, call your bank or credit-card company before your trip to ask about these fees.

If receipts show your credit-card number, don't toss these thoughtlessly. If your cards are lost or stolen, see page 276 for advice on what to do.

SLEEPING

I favor accommodations (and restaurants) handy to your sightseeing activities. Rather than list hotels scattered throughout a city, I choose two or three favorite neighborhoods and recommend the best accommodations values in each, from $15 bunk beds to fancy-for-my-book $250 doubles.

Hotel prices in Prague are at Western European levels, but once you get out of the city, you'll pay half as much for a similar room. Plan on spending $100–200 per hotel double in Prague, and $40–90 in smaller towns. A triple is much cheaper than a double and a single. Traveling alone can be expensive: A single room is often only 20 percent cheaper than a double. The price is usually posted in the room. Breakfast is generally included (sometimes continental, but often buffet).

I look for places that are friendly; clean; a good value; located in a central, safe, quiet neighborhood; English-speaking; and not mentioned in other guidebooks. I'm more impressed by a handy

Sleep Code

(20 Kč = about $1)

To help you sort easily through the listings, I've divided the rooms into three categories based on the price for a standard double room with bath:

$$$ **Higher Priced**
$$ **Moderately Priced**
$ **Lower Priced**

To give maximum information in a minimum of space, I use the following code to describe the accommodations. Prices listed are per room, not per person. Unless otherwise noted, English is spoken and breakfast is included. You can assume a hotel takes credit cards unless you see "cash only" in the listing.

When there is a range of prices in one category, that means the price fluctuate with the season; the prices and seasons are posted at or near the hotel desk.

S = Single room (or price for one person in a double).
D = Double or twin. Double beds are usually big enough for non-romantic couples.
T = Triple (often a double bed with a single).
Q = Quad (usually two double beds).
b = Private bathroom with toilet and shower or tub.
s = Private shower or tub only (the toilet is down the hall).

According to this code, a couple staying at a "Db-2,700 Kč" hotel in Prague would pay a total of 2,700 Czech crowns (about $135) for a double room with a private bathroom. The staff speaks English and credit cards are accepted.

location and a fun-loving philosophy than hair dryers and shoeshine machines. I also like local character and simple facilities that don't cater to American "needs." Obviously, a place meeting every criterion is rare, and all of my recommendations fall short of perfection—sometimes miserably. But I've listed the best values for each price category, given the above criteria. I've also thrown in a few hostels, private rooms, and other cheap options for budget travelers.

The prices listed in this book are generally valid for peak season, but may go up during major holidays (see page 7) and festivals (page 292). Prices can soften off-season, for stays of two nights or longer, or for payment in cash (rather than by credit card). Always mention that you found the place through this book—many of the hotels listed offer special deals to our readers.

For environmental reasons, towels are often replaced in hotels only when you leave them on the floor. In cheaper places, they aren't replaced at all, so hang them up to dry and reuse.

Before accepting a room, confirm your understanding of the complete price. The only tip my recommended hotels would like is a friendly, easygoing guest. And, as always, I appreciate feedback on your hotel experiences.

Private Rooms

A cheap option in the Czech Republic is a room in a private home (called "pension," sometimes advertised with the German phrase *Zimmer frei*, "room free," meaning vacancy). These places are inexpensive, at least as comfortable as a cheap hotel, and a good way to get some local insight. The boss changes the sheets, so people staying several nights are most desirable—and stays of less than three nights are often charged up to 30 percent more.

Hostels

For $15–20 a night, you can stay at a youth hostel. Travelers of any age are welcome, as long as they don't mind dorm-style accommodations and lots of traveling friends. Cheap meals are sometimes available, and kitchen facilities are usually provided for do-it-yourselfers. Expect crowds in the summer, snoring, and lots of youth groups giggling and making rude noises while you try to sleep. Family rooms and doubles are often available on request; unlike in Western Europe, many hostels in the Czech Republic are in university dorms where two- or three-person rooms are the norm. Hosteling is ideal for those traveling single: Prices are per bed, not per room, and you'll have an instant circle of friends. More and more hostels are getting their business acts together, taking credit-card reservations over the phone and leaving sign-in forms on the door for each available room. If you're serious about traveling cheaply, get a membership card (www.hihostels.com), carry your own sheets, and cook in the members' kitchens.

Making Reservations

Given the quality of the gems I've found for this book, I'd recommend that you reserve your rooms in advance, either directly with the hotel or through one of Prague's room-booking services (see page 112). Book several weeks ahead, or as soon as you've pinned down your travel dates. Note that some holidays merit your making reservations far in advance (see "Major Holidays and Weekends" sidebar on page 7).

Some travelers make reservations as they travel, calling hotels or B&Bs a few days to a week before their visit. If you prefer the flexibility of traveling without any reservations at all, you'll have greater success snaring rooms if you arrive at your destination early in the day. When you anticipate crowds, call hotels around 9:00 on the day you plan to arrive, when the hotel clerk knows who'll be checking out and just which rooms will be available.

To make a reservation in advance, contact hotels directly by email, phone, or fax. Email is the clearest and most economical way to make a reservation. In addition, many hotel websites now have online reservation forms. If phoning from the US, be mindful of time zones (see page 10). Most hotels listed are accustomed to English-only speakers.

To ensure you have all the information you need for your reservation, use the form in this book's appendix (also at www .ricksteves.com/reservation).

When you request a room for a certain time period, use the European style for writing dates: day/month/year. Hoteliers need to know your arrival and departure dates. For example, for a two-night stay in July I would request: "2 nights, arrive 16/07/08, depart 18/07/08." Consider in advance how long you'll stay; don't just assume you can extend your reservation for extra days once you arrive.

If you don't get a reply to your email or fax, it usually means the hotel is already fully booked.

If the response from the hotel gives its room availability and rates, it's not a confirmation. You must tell them that you want that room at the given rate.

The hotelier will sometimes request your credit-card number for a one-night deposit. While you can email your credit-card information (I do), some people prefer to share that personal info via phone call, fax, or secure online reservation form (if the hotel has one on its website).

If you must cancel your reservation, it's courteous to do so with as much advance notice as possible (simply make a quick phone call or send an email). Family-run hotels and B&Bs lose money if they turn away customers while holding a room for someone who doesn't show up. Understandably, some hoteliers bill no-shows for one night. Hotels in larger cities such as Prague sometimes have strict cancellation policies (for example, you might lose a deposit if you cancel within two weeks of your reserved stay, or you might be billed for the entire visit if you leave early); ask about cancellation policies before you book.

Always reconfirm your room reservation a few days in advance from the road. Most places will hold a room until 16:00, but if you'll be arriving later, let them know.

On the small chance that a hotel loses track of your reservation, bring along a hard copy of their emailed or faxed confirmation.

Introduction

EATING

You'll find that the local cafés, cuisine, beer, and wine are high-lights of your Czech adventure. This is affordable sightseeing for your palate.

When restaurant-hunting, choose a spot filled with locals, not the place with the big neon signs boasting "We Speak English and Accept Credit Cards." Incredible deals abound in the Czech Republic, where locals routinely eat well for $5. Venturing even a block or two off the main drag leads to authentic, higher-quality food for less than half the price of the tourist-oriented places. Most restaurants tack a menu onto their door for browsers and have an English menu inside. Most Czech restaurants are open Sunday through Thursday 11:00–22:00, and Friday and Saturday 11:00–24:00. Only a rude waiter will rush you. Good service is relaxed (slow to an American). You can stay in a pub as long as you want—no one will bring you the *účet* (bill) until you ask for it: *"Pane vrchní, zaplatím!"* (PAH-neh VURCH-nee zah-plah-TEEM; "Mr. Waiter, now I pay!"). The service charge is included in the bill but it's customary to tip 5–10 percent (for more on tipping, see page 277). Remember that in Prague, it's smart to pay cash for your meals rather than let your credit card leave your sight.

When you're in the mood for something halfway between a restaurant and a picnic, look for take-out food stands, bakeries (with sandwiches and small pizzas to go), delis with stools or a table, department-store cafeterias, salad bars, or simple little eateries for fast and easy sit-down restaurant food.

Czech Food

Czech cuisine is heavy, hearty, and tasty. Expect lots of meat, potatoes, and cabbage. Still, there's more variety than you might expect. Ethnic restaurants provide a welcome break from Slavic fare. Seek out vegetarian, Italian, or Chinese—these are especially good in bigger towns such as Prague, Olomouc, Český Krumlov, and Kutná Hora.

A Czech restaurant is a social place where people come to relax. Tables are not private. You can ask to join someone, and you will most likely make some new friends. After a sip of beer, ask for the *jídelní lístek* (menu).

Soups: *Polévka* (soup) is the most essential part of a meal. The saying goes: "The soup fills you up, the dish plugs it up." Some of the thick soups for a cold day are *zelná* or *zelňačka* (cabbage), *čočková* (lentil), *fazolová* (bean), and *dršťková* (tripe—delicious if fresh, chewy as gum if not). The lighter soups are *hovězí* or *slepičí vývar s nudlemi* (beef or chicken broth with noodles), *pórková* (leek), and *květáková* (cauliflower).

Bread: *Pečivo* (bread) is either delivered with the soup or you need to ask for it; it's always charged separately depending on how many *rohlíky* (rolls) or slices of *chleba* (yeast bread) you eat.

Main Dishes: These are divided into *hotová jídla* (quick, ready-to-serve standard dishes, in some places available only during lunch hours, 11:30–14:30) and the more specialized *jídla na objednávku* or *minutky* (plates prepared when you order). Even the supposedly quick *hotová jídla* will take longer than the fast food you're used to back home.

Hotová jídla (ready-to-serve dishes) come with set garnishes. The standard menu across the country includes *smažený řízek s bramborem* (fried pork fillet with potatoes), *svíčková na smetaně s knedlíkem* (beef tenderloin in cream sauce with dumplings), *vepřová s knedlíkem a se zelím* (pork with dumplings and cabbage), *pečená kachna s knedlíkem a se zelím* (roasted duck with dumplings and cabbage), *maďarský guláš s knedlíkem* (the Czech version of Hungarian goulash), and *pečené kuře s bramborem* (roasted chicken with potatoes). In this landlocked country, fish options are limited to *kapr* (carp) and *pstruh* (trout), prepared in a variety of ways and served with potatoes or fries. Vegetarians can go for the delicious *smažený sýr s bramborem* (fried cheese with potatoes) or default for *čočka s vejci* (lentils with fried egg). If you are spending the night out with friends, have a beer and feast on the huge *vepřové koleno s hořčicí a křenem* (pork knuckle with mustard and horseradish sauce) with *chleba* (yeast bread).

The range of the *jídla na objednávku* (meals prepared to order) depends on the chef. You choose your starches and garnishes, which are charged separately.

Salad: *Šopský salát,* like a Greek salad, is usually the best salad option (a mix of tomatoes, cucumbers, peppers, onion, and feta cheese with vinegar and olive oil). The waiter will bring it with the main dish, unless you specify that you want it before.

Dessert: For *moučník* (dessert), there are *palačinka* (crêpes served with fruit or jam), *lívance* (small pancakes with jam and curd), or *zmrzlinový pohár* (ice-cream sundae). Many restaurants will offer different sorts of *koláče* (pastries) and *štrůdl* (apple strudel), but it's much better to get these directly from a bakery.

Beverages: No Czech meal is complete without a cup of strong *turecká káva* (Turkish coffee—finely ground coffee that only partly dissolves, leaving "mud" on the bottom, drunk without milk). Although espressos and instant coffees have made headway in the past few years, many Czechs regard them as a threat to their culture.

A good alternative to a beer is *minerálka* (mineral water). These healthy waters have a high mineral content. They're naturally carbonated because they come from the springs in the many Czech spas (Mattoni, the most common brand, is from Carlsbad). If you want plain water, ask for *voda bez bublinek* (water without bubbles). Tap water is generally not served. Water comes bottled and generally costs more than beer.

Bohemia is beer country (see sidebar, page 125), with Europe's best and cheapest brew. Locals also like the herb liquor *becherovka.* Moravians prefer wine and *slivovice* (SLEE-voh-veet-seh)—a plum brandy so highly valued that it's the de facto currency of the Carpathian Mountains (often used for bartering with farmers and other mountain folk). *Medovina* ("honey wine") is mead.

In bars and restaurants, you can go wild with memorable liqueurs, most of which cost about a dollar a shot. Experiment. *Fernet,* a bitter drink made from many herbs, is the leading Czech aperitif. Absinthe, made from wormwood and herbs, is a watered-down version of the hallucinogenic drink that's illegal in much of Europe. It's famous as the muse of many artists (including Henri de Toulouse-Lautrec in Paris more than a century ago). *Becherovka,* made of 13 herbs and 38 percent alcohol, was used to settle upset aristocratic tummies and as an aphrodisiac. This velvety drink remains popular today. *Becherovka* and tonic mixed together is nicknamed *beton* ("concrete"). If you drink three, you'll find out why.

TRAVELING AS A TEMPORARY LOCAL

We travel all the way to Europe to enjoy differences—to become temporary locals. You'll experience frustrations. Certain truths that we find "God-given" or "self-evident," such as cold beer, ice in drinks, bottomless cups of coffee, hot showers, and bigger being better, are suddenly not so true. One of the benefits of travel is the eye-opening realization that there are logical, civil, and even better alternatives.

Americans tend to be noisy in public places, such as restaurants and trains. My Czech friends place a high value on speaking quietly in these same places. Listen while on the bus or in a restaurant—the place can be packed, but the decibel level is low. Try to remember this nuance, and soften your speaking voice as a way of respecting their culture.

How Was Your Trip?

Were your travels fun, smooth, and meaningful? If you'd like to share your tips, concerns, and discoveries, please fill out the survey at www.ricksteves.com/feedback. I value your feedback. Thanks in advance—it helps a lot.

If there is a negative aspect to the image Europeans have of Americans, it's that we are big, loud, aggressive, impolite, rich, superficially friendly, and a bit naive.

Given our reluctance to work with the world on climate change issues, Europeans don't respond well to Americans complaining about being too hot or too cold. Bring a sweater in winter, and in summer, be prepared to sweat a little like everyone else.

While Europeans look bemusedly at some of our Yankee excesses—and worriedly at others—they nearly always afford us individual travelers all the warmth we deserve. Judging from all the happy feedback I receive from travelers who have used this book, it's safe to assume you'll enjoy a great, affordable vacation—with the finesse of an independent, experienced traveler.

Thanks, and happy travels!

BACK DOOR TRAVEL PHILOSOPHY
From *Rick Steves' Europe Through the Back Door*

Travel is intensified living—maximum thrills per minute and one of the last great sources of legal adventure. Travel is freedom. It's recess, and we need it.

Experiencing the real Europe requires catching it by surprise, going casual..."Through the Back Door."

Affording travel is a matter of priorities. (Make do with the old car.) You can travel—simply, safely, and comfortably—nearly anywhere in Europe for $100 a day plus transportation costs. In many ways, spending more money only builds a thicker wall between you and what you came to see. Europe is a cultural carnival, and, time after time, you'll find that its best acts are free and the best seats are the cheap ones.

A tight budget forces you to travel close to the ground, meeting and communicating with the people, not relying on service with a purchased smile. Never sacrifice sleep, nutrition, safety, or cleanliness in the name of budget. Simply enjoy the local-style alternatives to expensive hotels and restaurants.

Extroverts have more fun. If your trip is low on magic moments, kick yourself and make things happen. If you don't enjoy a place, maybe you don't know enough about it. Seek the truth. Recognize tourist traps. Give a culture the benefit of your open mind. See things as different but not better or worse. Any culture has much to share.

Of course, travel, like the world, is a series of hills and valleys. Be fanatically positive and militantly optimistic. If something's not to your liking, change your liking. Travel is addictive. It can make you a happier American as well as a citizen of the world. Our Earth is home to six and a half billion equally important people. It's humbling to travel and find that people don't envy Americans. Europeans like us, but, with all due respect, they wouldn't trade passports.

Globe-trotting destroys ethnocentricity. It helps you understand and appreciate different cultures. Regrettably, there are forces in our society that want you dumbed down for their convenience. Don't let it happen. Thoughtful travel engages you with the world—more important than ever these days. Travel changes people. It broadens perspectives and teaches new ways to measure quality of life. Rather than fear the diversity on this planet, travelers celebrate it. Many travelers toss aside their hometown blinders. Their prized souvenirs are the strands of different cultures they decide to knit into their own character. The world is a cultural yarn shop, and Back Door travelers are weaving the ultimate tapestry. Join in!

CZECH REPUBLIC

Česká Republika

The Czech Republic is geographically small. In a quick visit, you can enjoy a fine introduction while still packing in plenty of surprises.

Despite their difficult 20th-century experience, the Czechs managed to preserve their history. In Czech towns and villages, you'll find a simple joy of life—a holdover from the days of the Renaissance. The deep spirituality of the Baroque era still shapes the national character. The magic of Prague, the beauty of Český Krumlov, and the lyrical quality of the countryside relieve the heaviness caused by the turmoil that passed through here. Get beyond Prague and explore the country's medieval towns. These rugged woods and hilltop castles will make you feel as if you're walking through the garden of your childhood dreams.

Of the Czech Republic's three main regions—Bohemia, Moravia, and small Silesia—the best known is Bohemia. It has nothing to do with beatnik bohemians, but with the Celtic tribe of Boheia that inhabited the land before the coming of the Slavs. A long-time home of the Czechs, Bohemia is circled by a naturally fortifying ring of mountains and cut down the middle by the Vltava River, with Prague as its capital. The wine-growing region of Moravia (to the east) is more hilly, Slavic, and colorful.

Tourists often conjure up images of Bohemia when they think of the Czech Republic. But the country consists of more than rollicking beer halls and gently rolling landscapes. It's also about dreamy wine cellars and fertile Moravian plains, with the rugged Carpathian Mountains on the horizon. Politically and geologically, Bohemia and Moravia are two distinct regions. The soils and climates in which the hops and wine grapes grow are very different...and so are the two regions' mentalities. The boisterousness of the Czech polka contrasts with the melancholy of the Moravian ballad; the political viewpoint of the Prague power broker is at

Czech Republic Almanac

Birth of Two Nations: The nation of Czechoslovakia—formed after World War I, and dominated by the USSR after World War II—split on January 1, 1993, into two separate nations: the Czech Republic (Česká Republika) and Slovakia.

Population: 10.3 million people. About 95 percent are ethnic Czechs, who speak Czech. Unlike some of their neighbors (including the very Catholic Poles and Slovaks), Czechs are inclined to be agnostic: One in four is Roman Catholic, but the majority (60 percent) list their religion as unaffiliated.

Latitude and Longitude: 50°N and 15°E (similar latitude to Vancouver, British Columbia).

Area: 31,000 square miles (similar to South Carolina or Maine).

Geography: The Czech Republic is made up of three regions—Bohemia (Čechy), Moravia (Morava), and a small slice of Silesia (Slezsko). The climate is generally cool and partly cloudy.

Biggest Cities: Prague (the capital, 1.2 million), Brno (380,000), Ostrava (318,000), and Plzeň (165,000).

Economy: The gross domestic product equals $200 billion (similar to Indiana). The GDP per capita is $19,500 (less than half that of the average American). Some major money makers for the country are machine parts, cars and trucks, and beer (including Pilsner Urquell and the original Budweiser—called "Czechvar" in the US).

odds with the spirituality of the Moravian bard.

Only a tiny bit of Silesia—around the town of Opava—is part of the Czech Republic today; the rest of the region is in Poland and Germany. (The Hapsburgs lost traditionally Czech Silesia to Prussia in the 1740s, and 200 years later, Germany in turn ceded most of it to Poland.) People in Silesia speak a wide variety of dialects that mix Czech, German, and Polish. Perhaps due to their diverse genes and cultural heritage, women from Silesia are famous for being intelligent and beautiful.

Since 1989, when the Czechs won their independence from Soviet control, people are working harder—but the average monthly wage is still only about $1,000. Roads have been patched up, facades have gotten facelifts, and neighborhood grocery stores have been pushed out by supermarkets.

Delayed Marriages, Fewer Children, More Divorces

In communist times, it was routine to be married by age 22. Once a Czech person finished training school and (for men) the compulsory two-year military service, there was little to aspire

More than a third of trade is with next-door-neighbor Germany. Privatization of formerly government-run industries goes on.

Currency: 20 Czech crowns (*koruna*, Kč) = about $1.

Government: Until 1989, Czechoslovakia was a communist state under Soviet control. Today, the Czech Republic is a member of the European Union (since 2004) and a vibrant democracy, with 68 percent of its eligible population voting in the 2006 election. Its parliament is made up of 200 representatives elected every four years and 81 senators elected for six years. No single political party dominates. The two big parties—the conservative Civic Democrats and the left-of-center Social Democrats—each won just a third of the vote in the 2006 election. The other three parties—the Communists, Christian Democrats, and the Greens—hold enough sway that the leader of the winning party typically heads a coalition government. The president (currently Václav Klaus, a conservative) is selected every five years by the legislators.

Flag: The Czech flag is red (bottom), white (top), and blue (a triangle along the hoist side).

The Average Czech: The average Czech has 1.2 kids (slowly rising after the sharp decline that followed the end of communism), will live 76 years, and has one television in the house.

to. Everyone was assigned essentially the same mediocre job ("They pretended to pay us, we pretended to work") with little hope of career progress—unless you were willing to cut ties with your friends by entering the Communist Party. Children (and summer homes) were the only way for people to project their dreams. Parenting was subsidized. In the countryside, young families were guaranteed housing, and in cities, flats were allocated according to long waiting lists that gave priority to married couples with children.

Today, many more options are available to young people—work, study, travel. Shacking up is no longer a problem; you need money, rather than a marriage certificate, to get a place to live. So most young adults wait until about age 30 to get married. Fewer Czechs are having children, although no one can say they lack incentives: The state pays a premium of one month's wage for every birth, and one parent is entitled to up to three years of paid maternity leave, without risk of losing his or her job. Try telling the Czechs about your one-month maternity leave without pay... they'll think you're crazy.

Without much need for a marriage certificate, more Czechs

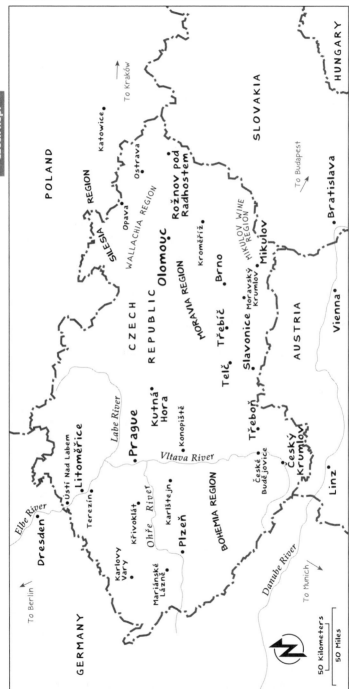

are getting divorced. In 2007, the prime minister and the head of the main opposition party brought media attention to the rising divorce rate—both left their wives for younger girlfriends.

New Freedom, Old Traditions

Most young Czechs are caught up in the new freedom. Everyone wants to travel—to the practical West to study law, or to the mystical East to learn to speak Tamil. They want to work for big bucks at a multinational investment bank, or for a meager salary at a non-profit organization operating in Afghanistan. People's dreams are within reach.

Yet even faced with a bright future, some locals maintain a healthy dose of pessimism and are reluctant to dive headlong into the Western rat race. Things still go a little slower here, and people find pleasure in simple things.

Ninety percent of the tourists who visit the Czech Republic see only Prague. But if you venture outside the capital, you'll enjoy traditional towns and villages, great prices, a friendly and gentle countryside dotted by nettles and wild poppies, and almost no Western tourists. Since the time of the Hapsburgs, fruit trees have lined the country roads for everyone to share. Take your pick.

PRAGUE

ORIENTATION

It's amazing what almost two decades of freedom can do. Prague has always been historic. Now it's fun, too. No other place in Europe has become so popular so quickly. And for good reason: Prague—the only Central European capital to escape the bombs of the last century's wars—is one of Europe's best-preserved cities. It's filled with sumptuous Art Nouveau facades, offers tons of cheap Mozart and Vivaldi concerts, and brews the best beer in Europe. Beyond its architecture and traditional culture, it's an explosion of pent-up entrepreneurial energy jumping for joy after 40 years of communist rule. Its low prices can cause you to jump for joy, too. Travel in Prague is like travel in Western Europe... 15 years ago and (except for hotels) for half the price.

Planning Your Time

A week in Prague is plenty of time to get a solid feel for the city and enjoy excursions to Český Krumlov and Kutná Hora. If you're in a rush, you need a minimum of two full days (with three nights, or two nights and a night train) for a good introduction to the city. From Munich, Berlin, and Vienna, Prague is a four- to six-hour train ride by day (you also have the option of a longer night train from Munich). From Budapest, Warsaw, or Kraków, you can take a handy overnight train.

With two days in Prague, I'd spend one morning seeing the castle and another morning in the Jewish Quarter. Use your afternoons for loitering around the Old Town, Charles Bridge, and the Little Quarter, and split your nights between beer halls and live music. Keep in mind that Jewish Quarter sights close on Saturday. Some museums, mainly in the Old Town, are closed on Monday.

OVERVIEW

Prague unnerves many travelers—it's behind the former Iron Curtain, and you've heard stories of rip-offs and sky-high hotel prices (both are real problems, but avoidable if you're smart). Despite your fears, Prague is charming, safe, and ready to show you a good time. The language barrier is tiny. It seems like every well-educated young person speaks English.

Locals call their town "Praha" (PRAH-hah). It's big, with 1.2 million people, but focus on its relatively compact old center during a quick visit. As you wander, take advantage of brown street signs directing you to tourist landmarks. Self-deprecating Czechs note that while the signs are designed to help tourists (locals never use them), they're only printed in Czech. Still—thanks to the little icons—the signs can help smart visitors who are sightseeing on foot.

The Vltava River divides the west side (Castle Quarter and Little Quarter) from the east side (New Town, Old Town, Jewish Quarter, Main Train Station, and most of the recommended hotels).

Prague addresses come with references to a general zone. Praha 1 is in the old center on either side of the river. Praha 2 is in the new city, southeast of Wenceslas Square. Praha 3 and higher indicate a location farther from the center. Virtually everything I list is in Praha 1 (unless noted otherwise).

Tourist Information

TIs are at several key locations: **Old Town Square** (in the Old Town Hall, just to the left of the Astronomical Clock; Easter–Oct Mon–Fri 9:00–19:00, Sat–Sun 9:00–18:00; Nov–Easter Mon–Fri 9:00–18:00, Sat–Sun 9:00–17:00; tel. 224-482-018), **Main Train Station** (generally same hours as Old Town Square TI, but closed Sun), and the castle side of **Charles Bridge** (Easter–Oct daily 10:00–18:00, closed Nov–Easter). For general tourist information in English, dial 12444 (Mon–Fri 8:00–19:00) or check the TIs' useful website: www.prague-info.cz.

The TIs offer maps, phone cards, a useful transit guide, information on guided walks and bus tours, and bookings for private guides, concerts, hotel rooms, and rooms in private homes.

Orientation

Several monthly event guides—all of them packed with ads—include the *Prague Guide* (29 Kč), *Prague This Month* (free), and *Heart of Europe* (free, summer only). The English-language weekly *Prague Post* newspaper is handy for entertainment listings and current events (60 Kč at newsstands).

Arrival in Prague

As soon as you arrive, be sure to buy a city map, with trams and Metro lines marked and tiny sketches of the sights drawn in for ease in navigating (30–70 Kč, many different brands; sold at kiosks, exchange windows, and tobacco stands). It's a mistake to try doing Prague without a good map—you'll refer to it constantly. The *Kartografie Praha* city map, which shows all the tram lines and major landmarks, includes a castle diagram and a street index. It comes in two versions: 1:15,000 covers the city center, and 1:25,000 includes the whole city. The city center map is easier to navigate, and sufficient unless you're staying in the suburbs.

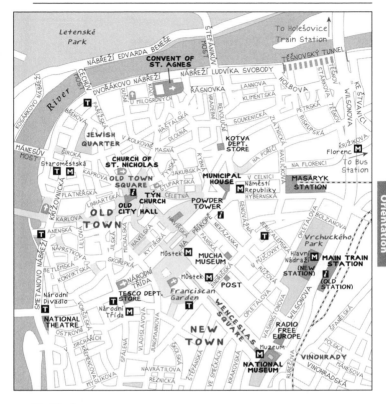

By Train

Prague has two international train stations. The Main Station (Hlavní Nádraží) serves all trains from Frankfurt, Munich, Salzburg, and Kraków; some trains from Vienna and Budapest; and most trains within the Czech Republic. The secondary station (Nádraží Holešovice, located north of the river) handles all trains from Berlin, most trains from Vienna and Budapest, and the high-speed SC Pendolino trains. Two smaller stations, Masaryk and Smíchov, connect with regional destinations. (For information on getting to Prague, see the Transportation Connections chapter, page 150.)

Upon arrival, get money. The stations have ATMs (best rates) and exchange bureaus (rates are generally bad, but can vary—compare by asking at two windows what you'll get for $100, but keep in mind that many of the windows are run by the same company). Then buy your map and confirm your departure plans. Those arriving on an international train may be met at the tracks by room hustlers, trying to snare tourists for cheap rooms. These can be a good value.

Main Station (Hlavní Nádraží): This station's low-ceilinged hall contains a fascinating mix of travelers, kiosks, gamblers,

Prague at a Glance

Activities

▲▲Self-Guided Tram Tour Quick, scenic, and handy overview of the city and its excellent transit system.

▲▲Tourist Concerts Good yet affordable concerts in sumptuous venues (daily from late afternoon to early evening).

▲▲Local Guides A worthwhile two- to three-hour tour of this complex city by a hired, hardworking young guide.

▲Paddle the River An hour's paddle on the river on a hot sunny day: peaceful, scenic, memorable...and good exercise.

In the Old Town

▲▲▲Old Town Square Colorful, magical main square of Old World Prague, with dozens of colorful facades, the dramatic Jan Hus Memorial, looming Týn Church, and fanciful Astronomical Clock. **Hours:** Týn Church generally open 10:00–13:00 & 15:00–17:00; clock strikes on the hour 8:00–21:00, until 20:00 in winter; clock tower open Tue–Sun 9:00–17:30, Mon 11:00–17:30.

▲▲▲Charles Bridge An atmospheric, statue-lined bridge that connects the Old Town to the Little Quarter and Prague Castle. **Hours:** Always open and crossable, though under renovation.

▲▲▲Jewish Quarter The best Jewish sight in Europe, featuring various synagogues and an evocative cemetery. **Hours:** April–Oct Sun–Fri 9:00–18:00, Nov–March Sun–Fri 9:00–16:30, always closed Sat.

▲▲Museum of Medieval Art The best Gothic art in the land, at St. Agnes Convent. **Hours:** Tue–Sun 10:00–18:00, closed Mon.

▲Havelská Market Colorful open-air market that sells crafts and produce. **Hours:** Daily 9:00–18:00.

▲Klementinum National Library's lavish Baroque Hall and Observatory Tower (with views), open by 45-minute tour only. **Hours:** Mon–Fri 14:00–19:00, Sat–Sun 10:00–19:00, less off-season.

In the New Town
▲▲**Wenceslas Square** Lively boulevard at the heart of modern Prague. **Hours:** Always open.

▲▲**Mucha Museum** Likeable collection of Art Nouveau works by Czech artist Alfons Mucha. **Hours:** Daily 10:00–18:00.

▲▲**Municipal House** Pure Art Nouveau architecture, including Prague's largest concert hall and several eateries. **Hours:** Daily 10:00–18:00.

▲▲**Museum of Communism** The rise and fall of the regime, from start to Velvet finish. **Hours:** Daily 9:00–21:00.

In the Little Quarter
Church of St. Nicholas Jesuit centerpiece of Little Quarter Square, with ultimate High Baroque decor and a climbable bell tower. **Hours:** Church—daily 9:00–17:00; tower—April–Oct daily 10:00–18:00, closed Nov–March.

Petřín Hill Little Quarter hill with public art, a funicular, a replica of the Eiffel Tower, and the quirky museum of a nonexistent Czech hero. **Hours:** Funicular—daily 8:00–22:00; tower and museum—daily 10:00–22:00.

In the Castle Quarter
▲▲▲**St. Vitus Cathedral** The Czech Republic's most important church, featuring a climbable tower and a striking stained-glass window by Art Nouveau artist Alfons Mucha. **Hours:** Daily April–Oct 9:00–17:00, Nov–March 9:00–16:00, but closed Sunday mornings year-round for Mass.

▲▲**Prague Castle** Traditional seat of Czech rulers, with St. Vitus Cathedral (see above), Old Royal Palace, Basilica of St. George, shop-lined Golden Lane, and lots of crowds. **Hours:** Castle sights—daily April–Oct 9:00–17:00, Nov–March 9:00–16:00; castle grounds—daily 5:00–23:00.

▲**Strahov Monastery and Library** Baroque center of learning, with ornate reading rooms and old-fashioned science exhibits. **Hours:** Daily 9:00–12:00 & 13:00–17:00.

Toy and Barbie Museum Several centuries of toys, starring an army of Barbies. **Hours:** Daily 9:30–17:30.

Daily Reminder

Sunday: The St. Vitus Cathedral at Prague Castle is closed Sunday morning for Mass. Some stores have shorter hours or are closed.

Monday: The major sights—such as Prague Castle and the Jewish Quarter—are open, but a number of the lesser sights are closed, including the Bethlehem Chapel, Museum of Czech Cubism, House at the Golden Ring, Loreta Church, Sternberg Palace, Convent of St. George, and Museum of Medieval Art.

If you're day-tripping today, only Terezín is open. Kutná Hora's Sedlec Bone Church and the three castles—Konopiště, Karlštejn, and Křivoklát—are closed.

In Prague's Old Town, musicians have a jam session at 17:00 at St. Martin in the Wall, and the cover is free at Roxy's music club, where concerts start at 20:00.

Tuesday–Friday: All sights are open.

Saturday: The Jewish Quarter sights are closed. In nearby Terezín, the Crematorium is closed.

Crowd-Beating Tips: Visit Prague Castle either first thing in the morning (be at St. Vitus Cathedral at 9:00—except Sun morning, when it's closed for Mass) or before it closes (17:00 in summer, 16:00 in winter). Hiring your own local guide for a historic walk is relatively cheap and allows you to choose a time (evening or early morning) and route that avoids crowds.

Summer Activities: Outdoor movies on Střelecký Island are shown at about 21:00 from mid-July through early September (see page 83). And a paddle down the river is always fun in warm weather.

Evening Activities: Prague Castle's grounds stay open until 23:00, and the shop-lined Golden Lane is free and empty after 18:00. Concerts in the National Theatre, Municipal House, and Rudolfinum feature superb artists at bargain prices (see the Entertainment chapter).

Orientation

loitering teenagers, and older riffraff. The creepy station ambience is the work of communist architects, who expanded a classy building to make it just big, painting it the compulsory dreary gray with reddish trim. An ATM is near the subway entrance. The station's baggage-storage counter is reportedly safer than the lockers.

At the Wasteels travel office, Jaroslav and Jaromír offer a helpful and friendly service. You can drop by here upon arrival to get a transit ticket without using the ATM (they take euro coins), and you can confirm and buy your outbound train tickets. They can help you figure out train connections, and they sell train tickets to

Prague Landmarks

English	Czech	Pronounced
Main Train Station	*Hlavní Nádraží*	hlav-NEE NAH-drah-zhee
Old Town	*Staré Město*	STAH-reh myehs-toh
Old Town Square	*Staroměstské Náměstí*	STAR-roh-myehst-skeh NAH-myehs-tee
New Town	*Nové Město*	NOH-vay myehs-toh
Little Quarter	*Malá Strana*	MAH-lah strah-nah
Jewish Quarter	*Josefov*	YOO-zehf-fohf
Castle Quarter	*Hradčany*	HRAD-chah-nee
Charles Bridge	*Karlův Most*	KAR-loov most
Wenceslas Square	*Václavské Náměstí*	VAHT-slahf-skeh NAH-myehs-tee
Vltava River	*Vltava*	VUL-tah-vah

anywhere in Europe—with domestic stopovers if you like—along with tickets for fast local trains and cheap phone cards (no commission; Mon–Fri 9:00–17:00 or later, Sat 9:00–16:00, closed Sun, tel. 972-241-954, www.wasteels.cz). You can even leave your bags here for a short time.

The information office for Czech Railways (downstairs on the left) is less helpful, and the ticket windows downstairs don't give schedule information. The windows marked *vnitrostátní* sell tickets within the Czech Republic.

The AVE office on the main floor books rooms in hotels and pensions, and sells taxi vouchers—for trips into town—at double the fair rate, but still better than you'd get directly from the cabbies themselves (daily 6:00–23:00; with your back to the tracks, walk down to the orange ceiling and past the "Meeting Point"—their office is in the left corner by the exit to the taxis; tel. 251-551-011, fax 251-555-156, www.avetravel.cz, ave@avetravel.cz).

If you're killing time at the station (or for a wistful glimpse of a more genteel age), go upstairs into the Art Nouveau hall. Here, under an elegant dome, you can sip coffee, enjoy music from the 1920s, watch boy prostitutes looking for work, and see new arrivals spilling into the city.

The station was originally named for Emperor Franz Josef. Later, it was renamed for President Woodrow Wilson (see the commemorative plaque in the main exit hall leading away from the tracks), because his promotion of self-determination led to the creation of the free state of Czechoslovakia in 1918. Under

Prague's Four Towns

Until about 1800, Prague was actually four distinct towns with four town squares, all separated by fortified walls. Each town had a unique character, which came from the personality of the people who initially settled it. Today, much of Prague's charm survives in the distinct spirit of each of its towns.

Castle Quarter (Hradčany): Since the ninth century, when the first castle was built on the promontory overlooking a ford across the Vltava River, Castle Hill has been occupied by the ruling class. When Christianity arrived in the Czech lands, this hilltop—oriented along an east–west axis—proved a perfect spot for a church and, later, the cathedral (which, according to custom, must be built with the altar pointing east). Finally, the nobles built their representative palaces in proximity to the castle to compete with the Church for influence on the king. Even today, you feel like clip-clopping through this neighborhood in a fancy carriage. The Castle Quarter—which hosts the offices of the president and the foreign minister—has high art and grand buildings, little commerce, and few pubs.

Little Quarter (Malá Strana): This Baroque town of fine palaces and gardens rose from the ashes of a merchant settlement that burned down in the 1540s. The Czech and European nobility who settled here took pride in the grand design of their gardens. In the 1990s, after decades of decay, the gardens were carefully restored. While some are open only to the successors of the former nobility—including the Czech Parliament and the American, German, and Polish Embassies—many are open to visitors.

Old Town (Staré Město): Charles Bridge connects the Little Quarter with the Old Town. A boomtown since the 10th century, this area has long been the busy commercial quarter—filled with merchants, guilds, and supporters of Jan Hus (who wanted a Czech-style Catholicism). Trace the walls of this town in the modern road plan (the Powder Tower is a remnant of a wall system that completed a fortified ring, half provided by the river). The marshy area closest to the bend—least inhabitable and therefore allotted to the Jewish community—became the ghetto (today's Josefov, or Jewish Quarter).

the communists (who weren't big fans of Wilson), it was bluntly renamed simply Hlavní Nádraží— "Main Station."

Even though the Main Station is basically downtown, it can be a little tricky to get to your hotel. The biggest challenge is that the **taxi** drivers at the train station are a gang of no-neck mafia thugs who wait around to charge an arriving tourist five times the regular rate. To get an honest cabbie, I'd walk a few blocks and

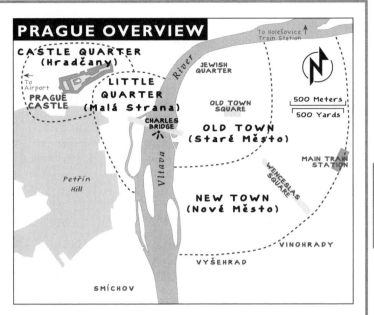

New Town (Nové Město): The New Town rings the Old Town—cutting a swath from riverbank to riverbank—and is fortified with Prague's outer wall. In the 14th century, the king created this town, tripling the size of what would become Prague. Wenceslas Square was once the horse market of this busy working-class district. Even today, the New Town is separated from the Old Town by a "moat" (the literal meaning of the street called Na Příkopě). As you cross bustling Na Příkopě, you leave the glass and souvenir shops behind, and you enter a town of malls and fancy shops that cater to locals and visitors alike.

The Royal Way: Cutting through the four towns—from St. Vitus Cathedral down to the Charles Bridge, and then from the bridge to the Powder Tower—is the Royal Way (Královská Cesta), the ancient path of coronation processions. Today, this city spine is marred by tacky trinket shops and jammed by tour groups. Use it for orientation only—try to avoid it if you want to see the real Prague.

hail one off the street; pay a premium for a voucher at the AVE office (see above); or call AAA Taxi (tel. 233-113-311) or City Taxi (tel. 257-257-257). A taxi should get you to your hotel for no more than 200 Kč (see "Getting Around Prague," page 41).

A better option may be to take the **Metro.** It's dirt-cheap and easy, with very frequent departures. Once you're on the Metro, you'll wonder why you would ever bother with a taxi (inside station, look for the red M with two directions: Háje or Letňany). To get to hotels in the Old Town, catch a Háje-bound train to the Muzeum stop, then transfer to the green line (direction: Dejvická) and get off at either Můstek or Staroměstská; these stops straddle the Old Town. Or, if your hotel is close enough, consider **walking** (Wenceslas Square, a downtown landmark, is about a 10-minute walk away—turn left out of the station and follow Wilsonova street to the huge National Museum).

Holešovice Station (Nádraží Holešovice): This station, slightly farther from the center, is suburban mellow. The main hall has all the services of the Main Station in a more compact area. On the left are international and local ticket windows (open 24 hours), an information office, and an AVE office with last-minute accommodations (daily 12:00–20:00, tel. 972-224-660). On the right is a little-frequented café with Internet access (1 Kč/min, daily 8:00–19:30). Two ATMs are immediately outside the first glass doors, and the Metro is 50 yards to the right (follow signs toward *Vstup*, which means "entrance"; it's three stops to Hlavní Nádraží—the Main Station—or four stops to the city-center Muzeum stop). Taxis and trams are outside to the right (allow 200 Kč for a cab to the center). The airport bus (45 Kč, runs 2/hr) is outside to the left.

By Plane

Prague's modern, tidy, low-key **Ruzyně Airport,** located 12 miles (about 30 min) west of the city center, is as user-friendly as any airport in Western Europe or the US. The airport has ATMs (avoid the change desks); desks promoting their transportation services (such as city transit and shuttle buses); kiosks selling city maps and phone cards; and a tourist service with few printed materials. Airport info: tel. 220-113-314, operator tel. 220-111-111.

Getting to and from the airport is easy. Leaving the airport, you have four options:

Dirt Cheap: Take bus #119 to the Dejvická Metro station, or #100 to the Zličín Metro station (20 min), then take the Metro into the center (20 Kč, info desk in airport arrival hall).

Cheap: Take the Čedaz minibus shuttle to Náměstí Republiky, across from Kotva department store (daily 5:30–21:30, 2/hr, pay 120 Kč directly to driver, info desk in arrival hall).

Moderate: Take a Čedaz minibus directly to your hotel, with a couple of stops likely en route (480 Kč for a group of up to four, tel. 220-114-286).

Expensive: Catch a taxi. Cabbies wait at the curb directly in front of the arrival hall. Airport taxi cabbies are honest but more expensive. Carefully confirm the complete price before getting in. It's a fixed rate of 600–700 Kč, with no meter.

Helpful Hints

Medical Help: A 24-hour pharmacy is at Palackého 5 (a block from Wenceslas Square, tel. 224-946-982). For standard assistance, there are two state hospitals in the center: the **General Hospital** (open daily 24 hours, moderate wait time, right above Karlovo Náměstí at U Nemocnice 2, Praha 2, use entry G, tel. 224-962-564); and the **Na Františku Hospital** (on the embankment next to Hotel InterContinental, Na Františku 1, go to the main entrance, for English assistance call Mr. Hacker between 8:00–14:00, tel. 222-801-278 or tel. 222-801-371—serious problems only). The reception staff may not speak English, but doctors do.

For better-than-standard assistance in English (including dental service), consider the top-quality **Hospital Na Homolce** (less than 1,000 Kč for an appointment, from 8:00–16:00 call 252-922-146, for after-hours emergencies call 257-211-111; bus #167 from Anděl Metro station, Roentgenova 2, Praha 5). The **Canadian Medical Care Center** is a small, private clinic with English-speaking Czech staff at Veleslavínská 1 in Praha 6 (3,000 Kč for an appointment, 4,500 Kč for a house call, halfway between the city and the airport, tel. 235-360-133, after-hours emergency tel. 724-300-301).

Internet Access: Internet cafés are well-advertised and scattered through the Old and New Towns. Consider **Bohemia Bagel** near the Jewish Quarter (see page 130). **Káva Káva Káva Coffee,** on the boundary between the Old and New Towns, is in the Platýz courtyard off Národní 37.

Bookstore: For some good bookstores in Prague, see page 139 in the Shopping chapter.

Laundry: A full-service laundry near most of the recommended hotels is at Karolíny Světlé 11 (200 Kč/8-pound load, wash and dry in 2 hours, Mon–Fri 7:30–19:00, closed Sat–Sun, 200 yards from Charles Bridge on Old Town side). Or surf the Internet while your undies tumble-dry at Korunní 14 (160 Kč/load wash and dry, Internet access-2 Kč/min, daily 8:00–20:00, near Náměstí Míru Metro stop, Praha 2).

Local Help: Magic Praha is a tiny travel service run by hard-working Lída Jánská. A charming Jill-of-all-trades who takes her clients' needs seriously, she's particularly helpful with accommodations and transfers throughout the Czech Republic, as well as private tours and side-trips to historic towns (tel. 235-325-170, mobile 604-207-225, www.magicpraha.cz, magicpraha@magicpraha.cz). Lída also speaks Spanish and Portuguese.

Car Rental: All of the biggies have offices in Prague (check each company's website, or ask at the TI). For a local alternative,

Rip-Offs in Prague

Prague's new freedom comes with new scams. There's no particular risk of violent crime, but green, rich tourists do get taken by con artists. Simply be on guard, particularly when traveling on trains (thieves thrive on overnight trains), changing money (tellers with bad arithmetic and inexplicable pauses while counting back your change), dealing with taxis (see "By Taxi," page 44), paying in restaurants (see Eating chapter, page 123), and in seedy neighborhoods.

Anytime you pay for something, make a careful note of how much it costs, how much you're handing over, and how much you expect back. Count your change. Someone selling you a phone card marked 190 Kč might first tell you it's 790 Kč, hoping to pocket the difference. If you call his bluff, he'll pretend that it never happened.

Plainclothes policemen "looking for counterfeit money" are con artists. Don't show them any cash or your wallet. If you're threatened with an inexplicable fine by a "policeman," conductor, or other official, you can walk away, scare him away by saying you'll need a receipt (which real officials are legally required to provide), or ask a passerby if the fine is legit. On the other hand, do not ignore the plainclothes inspectors on the Metro and trams who have shown you their badges.

Pickpockets can be little children or adults dressed as professionals—or even as tourists. They target Western visitors. Many thieves drape jackets over their arms to disguise busy fingers.

consider **Alimex,** which features a wide variety of new vehicles (tel. 233-350-001, toll-free tel. 800-150-170, www.alimexcr.cz). The cheapest model, a Škoda Fabia, is a great value (450 Kč/day with basic insurance, plus 238 Kč/day for full theft and damage insurance; additional fees: 500-Kč tax for airport pickup, 357 Kč for delivery to your hotel; discounts if you book online, smart to reserve up to a week ahead in peak season). Note that the cheapest cars sometimes have giant ads pasted on the side. They have branches at the airport (daily 8:00–22:00) and near the Holešovice Station (daily 8:00–18:00).

Best Views: Enjoy the "Golden City of a Hundred Spires" during the early evening, when the light is warm and the colors are rich. Good viewpoints include the terrace at the Strahov Monastery (above the castle), the top of St. Vitus Cathedral (at the castle), the top of either tower on Charles Bridge, the Old Town Square clock tower (has an elevator), the Restaurant u Prince Terrace (see page 130), and the steps of the National Museum overlooking Wenceslas Square.

Thieves work the crowded and touristy places in teams. They use mobile phones to coordinate their bumps and grinds. Be careful if anyone creates a commotion at the door of a Metro or tram car (especially around the Národní Třída and Vodičkova tram stops, or on the made-for-tourists trams #22 and #23)—it's a smoke-screen for theft.

Car theft is also a big problem in Prague (many Western European car-rental companies don't allow their rentals to cross the Czech border). Never leave anything valuable in your car—not even in broad daylight on a busy street.

The sex clubs on Skořepka street, just south of Havelská Market, routinely rip off naive tourists and can be dangerous. They're filled mostly with young Russian women and German and Asian men. Lately this district has become the rage for British "stag" parties, for guys who are happy to fly cheaply to get to cheap beer and cheap thrills.

This all sounds intimidating. But Prague is safe. It has its share of petty thieves and con artists, but very little violent crime. Don't be scared—just be alert.

Getting Around Prague

You can walk nearly everywhere. But after you figure out the public transportation system, the Metro is slick, the trams fun, and the taxis quick and easy. For details, pick up the handy transit guide at the TI. City maps show the tram, bus, and Metro lines.

By Metro and Train

Affordable and excellent public transit is perhaps the best legacy of the communist era (locals ride all month for 460 Kč). The three-line Metro system is handy and simple, but doesn't always get you right to the tourist sights (landmarks such as the Old Town Square and Prague Castle are several blocks from the nearest Metro stops). The trams rumble by every two or three minutes and take you just about anywhere.

Tickets: The trams and Metro work on the same tickets (but expect price increases):

- 20-minute basic ticket with limited transfer options—14 Kč *základní s omezenou přestupností*. With this ticket, no transfers are allowed on trams and buses, but on the Metro, you can go up to five stops with one transfer (not valid for night trams or night buses).

- 75-minute transfer ticket with unlimited transfers *(základní přestupní)*—20 Kč.
- 24-hour pass *(jízdenka na 24 hodin)*—80 Kč.
- 3-day pass *(jízdenka na 3 dny)*—220 Kč.
- 7-day pass *(jízdenka na 7 dní)*—280 Kč.

Buy tickets from your hotel, at newsstand kiosks, or from automated machines (select ticket price, then insert coins). For convenience, buy all the tickets that you think you'll need—but estimate conservatively. Remember, Prague is a great walking town, so unless you're commuting from a hotel far outside the center, you will likely find that individual tickets work best. Be sure to validate your ticket on the tram, bus, or Metro by sticking it in the machine (which stamps a time on it—watch locals and imitate). Inspectors routinely ambush ticketless riders (including tourists) and fine them 500 Kč on the spot.

Tips: Navigate by signs that list the end stations. When you come to your stop, push the yellow button if the doors don't automatically open. Although it seems that all Metro doors lead to the neighborhood of Výstup, that's simply the Czech word for "exit." When a tram pulls up to a stop, two different names are announced: first, the name of the stop you're currently at, followed by the name of the stop that's coming up next. Confused tourists, thinking they've heard their stop, are notorious for rushing off the tram one stop too soon. Trams run every 5–10 minutes in the daytime (a schedule is posted at each stop). The Metro closes at midnight, and the nighttime tram routes (identified with white numbers on blue backgrounds at tram stops) run all night at 30-minute intervals. There's more information and a complete route planner at www.dp-praha.cz.

Handy Trams: Trams #22 and #23 are practically made for sightseeing, using the same route to connect the New Town with

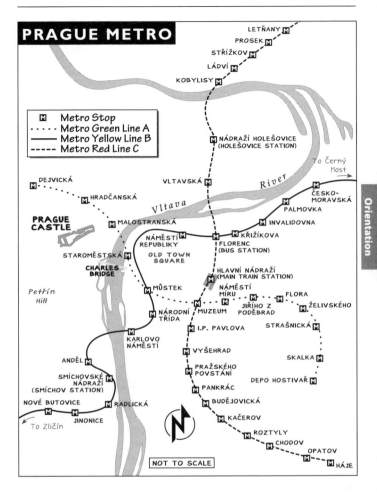

PRAGUE METRO

LETŇANY M
PROSEK M
STŘÍŽKOV M
LÁDVÍ M
KOBYLISY M

M Metro Stop
· · · · Metro Green Line A
——— Metro Yellow Line B
- - - - Metro Red Line C

M NÁDRAŽÍ HOLEŠOVICE
(HOLEŠOVICE STATION)

To Černý Most →

M DEJVICKÁ
VLTAVSKÁ M
River

M HRADČANSKÁ
Vltava
ČESKO-MORAVSKÁ
PALMOVKA

PRAGUE CASTLE
M MALOSTRANSKÁ
M INVALIDOVNA

NÁMĚSTÍ REPUBLIKY M
M KŘIŽÍKOVA
STAROMĚSTSKÁ M
FLORENC (BUS STATION)
CHARLES BRIDGE
OLD TOWN SQUARE

HLAVNÍ NÁDRAŽÍ (MAIN TRAIN STATION) M

Petřín Hill
M MŮSTEK
NÁMĚSTÍ MÍRU M
FLORA
JIŘÍHO Z PODĚBRAD M
ŽELIVSKÉHO
NÁRODNÍ TŘÍDA
MUZEUM M
M I.P. PAVLOVA
STRAŠNICKÁ M
KARLOVO NÁMĚSTÍ M
VYŠEHRAD M
SKALKA M
ANDĚL M
PRAŽSKÉHO POVSTÁNÍ M
DEPO HOSTIVAŘ M
SMÍCHOVSKÉ NÁDRAŽÍ (SMÍCHOV STATION) M
PANKRÁC M
NOVÉ BUTOVICE M
M RADLICKÁ
BUDĚJOVICKÁ M
M JINONICE
KAČEROV M
← To Zličín
ROZTYLY M
CHODOV M
OPATOV
M HÁJE

NOT TO SCALE

the Castle Quarter (see my "Self-Guided Tram Tour," later in this chapter, and find the line marked on the color map at beginning of this book). The trams use some of the same stops as the Metro (making it easy to get to—or travel on from—the tram route). Of the many stops these trams make, the most convenient are two in the New Town (Národní Třída Metro stop, between the bottom of Wenceslas Square and the river; and Národní Divadlo, at the National Theatre), one stop in the Little Quarter (Malostranská Metro stop), and three stops above Prague

Castle (Královský Letohrádek, Pražský Hrad, and Pohořelec; for details, see "Getting to Prague Castle—By Tram" on page 94).

By Taxi

Prague's taxis—notorious for hyperactive meters—are being tamed. New legislation is in place to curb crooked cabbies, and police will always take your side in an argument. Many cabbies are crooks who consider it a good day's work to take one sucker for a ride. You'll make things difficult for a dishonest cabbie by challenging an unfair fare.

While most hotel receptionists and guidebooks advise that you avoid taxis, I find Prague to be a great taxi town and use them routinely. With the local rate, they're cheap (read the rates on the door: drop charge starts at 36 Kč; per-kilometer charge—29 Kč; and waiting time per minute—5 Kč). The key is to be sure the cabbie turns on the meter at the #1 tariff (look for the word *sazba,* meaning "tariff," on the meter). Avoid cabs waiting at tourist attractions and train stations. To improve your odds of getting a fair meter rate—which starts only when you take off—call for a cab (or have your hotel or restaurant call one for you). AAA Taxi (tel. 233-113-311) and City Taxi (tel. 257-257-257) are the most likely to have English-speaking staff—and honest cabbies. I also find that hailing a passing taxi usually gets me a decent price.

If a cabbie surprises you at the end with an astronomical fare, simply pay 200 Kč, which should cover you for a long ride anywhere in the center. Then go into your hotel. On the miniscule chance that he follows you, the receptionist will back you up.

TOURS

Walking Tours

Many small companies offer walking tours of the Old Town, the castle, and more. For the latest, pick up the walking tour fliers at the TI. Since guiding is a routine side-job for local university students, you'll generally get hardworking young guides at good prices. While I'd rather go with my own private guide (see below), public walking tours are cheaper, cover themes you might not otherwise consider, connect you with other English-speaking travelers, and allow for spontaneity. **Prague Walks** is as good as any (250–1,000 Kč, 1.5–6 hours; tours depart at 11:00, 14:00, and 19:00 from Astronomical Clock; tel. 222-322-309, mobile 608-339-099, www.praguewalks.com, pwalks@comp.cz). By request, they can organize a clever Good Morning Walk, which starts at 8:00 (April–Aug only), before the crowds hit.

Orientation

Private Guides

In Prague, hiring a local guide is particularly smart—they're twice as helpful for half the price compared to guides in Western Europe. Because prices are usually per hour (not per person), small groups can inexpensively hire a guide for several days. Guides meet you wherever you like, and tailor the tour to your interests. Visit their websites in advance for details on various walks, airport transfers, countryside excursions, and other services offered, and then make arrangements by email.

Šárka Kačabová and her team of guides have a knack for making popular Czech culture easily comprehensible in a short time (400 Kč/hr for one or two people, 600 Kč/hr for three or more, mobile 777-225-205, www.prague-guide.info, saraguide @volny.cz). **Katka Svobodová,** an anthropologist and historian, is a hardworking guide who knows her stuff and speaks excellent English (400 Kč/hr, 3-hour minimum, mobile 603-181-300, www .praguewalker.com, katerina@praguewalker.com). **Jana Hronková** has a natural style—a welcome change from the more strict professionalism of some of the busier guides (mobile 732-185-180, janahronkova@hotmail.com).

My readers have recommended **Renata Blažková,** who has a special interest in the history of Prague's Jewish Quarter (tel. 222-716-870, mobile 602-353-186, blazer@volny.cz) and **Martin Bělohradský,** whose main area of expertise lies in fine arts and architecture (martinb@uochb.cas.cz, mobile 723-414-565).

Athos Travel's licensed guides can lead you on a general sightseeing tour or fit the walk to your interests: music, Art Nouveau, architecture, and more (1–5 people—700 Kč/hr, more than 5 people—800 Kč/hr, arrange tour at least 24 hours in advance, tel. 241-440-571, www.athos.cz, info@athos.cz).

The **TI** also has plenty of private guides (rates for a 3-hour tour: 1,200 Kč/1 person, 1,400 Kč/2 people, 1,600 Kč/3 people, 2,000 Kč/4 people; desk at Old Town Square TI, arrange and pay in person at least 2 hours in advance, tel. 224-482-562, guides@pis.cz). For a listing of more private guides, see www.guide-prague.cz.

Jewish-Themed Tours: Sylvie Wittmann, a native Czech Jew, has developed a diverse group of knowledgeable guides who aspire to bring Jewish traditions back to life in Prague. Consider her three-hour walking tour of the Jewish Quarter (630 Kč includes entry to the synagogues of the Jewish Museum, May–Oct Sun–Fri at 10:30 and 14:00, Nov–April Sun–Fri at 10:30 only, no tours on Sat) or her six-hour trip to Terezín Concentration Camp (1,150 Kč includes transportation and all entries, departs May–Oct daily at 10:00; mid-March–April and Nov–Dec no Mon, Wed, or Fri tours; Jan–mid-March by appointment only). All tours require prior reservation and meet in front of Hotel

InterContinental at the end of Pařížská street (tel. & fax 222-252-472, mobile 603-168-427, www.wittmann-tours.com, sylvie @wittmann-tours.com). Sylvie also offers trips to lesser-known destinations, as well as tours of the Czech Republic and Eastern Europe from a Jewish point of view.

Outside Prague: To get beyond sights listed in most guidebooks, call Thomas Zahn, who runs **Pathways Guided Travel.** Thomas, an American who married into the Czech Republic, specializes in helping Americans of Czech descent find their roots. On short notice, Thomas might be able to get you to the village where your ancestors emigrated from. But if you're serious about locating your actual ancestral home and maybe even meeting with newly discovered relatives, you'll need to call Thomas three to four months in advance so you both can begin the research. Thomas also organizes and leads creative, affordable (typically one- to two-day) excursions from Prague, during which you'll ideally learn how to navigate the off-the-beaten-track destinations in the Czech Republic by yourself. Thomas is raising his three children in the Czech Republic, and has good ideas about how to make Prague and the surrounding area fun for your kids. Explore Thomas' website for ways to connect with the Czech countryside (tel. 257-940-113, mobile 603-758-983, www.pathfinders.cz).

Bus Tours

While I generally recommend cheap big-bus orientation tours for an efficient, once-over-lightly look at great cities, Prague just isn't built for bus tours. In fact, most bus tours of the city are walking tours that use buses for pick-ups and transfers. The sightseeing core (Castle Quarter, Charles Bridge, and the Old Town) are not accessible by bus. So if you insist on a bus, you're playing basketball with a catcher's mitt.

Bus tours make more sense for day trips out of Prague. Several companies have kiosks on Na Příkopě where you can comparison-shop. **Premiant City Tours** offers 20 different tours, including Terezín Concentration Camp, Karlštejn Castle, and Český Krumlov (1,750 Kč, 10 hrs), and a river cruise. The tours feature live guides and depart from near the bottom of Wenceslas Square at Na Příkopě 23. Get tickets at an AVE travel agency, your hotel, on the bus, or at Na Příkopě 23 (tel. 224-946-922, mobile 606-600-123, www.premiant.cz). Tour salespeople are notorious for telling you anything to sell a ticket. Some tours, especially those heading into the countryside, can be in as many as four different languages. Hiring a private guide, many of whom can drive you around in their car, can be a much better value (see "Private Guides," page 45).

More Tours

Tram Tours—Prague's trams #22 and #23 are an easy way to get familiar with the city at very little cost (use the 20 Kč, 75-minute transfer ticket—see page 41, trams run every 5 minutes). Handy tram stops for this tour are located near the Národní Třída and Malostranská Metro stops (see below).

Cruises—Prague isn't ideal for a boat tour because you'll spend half the time waiting to go through the locks. Still, the hour-long

Vltava River cruises, which leave from near the castle end of Charles Bridge about hourly, are scenic and relaxing, though not informative (100–150 Kč).

▲**Paddleboat Cruises**—Renting a rowboat or paddleboat on the island by the National Theatre is a better way to enjoy the river. You'll float at your own pace among the swans and watch local lovers cruise by in their own paddleboats (40–60 Kč/hr, bring photo ID for deposit).

Orientation

SELF-GUIDED TRAM TOUR

▲▲Welcome to Prague: Trams #22 and #23

Trams #22 and #23 both make a fine Prague orientation joy-ride. They run exactly the same route (although #23 is often less crowded) roughly every five minutes, and you can hop on and off as you like (20-Kč transfer ticket valid 75 min—see page 41 for more about tram tickets). There are more seats and less traffic early and late. Be warned: Thieves like this route as much as the tourists.

Catch the tram in the New Town and ride it over the river, through the Little Quarter, and up to the castle (stop: Pohořelec). You'll see how easy it is to use the trams, get the lay of the land, and zip effortlessly up to the castle (saving lots of sweat or a 200-Kč taxi ride).

Start at the **Národní Třída** stop (facing the Metro stop of the same name, catch the tram closest to the Metro, on the same side of the street as the Tesco department store). The tram will turn and rattle along National street (Národní Třída).

At the next stop, **Národní Divadlo,** you'll see Café Slavia facing the National Theatre, just before the tram crosses the river. Survey the boat-rental scene (island with rental wharfs) and the romantic beach island, and enjoy a great castle view. The Dancing House (while hard to see) is 400 yards upstream.

The next stop, **Újezd,** faces a park. See the Monument to Victims of Communism Who Survived—with devoured spirits on the steps (uphill at the corner, described on page 91). A funicular leads to the Eiffel-like Petřín Tower.

The tram then heads north from the **Hellichova** stop, paralleling Kampa Island on the river side (to the right). On the inland side, the tram passes St. Mary the Victorious Church, popular with pilgrims for its Infant Jesus of Prague. Entering the Little Quarter, the tram goes uphill to the American Embassy (with the flag).

The tram stops next at **Malostranské Náměstí,** on the Little Quarter's main square, dominated by the Church of Saint Nicholas. From here you can hike up Nerudova street to Prague Castle. Charles Bridge is just 100 yards away—catch a peek-a-boo view through the gate.

Fifteen yards beyond the **Malostranská** Metro stop (also a tram stop) is the entry to the Wallenstein Palace Garden. Past the park, with its memorial to World War II freedom fighters, a bridge leads across the Vltava River to Josefov, the Jewish Quarter. The tram now enters the longest stretch between stations—perfect for ticket checkers to reveal themselves and catch anyone traveling without a valid ticket.

Immediately across the street from the **Královský Letohrádek** stop is the Royal Summer Palace, the Royal Gardens leading fragrantly to Prague Castle (and a public WC). On the tram side of the street is one of the few preserved gates of Prague's Baroque fortification system.

Jump out at the **Pražský Hrad** stop for the direct route to the castle entrance. Or stay on as the tram winds past the **Brusnice** stop through a greenbelt built along the top of the city wall (only remnants survive).

The next stop, **Pohořelec,** is my preferred approach to the castle and the closest stop to the Strahov Monastery. Hop out here, and it's all downhill. Or catch a tram going the opposite direction to do this trip in reverse.

Extending the Route: You could start this tour earlier at the Náměstí Míru stop (four stops before Národní Třída), next to several recommended places to eat and sleep. And you could get off later at the Břevnovský Klášter stop (five stops after Pohořelec, tram #22 only) at the peaceful Břevnov Monastery, next to two recommended hotels.

THE OLD TOWN

Staré Město

From Prague's dramatic centerpiece, the Old Town Square, sightseeing options fan out in all directions. Get oriented on the square before venturing onward. You can find out about Jewish heritage in the Jewish Quarter (Josefov), a few blocks from the Old Town Square. Closer to the square, you'll find the quaint and historic Ungelt courtyard and Celetná street, which leads to the Museum of Czech Cubism and the landmark Estates Theatre. If you're intrigued by Jan Hus, the preacher and martyr, look for his pulpit in the chapel on Bethlehem Square. Nearby, Karlova street funnels all the tourists to the famous Charles Bridge. All of the sights described here are within a five-minute walk of the magnificent Old Town Square.

▲▲▲Old Town Square (Staroměstské Náměstí)

The focal point for most visits, Prague's Old Town Square is one of the top sights. This has been a market square since the 11th cen-

tury. It became the nucleus of the Old Town (Staré Město) in the 13th century, when its Town Hall was built. Today, the old-time market stalls have been replaced by outdoor cafés and touristy horse buggies. But under this shallow surface, the square hides a magic power to evoke the history that has passed through here. The square's centerpiece is a memorial to Jan Hus.

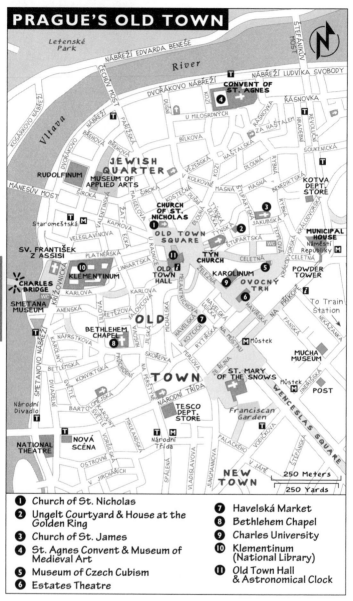

PRAGUE'S OLD TOWN

Letenské Park

NÁBŘEŽÍ EDVARDA BENEŠE

River

Vltava

DVOŘÁKOVO NÁBŘEŽÍ

NÁBŘEŽÍ LUDVÍKA SVOBODY

CONVENT OF ST. AGNES ❹

U MILOSRDNÝCH

ŘÁSNOVKA

BÍLKOVA

JEWISH QUARTER

RUDOLFINUM

MUSEUM OF APPLIED ARTS

ŠIROKÁ

Staroměstská Ⓜ

VELESLAVÍNOVA

SV. FRANTIŠEK Z ASSISI

KLEMENTINUM ❿

CHARLES BRIDGE

SMETANA MUSEUM

CHURCH OF ST. NICHOLAS ❶

OLD TOWN SQUARE

OLD TOWN HALL ⓫

TÝN CHURCH

KAROLINUM ❺

OVOCNÝ TRH ❻

KOTVA DEPT. STORE

MUNICIPAL HOUSE
Náměstí Republiky Ⓜ

POWDER TOWER

To Train Station

BETHLEHEM CHAPEL ❽

OLD TOWN

HAVELSKÁ MARKET ❼

Můstek Ⓜ

MUCHA MUSEUM

ST. MARY OF THE SNOWS

Můstek Ⓜ

POST

Národní Divadlo

TESCO DEPT. STORE

Franciscan Garden

WENCESLAS SQUARE

NATIONAL THEATRE

NOVÁ SCÉNA

Národní Třída Ⓜ

NEW TOWN

250 Meters
250 Yards

❶ Church of St. Nicholas
❷ Ungelt Courtyard & House at the Golden Ring
❸ Church of St. James
❹ St. Agnes Convent & Museum of Medieval Art
❺ Museum of Czech Cubism
❻ Estates Theatre
❼ Havelská Market
❽ Bethlehem Chapel
❾ Charles University
❿ Klementinum (National Library)
⓫ Old Town Hall & Astronomical Clock

Jan Hus and Martin Luther

The word *catholic* means "universal." The Roman Catholic Church—in many ways the administrative ghost of the Roman Empire—is the only organization to survive from ancient times. For more than a thousand years, it enforced its notion that the Vatican was the sole interpreter of God's word on earth, and the only legitimate way to be a Christian was as a Roman Catholic.

Jan Hus (c. 1369–1415) lived and preached a century before Martin Luther. Both were college professors, as well as priests. Both drew huge public crowds as they preached in their university chapels. Both condemned Church corruption and promoted a local religious autonomy. Both helped establish their national languages. (Hus gave the Czech alphabet its unique accent marks so that the letters could fit the sounds.) And both got in big trouble.

While Hus was burned, Luther survived. Thanks to the new printing press, invented by Gutenberg, Luther was able to spread his message cheaply and effectively. Since Luther was high-profile and German, killing him would have caused major political complications. While Hus may have loosened Rome's grip on Christianity, Luther orchestrated the Reformation that finally broke it. Today, both are honored as national heroes as well as religious reformers.

Jan Hus Memorial

This monument, erected in 1915 (500 years after the Czech reformer's martyrdom by fire), symbolizes the long struggle for Czech freedom (see sidebar above).

Walk around the memorial. Jan Hus stands tall between two groups of people: victorious Hussite patriots and Protestants defeated by the Hapsburgs in 1620. One of the patriots holds a chalice (cup); in the medieval Church, only priests could drink the wine at Communion. Since the Hussites fought for their right to take both the wine and the bread, the cup is their symbol. Hus looks proudly at the Týn Church (described below), which became the headquarters and leading church of his followers. A golden chalice once filled the now-empty niche under the gold bas-relief of the Virgin Mary on the church's facade. After the Hapsburg (and, therefore, Catholic) victory over the Czechs in 1620, the Hussite chalice was melted down and made into the image of Mary that shines from that spot high over the square today.

Behind the statue of Jan Hus, the bronze statue of a mother with her children represents the ultimate rebirth of the Czech nation. Because of his bold stance for independence in the way common people worship God, Hus was excommunicated and burned in Germany a century before the age of Martin Luther.

Old Town Square Orientation Spin-Tour

Whirl clockwise to get a look at Prague's diverse architectural styles: Gothic, Renaissance, Baroque, Rococo, and Art Nouveau. Start with the green domes of the Baroque **Church of St. Nicholas.** Originally Catholic, now Hussite, this church is a popular venue for concerts. (There's another green-domed Church of St. Nicholas—also popular for concerts—by the same architect, across the Charles Bridge in the Little Quarter.) The Jewish Quarter (Josefov) is a few blocks behind the church, down the uniquely tree-lined Pařížská—"Paris street." (For more on the Jewish Quarter, see page 65.) Pařížská, an eclectic cancan of mostly Art Nouveau facades, leads to a bluff that once sported a 100-foot-tall stone statue of Stalin. Demolished in 1962 after Khrushchev exposed Stalin's crimes, it was replaced in 1991 by a giant ticking **metronome**—partly to commemorate Prague's centennial exhibition (the 1891 exhibition is remembered by the Little Quarter's Eiffel-esque Petřín Tower), and partly to send the message that for every power, there's a time to go.

Spin to the right, past the Hus Memorial and the fine yellow Art Nouveau building. The large Rococo palace on the right (with a public WC in the courtyard) is part of the **National Gallery;** the temporary exhibits here are often the best in town.

To the right, you can't miss the towering, Gothic **Týn Church** (pronounced "teen"), with its fanciful spires flanking the gold bas-

relief of Mary. For 200 years after Hus' death, this was Prague's leading Hussite church (described in more detail below). A narrow lane leading to the church's entrance passes the **Via Musica,** the most convenient ticket office in town (see page 140). Behind the Týn Church is a gorgeously restored medieval courtyard called **Ungelt** (see page 55). The row of pastel houses in front of Týn Church has a mixture of Gothic, Renaissance, and Baroque facades. To the right of these buildings, shop-lined **Celetná street** leads to a square called Ovocný Trh (with the Estates Theatre and Museum

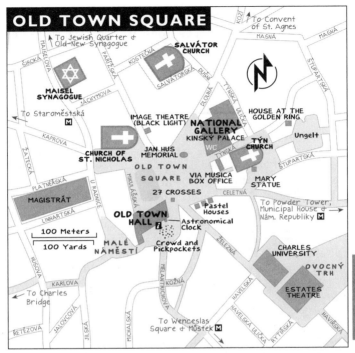

of Czech Cubism—see page 57), and beyond that, to the Municipal House and Powder Tower in the New Town (see page 80).

Continue spinning right—with more gloriously colorful architecture—until you reach the pointed 250-foot-tall spire marking the 14th-century **Old Town Hall** (which has the only

elevator-accessible tower in town—described later in this chapter). The chunk of pink building attached to the tower of the Neo-Gothic City Hall is the town's memorial to bad losers. The building once stretched all the way to the Church of St. Nicholas. Then, in the last days of World War II (May 1945), German tanks knocked off this landmark—to the joy of many Prague citizens who considered it an ugly, oversized 19th-century stain on the medieval square. Across the square from the Old Town Hall (opposite the Astronomical Clock), touristy **Melantrichova street** leads directly to the New Town's Wenceslas Square (see page 72), passing the craft-packed Havelská Market (see page 58) along the way.

Twenty-Seven Crosses

Embedded in the pavement at the base of the Old Town Hall tower (near the snack stand), you'll see white inlaid crosses marking the spot where 27 Protestant nobles, merchants, and intellectuals were beheaded in 1621 after rebelling against the Catholic Hapsburgs. The execution ended Czech independence for 300 years—and it's still one of the grimmest chapters in its history.

▲▲Astronomical Clock

Join the gang for the striking of the hour on the Town Hall clock (daily 8:00–21:00, until 20:00 in winter). As you wait, see if you

can figure out how the clock works.

With revolving disks, celestial symbols, and sweeping hands, this clock keeps several versions of time. Two outer rings show the hour: Bohemian time (gold Gothic numbers on black background, counts from sunset—find the zero, between 23 and 1...supposedly the time of tonight's sunset) and modern time (24 Roman numerals, XII at the top being noon, XII at the bottom being midnight). Five hundred years ago, everything revolved around the earth (the fixed middle background—with Prague marking the center, of course).

To indicate the times of sunrise and sunset, arcing lines and moving spheres combine with the big hand (a sweeping golden sun) and the little hand (a moon that spins to show various stages). Look for the orbits of the sun and moon as they rise through day (the blue zone) and night (the black zone).

If this seems complex to us, it must have been a marvel 500 years ago. Because the clock was heavily damaged during World War II, much of what you see today is a reconstruction. The circle below (added in the 19th century) shows the signs of the zodiac, scenes from the seasons of a rural peasant's life, and a ring of saints' names—one for each day of the year, with a marker showing today's special saint (at top).

Four statues flanking the clock represent the 15th-century outlook on time and prejudices. A Turk with a mandolin symbolizes hedonism, a Jewish moneylender is greed, and the figure staring into a mirror stands for vanity. All these worldly goals are vain in the face of Death, whose hourglass reminds us that our time is unavoidably running out.

At the top of the hour (don't blink—the show is pretty quick): First, Death tips his hourglass and pulls the cord, ringing the bell;

then the windows open and the 12 apostles parade by, acknowledging the gang of onlookers; then the rooster crows; and then the hour is rung. The hour is often off because of daylight saving time (completely senseless to 15th-century clockmakers). At the top of the next hour, stand under the tower—protected by a line of banner-wielding concert salespeople in powdered wigs—and watch the tourists.

Clock Tour and Tower Climb: The main TI, to the left of the Astronomical Clock, contains an information desk and sells tickets for these two options: zipping up the Old Town Hall tower via elevator (60 Kč, Tue–Sun 9:00–17:30, Mon 11:00–17:30, fine views); or taking a 45-minute tour of the Old Town Hall, which includes a Gothic chapel and a close-up look at the inner guts of the Astronomical Clock (plus its statues of the 12 apostles; 50 Kč, 2/hr).

▲Týn Church

Though this church has a long history, it's most notable for its 200-year-stint as the leading church of the Hussite movement (generally open daily 10:00–13:00 & 15:00–17:00). It was Catholic before the Hussites, and returned to Catholicism after the Hussites were defeated. As if to insult Hus and his doctrine of simplicity, the church's once elegant and pure Gothic columns are now encrusted with noisy Baroque altars. While Gothic, the church interior is uncharacteristically bright because of its clear Baroque windowpanes and whitewash. Read the church's story (posted in English, rear-left side) for a Catholic spin on the church's events—told with barely a mention of Hus. The fine 16th-century carved John the Baptist altar (right aisle) is worth a look. As you enjoy this church, try to ignore its unwelcoming signs—other than the Catholic-slanted history, the only English words you'll see here are commands that tell you what not to do.

Outside, on the side of the church facing Celetná street, find a statue of St. Mary resting on a temporary column against the wall. The Catholics are still waiting for a chance to reinstall St. Mary in the middle of the Old Town Square, where she stood for about 250 years until being torn down in 1918 by a mob of anti-Hapsburg (and therefore anti-Catholic) demonstrators.

Behind Týn Church

▲Ungelt Courtyard (Týnský Dvůr)—Ever since the Old Town was established, the Ungelt courtyard—located directly behind the Old Town Square's Týn Church—has served as a hostel for foreign merchants, much like a Turkish caravanserai. Here the merchants (usually German) would store their goods and pay taxes before setting up stalls on the Old Town Square. Notice that there are only two entrances into the complex, for the purpose of guaranteeing the safety of goods and merchants. After decades of disuse, the courtyard had fallen into such disrepair by the 1980s that authorities considered demolishing it. Marvelously restored a few years ago, the Ungelt courtyard is now the most pleasant area in the Old Town for an outdoor coffee (such as at Ebel Coffee House—see page 132), sorting through wooden crafts, and paging through English books (at Anagram Bookshop, described on page 139). Although Prague has undoubtedly lost some of its dreamy character to the booming tourist industry, places such as Ungelt stand as testimony to the miracles that money can work. Had the communists stayed in power for a few more years, Ungelt would have been a black hole by now. Ungelt also reminds us that Prague, for most of its history, has been a cosmopolitan center quite alien to the rest of the country.

House at the Golden Ring (Dům u Zlatého Prstenu)—This medieval townhouse displays a delightful collection of 20th-century Czech art. Its exterior has rectangular sgraffiti etchings (designs scratched out of one layer, revealing a different-colored layer beneath). Since 1900, Czech artists have been refining the subtle differences between dream, myth, and ideal. The English descriptions of each room psychoanalyze this demanding art, and recall the fact that Prague in the 1930s and 1960s was at the forefront of the European avant-garde.

Notice the absence of Socialist Realism: The artists exhibited here chose deeply personal means of expression over regime-sponsored proclamations of universal optimism (90 Kč, Tue–Sun 10:00–18:00, closed Mon, just left of the entry into Ungelt courtyard as you approach it from the Old Town Square, Týnská 6, tel. 224-827-0224, www.citygalleryprague.cz). There's a lively-with-students café in the courtyard.

Church of St. James (Kostel Sv. Jakuba)—Perhaps the most beautiful church in the Old Town, the Church of St. James is just behind Ungelt courtyard. The Minorite Order has occupied this church and the adjacent monastery almost as long as merchants have occupied Ungelt. A medieval city was a complex phenomenon: Side-by-side, there existed commerce, brothels, and a life of contemplation. (I guess it's not that much different from today.)

Artistically, St. James (along with the Church of the Ascension of St. Mary at Strahov Monastery—see page 96) is a stunning example of how simple Gothic spaces could be transformed into sumptuous feasts of Baroque decoration. The blue light in the altar highlights one of Prague's most venerated treasures—the bejeweled Madonna Pietatis. Above the *pietà*, as if held aloft by hummingbird-like angels, is a painting of the martyrdom of St. James (free, daily 9:30–12:00 & 14:00–16:00).

As you leave, find the black and shriveled-up arm with clenched fingers (15 feet above and to the left of the door). According to legend, a thief attempted to rob the Madonna Pietatis from the altar, but his hand was frozen the moment he touched the statue. The monks had to cut off the arm in order for it to let go. The desiccated arm now hangs here as a warning—and the entire delightful story is posted nearby in English.

North of the Old Town Square, near the River

▲▲**Museum of Medieval Art**—The St. Agnes Convent houses the Museum of Medieval Art in Bohemia and Central Europe (1200–1550). The 14th century was Prague's Golden Age, and the religious art displayed in this Gothic space is a testament to the rich cultural life of the period. Each exquisite piece is well-lit and thoughtfully described in English. Follow the arrows on a chronological sweep through Gothic art history. The various Madonnas and saints were gathered here from churches all over Central Europe (100 Kč, Tue–Sun 10:00–18:00, closed Mon, two blocks northeast of the Spanish Synagogue, along the river at Anežská 12).

Princess Agnes founded this Clarist convent in the 13th century as the first hospital in Prague. Agnes was canonized by Pope John Paul II (who loved to promote the Slavic faithful) in 1989. Since local celebrations of her sainthood on November 26 coincided with the Velvet Revolution (the peaceful overthrow of the Communist government in 1989), Agnes has since been regarded as the patron of the renascent Czech democracy (you'll see her on the 50-Kč bill).

On Celetná Street, Toward the New Town

Celetná, a pedestrian-only street, is a convenient and relatively untouristy way to get from the Old Town Square to the New Town (specifically the Municipal House and Powder Tower, described on page 80). Along the way, at the square called Ovocný Trh, you'll find these sights.

Museum of Czech Cubism—Cubism was a potent force in Prague in the early 20th century. The fascinating Museum of Czech Cubism in the Black Madonna House (Dům u Černé Matky Boží) offers the complete Cubist experience: Cubist architecture (stand back and see how masterfully it makes its statement while mixing with its neighbors...then get up close and study the details), a great café (upstairs), a ground-floor shop, and, of course, a museum. On three floors, you'll see paintings, furniture, graphics, and architectural drafts by Czech Cubists. This building is an example of what has long been considered the greatest virtue of Prague's architects:

the ability to adapt their grandiose plans to the existing cityscape (museum entry-100 Kč, Tue–Sun 10:00–18:00, closed Mon, corner of Celetná and Ovocný Trh at Ovocný Trh 19, tel. 224-301-003). If you're not interested in touring the museum itself, consider a drink in the similarly decorated upstairs Grand Café Orient (see page 132).

Estates Theatre (Stavovské Divadlo)—Built by a nobleman in the 1770s, this Classicist building—gently opening its greenish walls onto Ovocný Trh—was the prime opera venue in Prague at a time when an Austrian prodigy was changing the course of music. Wolfgang Amadeus Mozart premiered *Don Giovanni* in this building, and personally directed many of his works here. Prague's theatergoers would whistle arias from Mozart's works on the streets the morning after they premiered. Today, part of the National Theatre group, the Estates Theatre, continues to produce *The Marriage of Figaro, Don Giovanni,* and occasionally *The Magic Flute.* For a more intimate encounter with Mozart, go to Villa Bertramka (see page 144).

On Melantrichova

▲**Havelská Market**—Skinny, tourist-clogged Melantrichova street leads directly from the Old Town Square's Astronomical Clock to the bottom of Wenceslas Square. But even along this most crowded of streets, a genuine bit of Prague remains: Havelská Market, offering crafts and produce. The open-air market was set up in the 13th century for the German trading community. Though heavy on souvenirs these days, the market still keeps hungry locals and vagabonds fed cheaply. It's ideal for a healthy snack; merchants are happy to sell a single vegetable or piece of fruit; and you'll find a washing fountain and plenty of inviting benches midway down the street. The market is also a fun place to browse for crafts. It's a homegrown, homemade kind of place; you'll often be dealing with the actual artist or farmer (market open daily 9:00–18:00, produce best on weekdays; more souvenirs, puppets, and toys on weekends). The many cafés and little eateries

The Old Town

Czechs and Indians

The German writer Karl May (who did not visit America until 1908, very late in his life) used the time he spent in prison for fraud to write stories about the fictional, noble Apache chief Winnetou and his German friend, Old Shatterhand—and ever since, the Czechs have been obsessed with Native Americans. Most kids spend summers in camps (as Boy Scouts and Girl Scouts), where they learn about the Native Americans' respect for nature, survival skills in the wilderness, courage, and the idealized noble spirit. A tune celebrating the Little Big Horn victory is one of the most popular sagas sung at campfires around the country. When Lance Armstrong, the famous cancer survivor, visited Prague's oncology ward in July 2004—just days after his unprecedented sixth consecutive victory in the rigorous Tour de France—child cancer patients rewarded their idol with the Native American name "Fast Wind." Prague's Náprstek Museum of Asian, African, and American Cultures actually displays attire worn by Lakota Chief Sitting Bull (Betlémské Náměstí 1).

circling the market offer a fine and relaxing vantage point from which to view the action.

Bethlehem Square (Betlémské Náměstí)

This sight sits on the charming, relatively quiet Bethlehem Square (Betlémské Náměstí), a pleasantly untouristy chunk of Old Town real estate.

Bethlehem Chapel (Betlémské Kaple)—Emperor Charles IV founded the first university in Central Europe, and this was the university's chapel. In about the year 1400, priest and professor Jan Hus preached from the pulpit here (see sidebar on page 51). While meant primarily for students and faculty, Hus' Masses were open to the public. Standing-room-only crowds of more than 3,000 were the norm when Hus preached. Hus proposed that the congregation should be more involved in worship (e.g., actually drink the wine at Communion) and have better access to the word of God through services and scriptures written in the people's language, not in Latin. The stimulating, controversial ideas debated at the university spread throughout the city and, after Hus' death at the stake, sparked the bloodiest civil war in Czech history.

Each subsequent age has interpreted Hus to its liking: For the Protestants, Hus was the founder of the first Protestant church (though he was actually an ardent Catholic); for the revolutionaries, this critic of the power of the Church was a proponent of social equality; for the nationalists, this Czech preacher was the defender

Prague's Charles University

Back in the 1300s, Charles University students studied the arts first, and only then proceeded to one of the other three faculties (medicine, law, and theology), of which theology was the most prestigious. Teaching was done in Latin, and the student body was cosmopolitan—Czechs made up only a fourth of all students.

During the chaotic period of Hussite reforms in the early 1400s, the university's policies were changed to give more power to the Czechs. In protest, many foreign students and professors left Prague and founded the first German university in Leipzig. Celebrated by Czech nationalists as a victory over foreigners, the new policies in fact reduced Charles University from a European center of learning to a provincial institution.

In the 1600s, the predominantly Protestant university was handed over to the Jesuits. But in the 1780s, Hapsburg Emperor Josef II abolished the Jesuit order, opened the university to non-Catholics, and changed the language of instruction from Latin to German. Czechs did not win the freedom to study in their own language until 1882, when the university split into two separate schools (the German school ceased to exist in 1945).

Today, the Old Town continues to live a double life as both a commercial center and a university campus. Though lined with souvenir stalls outside, many buildings hold classrooms that have been animated by lecturers for centuries. Some of the Old Town's most hidden courtyards have provided Czech scholars with their two most essential needs: good beer, and space for an inspiring conversation.

Charles University, always a center of Czech political thinking, has incited trouble and uprisings. Jan Hus initiated the reform of the Church here; the revolutions of 1618 and 1848 were sparked by university minds; and in the modern era, students rose up against totalitarian regimes in 1939, 1948, and 1968. The Germans closed down all Czech universities for the duration of

of the language; and for the communists, Hus was the first ideologue to preach the gospel of socialism.

Today's chapel is a 1950s reconstruction of the original. Try the unbelievably bad acoustics inside—they demonstrate the sloppy work sponsored by the communists (tiny upstairs exhibit and big chapel with English-info sheets available; entry-40 Kč; April–Oct daily 10:00–18:30; Nov–March Tue–Sun 10:00–17:30, closed Mon and frequently during university functions; Betlémské Náměstí, tel. 224-248-595).

The Klub Architektů restaurant, across from the entry, has a cave-like atmosphere inside, straw-chair seating outside, and good

World War II. Later, the communists fired professors unwilling to follow the party line and replaced them with applicants chosen on the basis of class background rather than ability. The Velvet Revolution, which swept communists out of power in November 1989, started as a student demonstration.

Although many professors returned to their classrooms after 1989, the education system itself has yet to escape the legacy of the authoritarian regimes. From an early age, students are taught to memorize rather than to think independently, knowledge is measured by facts rather than by the ability to use them, and even at the university level, few students dare to challenge the professor's view.

Charles University still attracts the best Czech and Slovak students. University education is, as in most of Europe, free in the Czech Republic, and student housing is heavily subsidized. You would expect that free admission would make education more accessible to students from poorer backgrounds. This is not always true. Without enough money in the education system, the state doesn't have the means to build more schools. The demand exceeds the supply, so only a third of the people who apply to high school ("gymnasium") are accepted, and only half of university applicants are admitted. Students from better-educated backgrounds tend to do better in a system that begins selecting students from the age of 10.

Teachers are poorly paid (even a tenured university professor barely gets by), and libraries are under-funded. Consequently, even students have campaigned for the introduction of moderate fees that would improve access to education and allow professors to spend less time on side jobs and more time on lecture preparation and research. The final verdict on school fees lies with the politicians, who often pay more attention to public opinion than to students and teachers.

food both in and out (see page 127).

The tiny **Family Museum of Postcards** is around the corner on Liliová street, which connects Bethlehem Square with Karlova. After learning how the Austrian Empire invented the postcard, you can buy your own early-20th-century specimen (entry-40 Kč, Tue–Sun 11:00–19:00, closed Mon, tel. 222-222-519).

From Old Town Square to Charles Bridge

Karlova Street—Karlova street winds through medieval Prague from the Old Town Square to the Charles Bridge (it zigzags...just follow the crowds). This is a commercial gauntlet, and it's here that the touristy feeding frenzy of Prague is most ugly. Street signs keep you on track, and *Karlův most* signs point to the bridge. Obviously, you'll find few good values on this drag. Two favorite places providing a quick break from the crowds are just a few steps off Karlova on Husova street: **Cream and Dream Ice Cream** (Husova 12) and **U Zlatého Tygra,** a colorful pub that serves great, cheap beer in a classic and untouristy setting (Husova 17; see page 126).

▲**Klementinum**—The Czech Republic's massive National Library borders touristy Karlova street. The contrast could not be starker: Step out of the most souvenir-packed stretch of Eastern Europe, and enter into the meditative silence of Eastern Europe's biggest library. The Klementinum was built to house a college in the 1600s by the Jesuits, who had been invited to Prague by the Catholic Hapsburgs to offset the influence of the predominantly Protestant Charles University nearby. The building was transformed into a library in the early 1700s, when the Jesuits took firm control of the university. Their books, together with the collections of several noble families (written in all possible languages...except Czech), form the nucleus of the National and University Library, which is now six-million-volumes strong. (Note that the Klementinum's Chapel of Mirrors is a popular venue for evening concerts.)

Library Tour and Tower Climb: While much of the Klementinum building is simply a vast library, its magnificent original Baroque Hall and Observatory Tower are open to the public by tour only (45 min, in English). You'll belly up to a banister at the end of the ornate library with its many centuries-old books, fancy ceilings with Jesuit leaders and saints overseeing the pursuit of knowledge, and Josef II—the enlightened Hapsburg emperor—looking on from the far end. Then you'll climb the Observatory Tower, learning how early astronomers charted the skies over Prague. The tour finishes with a grand Prague view from the top (100 Kč, departs on the hour Mon–Fri 14:00–19:00, Sat–Sun 10:00–19:00, shorter hours off-season, tel. 221-663-165 or 603-231-241; strolling down Karlova, turn at the intersection with Liliová through an archway into the Klementinum's courtyard).

▲▲▲Charles Bridge (Karlův Most)

Among Prague's defining landmarks, this much-loved bridge offers one of the most pleasant and entertaining 500-plus-yard strolls in Europe. Enjoy the bridge at different times of day. The bridge is most memorable early—before the crowds—and late, during that photographers' "magic hour" when the sun is low in the sky.

Charles Bridge Reconstruction

Talked about for many years, financed by the city of Prague, and scheduled to last over a decade, the long-overdue reconstruction of the Charles Bridge finally began in the summer of 2007, days after people celebrated the bridge's 650-year anniversary.

Aware of the blow that closing the entire bridge would deal to the tourist industry, the city chose a more costly and technologically challenging "chessboard" strategy. With this plan, only a partial section is closed at any time, allowing people to still use the bridge for crossing over. Moreover, to give everyone the opportunity to peek inside the centuries-old structure, and thus turn the bridge renovation into Prague's new attraction, the mayor requested (to the dismay of many archaeologists) that the construction site be at all times surrounded only by light, transparent fences.

The reconstruction is planned in two stages. In the first major stage—preceded by archaeological excavations and scheduled to be completed by 2010—gas lighting will return to the bridge, and the sewage system, insulation, and pavement will be installed. In the next stage, many of the deteriorated sandstone pieces will be replaced by new ones. In the past, builders often chose poor-quality sandstone, and this is precisely the mistake current workers want to avoid. To minimize impact on the nearby areas, most of the building materials will be transported by river.

At the Old Town end of the bridge, in a little square, is a statue of the bridge's namesake, **Charles IV.** This Holy Roman

Emperor (Karlo Quatro—the guy on the 100-Kč bill) ruled his vast empire from Prague in the 14th century. He's holding a contract establishing Prague's university (see sidebar on page 60), the first in Northern Europe. This statue was erected in 1848 to celebrate the university's 500th birthday. The women around Charles' pedestal symbolize the university's four subjects: the arts, medicine, law, and theology. (From the corner by the busy street, many think the emperor's silhouette makes it appear as if he's peeing on the tourists. Which reminds me, public WCs are in the passageway opposite the statue.)

Bridges had been built on this spot before, as the remnant

tower from Judith Bridge testifies (see the smaller of the two bridge towers at the far end). All were washed away by floods. After a major flood in 1342, Emperor Charles IV decided to commission an entirely new structure rather than repair the old one. Until the 19th century, this was Prague's only bridge that crossed the river.

Charles Bridge has long fueled a local love of legends—including one tied to numbers. According to medieval record, the bridge's foundation was laid in 1357. In the late 1800s, an amateur astronomer noticed a curious combination of numbers, leading to a popular theory about Charles IV. Charles is known to have been interested in numerology and astrology, and was likely aware of the significance of this date: the ninth of July at 5:31 in the morning. Written out in digits—as the year, month, day, hour, and minute—it's a numerical palindrome: 135797531. It's said that Charles must have chosen that precise moment (which also coincides with a favorable positioning of the earth and Saturn) to lay the foundation stone of the bridge. Further "corroboration" of this remarkable hypothesis was provided by the discovery that the end of the bridge on the Old Town side aligns perfectly with the tomb of St. Vitus (in the cathedral across the river) and the setting sun at summer solstice. In the absence of accurate 14th-century records, this intriguing proposition has delighted the modern Czech imagination. The number "135797531" is bound to remain celebrated as the adopted birthday of Prague's most beloved structure.

The magically aligned spot on the Old Town side is now occupied by the **bridge tower,** considered one of the finest Gothic gates anywhere. Contemplate the fine sculpture on the Old Town side of the tower, showing the 14th-century hierarchy of kings, bishops, and angels. Climbing the tower rewards you with wonderful views over the bridge (40 Kč, daily 10:00–19:00, as late as 22:00 in summer).

In the 17th century, there were no statues on the bridge—only a **cross,** which you can still see as part of the third sculpture on the right. The gilded Hebrew inscription celebrating Christ was paid for by a fine imposed on a Jew for mocking the cross.

The bronze Baroque statue depicting **John of Nepomuk**—a saint of the Czech people—draws a crowd (look for the guy with the five golden stars around his head, near the Little Quarter end of the bridge on the right). John of Nepomuk was a 14th-century priest to whom the queen confessed all her sins. According to a

17th-century legend, the king wanted to know his wife's secrets, but Father John dutifully refused to tell. He was tortured and eventually killed by being tossed off the bridge. When he hit the water, five stars appeared. The shiny plaque at the base of the statue depicts the heave-ho. Devout pilgrims—from Mexico and Moravia alike—touch the

engraving to make a wish come true. You get only one chance in life for this wish, so think carefully before you touch the saint. Notice the date on the inscription: This oldest statue on the bridge was unveiled in 1683, on the supposed 300th anniversary of the martyr's death.

The reason for John of Nepomuk's immense Baroque popularity and 1729 canonization remains contested. Some historians claim that at a time when the Czechs were being forcibly converted to Catholicism, Nepomuk became the rallying national symbol ("We will convert, but our patron must be Czech"). Others argue that Nepomuk was a propaganda figure used by Catholic leaders to give locals an alternative to Jan Hus. You'll find statues like this one on squares and bridges throughout the country. The actual spot of the much-talked-about heave-ho is a few steps farther away from the castle—find the five points of the Orthodox cross between two statues on the bridge railing.

Most of the other Charles Bridge statues date from the late 1600s and early 1700s. Today, half of them are replicas—the originals are in city museums, out of the polluted air. At the far end of Charles Bridge, you reach the **Little Quarter.** For sights in this neighborhood, see page 85.

▲▲▲Jewish Quarter (Josefov)

Prague's Jewish Quarter neighborhood and its well-presented, profoundly moving museum tell the story of this region's Jews. For me, this is the most interesting collection of Jewish sights in Europe, and well worth seeing. The Jewish Quarter is an easy walk from Old Town Square, up delightful Pařížská street (next to the green-domed Church of St. Nicholas).

As the Nazis decimated Jewish communities in the region, Prague's Jews were allowed to collect and archive their treasures here. While the archivists were ultimately killed in concentration

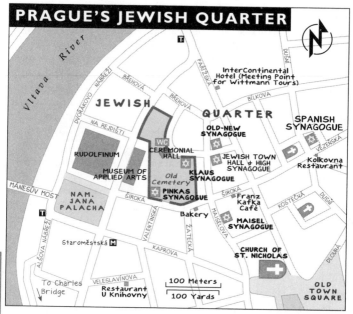

PRAGUE'S JEWISH QUARTER

InterContinental Hotel (Meeting Point for Wittmann Tours)

JEWISH QUARTER

OLD-NEW SYNAGOGUE

SPANISH SYNAGOGUE

RUDOLFINUM

CEREMONIAL HALL

JEWISH TOWN HALL + HIGH SYNAGOGUE

Kolkovna Restaurant

MUSEUM OF APPLIED ARTS

Old Cemetery

KLAUS SYNAGOGUE

PINKAS SYNAGOGUE

NAM. JANA PALACHA

Franz Kafka Café

Bakery

MAISEL SYNAGOGUE

Staroměstská

CHURCH OF ST. NICHOLAS

To Charles Bridge

Restaurant U Knihovny

100 Meters

100 Yards

OLD TOWN SQUARE

camps, their work survives. Seven sights scattered over a three-block area make up the tourists' Jewish Quarter. Six of the sights—all except the Old-New Synagogue—are called "The Museum" and are covered by one admission ticket. Your ticket comes with a map that locates the sights and lists admission appointments—the times you'll be let in if it's very busy. (Ignore the times unless it's really crowded.) You'll notice plenty of security (stepped up since 9/11).

Cost, Hours, Tours: To visit all seven sights, you'll pay 500 Kč (300 Kč for the six sights that make up the Museum, plus 200 Kč for the Old-New Synagogue—hours on page 70). Museum sights open April–Oct Sun–Fri 9:00–18:00; Nov–March Sun–Fri 9:00–16:30; closed year-round on Sat—the Jewish Sabbath—and on Jewish holidays. Each sight is thoroughly and thoughtfully described in English, making a guided tour unnecessary for most visitors. Occasional guided walks in English start at the Maisel Synagogue (50 Kč, 3 hours, tel. 222-317-191).

Cemetery: The Old Jewish Cemetery—with its tightly packed, topsy-turvy tombstones—is, for many, the most evocative part of the experience. Unfortunately, there's no ticket just to see the cemetery, and they've closed off most free viewpoints. If the 300-Kč museum ticket is too steep for you and you just want a free peek at the famous cemetery, climb the steps to the covered porch of the Ceremonial Hall (but don't rest your chin on the treacherous railing).

Planning Your Time: The most logical start (if you'll be seeing everything) is to buy your ticket at Pinkas Synagogue and visit this most powerful memorial of the museum complex first. From there, walk through the Old Jewish Cemetery, which leads to the Ceremonial Hall and Klaus Synagogue. After visiting those, head over to the Old-New Synagogue, have a coffee break (Pekařství bakery or Franz Kafka Café, both described on page 130, are nearby). Next, visit the museum-like Maisel Synagogue, and finally the Spanish Synagogue. (Note that Prague's fine Museum of Medieval Art, described on page 57, is only a few blocks from the Spanish Synagogue.)

Art Nouveau and the New Josefov: Going from sight to sight in the Jewish Quarter, you'll walk through perhaps Europe's finest Art Nouveau neighborhood. Make a point to enjoy the circa-1900 buildings with their marvelous trimmings and oh-wow entryways. While today's modern grid plan has replaced the higgledy-piggledy medieval streets of old, Široká ("Wide Street") was and remains the main street of the ghetto.

Pinkas Synagogue (Pinkasova Synagóga)

A site of Jewish worship for 400 years, this synagogue is a poignant memorial to the victims of the Nazis. The walls are covered

with the handwritten names of 77,297 Czech Jews who were sent from here to the gas chambers at Auschwitz and other camps. (As you ponder this sad sight, you'll hear the somber reading of the names alternating with a cantor singing the Psalms.) Hometowns are in gold and family names are in red, followed in black by the individual's first name, birthday, and last date known to be alive. Notice that families generally perished together. Extermination camps are listed on the east wall. Climb eight steps into the women's gallery. When the communists moved in, they closed the synagogue and erased virtually everything. With freedom, in 1989, the Pinkas Synagogue was reopened and the names were rewritten. (The names in poor condition near the ceiling are original.) Note that large tour groups may disturb this small memorial's compelling atmosphere between 10:00 and 12:00.

Upstairs is the **Terezín Children's Art Exhibit** (very well-described in English), displaying art drawn by Jewish children who were imprisoned at Terezín Concentration Camp and later perished. Terezín makes an emotionally moving day trip from Prague; it's easily accessible by local bus (see page 168) or tour bus (see page 46).

The Old Town

Prague's Jewish Heritage

The Jewish people from the Holy Land (today's Israel) were dispersed by the Romans 2,000 years ago. Over the centuries, their culture survived in enclaves throughout the world: "The Torah was their sanctuary which no army could destroy." Jews first came to Prague in the 10th century. The Jewish Quarter's main intersection (Maiselova and Široká streets) was the meeting point of two medieval trade routes.

During the Crusades in the 12th century, the pope declared that Jews and Christians should not live together. Jews had to wear yellow badges, and their quarter was walled in. It became a ghetto. In the 16th and 17th centuries, Prague had one of the biggest ghettos in Europe, with 11,000 inhabitants. Within its six gates, Prague's Jewish Quarter was a gaggle of 200 wooden buildings. It was said that "Jews nested rather than dwelled."

The "outcasts" of Christianity relied mainly on profits from money lending (forbidden to Christians) and community solidarity to survive. While their money bought them protection (the kings highly taxed Jewish communities), it was often also a curse.

Old Jewish Cemetery (Starý Židovský Hřbitov)

From the Pinkas Synagogue, you enter one of the most wistful scenes in Europe—Prague's Old Jewish Cemetery. As you wander among 12,000 evocative tombstones, remember that from 1439 until 1787, this was the only burial ground allowed for the Jews of Prague. Tombs were piled atop each other because of limited space, the sheer number of graves, and the Jewish belief that the body should not be moved once buried. With its many lay-

ers, the cemetery became a small plateau. And as things settled over time, the tombstones got crooked. The Hebrew word for cemetery means "House of Life." Many Jews believe that death is the gateway into the next world. Pebbles on the tombstones are "flowers of the desert," reminiscent of the old days when rocks were placed upon the sand gravesite to keep the body covered.

Throughout Europe, when times got tough and Christian debts to the Jewish community mounted, entire Jewish communities were evicted or killed.

In the 1780s, Emperor Josef II, motivated more by economic concerns than philanthropy, eased much of the discrimination against Jews. In 1848, the Jewish Quarter's walls were torn down, and the neighborhood—named Josefov in honor of the emperor who provided this small measure of tolerance—was incorporated as a district of Old Town.

In 1897, ramshackle Josefov was razed and replaced by a new modern town—the original 31 streets and 220 buildings became 10 streets and 83 buildings. This is what you'll see today: an attractive neighborhood of pretty, mostly Art Nouveau buildings, with a few surviving historic Jewish structures. By the 1930s, Prague's Jewish community was hugely successful, thanks largely to their ability to appreciate talent—a rare quality in the small Central European countries whose citizens, as the great Austrian novelist Robert Musil put it, "were equal in their unwillingness to let one another get ahead."

Of the 120,000 Jews living in the area in 1939, just 10,000 survived the Holocaust to see liberation in 1945. Today, only a few thousand Jews remain in Prague...but the legacy of their ancestors lives on.

Wedged under some of the pebbles are scraps of paper that contain prayers.

Ceremonial Hall (Obřadní Síň)

Leaving the cemetery, you'll find a Neo-Romanesque mortuary house built in 1911 for the purification of the dead (on left). It's filled with a worthwhile exhibition, described in English, on Jewish medicine, death, and burial traditions. A series of crude but instructive paintings (hanging on walls throughout the house) show how the "burial brotherhood" took care of the ill and buried the dead. As all are equal before God, the rich and poor alike were buried in embroidered linen shrouds similar to the one you'll see on display.

Klaus Synagogue (Klauzová Synagóga)

This 17th-century synagogue (also near the cemetery exit) is the final wing of a museum devoted to Jewish religious practices. Exhibits on the ground floor explain the Jewish calendar of festivals. The central case displays a Torah (the first five books of the Bible) and solid silver pointers used when reading—necessary since the Torah is not to be touched. Upstairs is an exhibit on the rituals of Jewish life (circumcisions, bar and bat mitzvahs, weddings, kosher eating, and so on).

Old-New Synagogue (Staronová Synagóga)

For more than 700 years, this has been the most important synagogue and the central building in Josefov. Standing like a bomb-hardened bunker, it feels as though it has survived plenty of hard times. Stairs take you down to the street level of the 13th century and into the Gothic interior. Built in 1270, it's the oldest synagogue in Eastern Europe (separate 200-Kč admission includes worthwhile 10-minute tour—ask about it, Sun–Thu 9:30–18:00, Fri 9:30–17:00, closed Sat). Snare an attendant, who is likely to love showing visitors around. The steep admission keeps many away, but even if you decide not to pay, you can see the exterior and a bit of the interior. (Go ahead...pop in and crane your cheapskate neck.)

The lobby (down the stairs, where you show your ticket) has two fortified old lockers—in which the most heavily taxed community in medieval Prague stored its money in anticipation of the taxman's arrival. As 13th-century Jews were not allowed to build, the synagogue was erected by Christians (who also built the St. Agnes Convent nearby). The builders were good at four-ribbed vaulting, but since that resulted in a cross, it wouldn't work for a synagogue. Instead, they made the ceiling using clumsy five-ribbed vaulting.

The interior is pure 1300s. The Shrine of the Ark in front is the focus of worship. The holiest place in the synagogue, it holds the sacred scrolls of the Torah. The old rabbi's chair to the right

remains empty (notice the thin black chain) out of respect. The red banner is a copy of the one that the Jewish community carried through town during medieval parades. Notice the yellow-pointed hat within the Star of David (on the banner), which the pope ordered all Jewish men to wear in 1215. Twelve is a popular number (e.g., windows), because it symbolizes the 12 tribes of Israel. The horizontal slit-like windows are an 18th-century addition, allowing women to view the male-only services.

Maisel Synagogue (Maiselova Synagóga)

This synagogue was built as a private place of worship for the Maisel family during the 16th-century Golden Age of Prague's Jews. Maisel, the financier of the Hapsburg king, had lots of money. The synagogue's interior is decorated Neo-Gothic. In World War II, it served as a warehouse for the accumulated treasures of decimated Jewish communities that Hitler planned to use for his "Museum of the Extinct Jewish Race." The one-room exhibit shows a thousand years of Jewish history in Bohemia and Moravia. Well-explained in English, topics include the origin of the Star of David, Jewish mysticism, the history of discrimination, and the creation of Prague's ghetto. Notice the eastern wall, with the Holy Ark containing the scroll of the Torah. The central case shows the silver ornamental Torah crowns that capped the scroll.

Spanish Synagogue (Španělská Synagóga)

Displays of Jewish history through the 18th, 19th, and tumultuous 20th centuries continue in this ornate, Moorish-style synagogue built in the 1800s. The upstairs is particularly intriguing, with circa-1900 photos of Josefov, an exhibit on the fascinating story of this museum and its relationship with the Nazi regime, and life in Terezín. The Winter Synagogue (also upstairs) shows a trove of silver worshipping aids gathered from countryside Jewish neighborhoods that were depopulated in the early 1940s, thus giving a sense of what the Nazis stockpiled.

THE NEW TOWN

Nové Město

Enough of pretty, medieval Prague—let's leap into the modern era. The New Town, with Wenceslas Square as its focal point, is today's urban Prague. This part of the city offers bustling boulevards and interesting neighborhoods. The New Town is the best place to view Prague's remarkable Art Nouveau art and architecture and to learn more about its recent communist past.

▲▲Wenceslas Square Self-Guided Walk

More a broad boulevard than a square (until recently, trams rattled up and down its park-like median strip), this city landmark is named for King Wenceslas—featured both on the 20-Kč coin and the equestrian statue that stands at the top of the boulevard. Wenceslas Square (Václavské Náměstí) functions as a stage for modern Czech history: The creation of the Czechoslovak state was celebrated here in 1918; in 1968, the Soviets suppressed huge popular demonstrations here; and, in 1989, more than 300,000 Czechs and Slovaks converged here to claim their freedom.

• *Starting near the Wenceslas statue at the top (Metro: Muzeum), look to the building crowning the top of the square...*

National Museum
(Národní Muzeum)

The museum stands grandly at the top. While its collection is dull, the building offers a powerful view, and the interior is richly decorated in the Czech Revival Neo-Renaissance style that heralded the 19th-century rebirth of the Czech nation. The light-colored patches in the

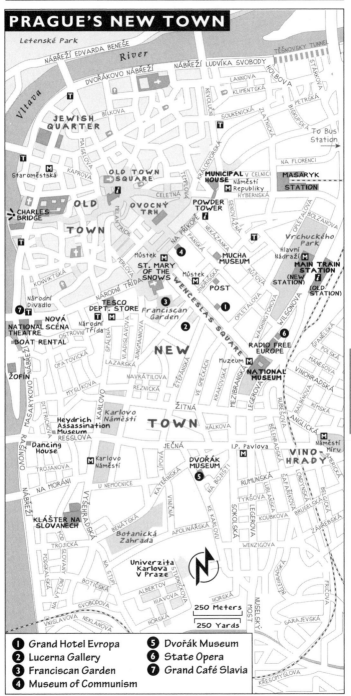

PRAGUE'S NEW TOWN

Letenské Park

NÁBŘEŽÍ EDVARDA BENEŠE

River

DVOŘÁKOVO NÁBŘEŽÍ

NÁBŘEŽÍ LUDVÍKA SVOBODY

TĚČNOVSKÝ TUNNEL

NÁBŘEŽÍ EDVARDA BENEŠE

LANNOVA

HOLBOVA

STÁRKOVA

KLIMENTSKÁ

REVOLUČNÍ

SOUKENICKÁ

ZLATNICKÁ

BISKUPSKÁ

PETRSKÁ

Vltava

JEWISH QUARTER

BÍLKOVA

KRÁLODVORSKÁ

NA FLORENCI

To Bus Station

MAISELOVA

KAPROVA

Staroměstská

OLD TOWN SQUARE

MUNICIPAL HOUSE

V CELNICI

Náměstí Republiky

MASARYK STATION

CELETNÁ

HYBERNSKÁ

OPLETALOVA

BOLZANOVA

CHARLES BRIDGE

OLD   TOWN

OVOCNÝ TRH

POWDER TOWER

PELANTRICH

NA PŘÍKOPĚ

NEKAZANKA

SENOVAZNÁ

Vrchuckého Park

Hlavní Nádraží

MAIN TRAIN STATION (NEW STATION)

Můstek

MUCHA MUSEUM

PANSKÁ

RŮZOVÁ

(OLD STATION)

ST. MARY OF THE SNOWS

Můstek

POST

JINDŘIŠSKÁ

OPLETALOVA

NÁRODNÍ TŘÍDA

PERLOVA

KONVIKTSKÁ

Národní Divadlo

TESCO DEPT. STORE

Franciscan Garden

WENCESLAS SQUARE

WILSONOVA

ŠPANĚLSKÁ

NOVÁ SCÉNA THEATRE

Národní Třída

OSTROVNÍ

VLADISLAVOVA

JUNGMANNOVA

NATIONAL THEATRE

SPÁLENÁ

NEW

VE SMEČKÁCH

RADIO FREE EUROPE

POLSKÁ

BOAT RENTAL

LAZARSKÁ

Muzeum

MÁNESOVA

MASARYKOVO NÁBŘEŽÍ

OPATOVICKÁ

ŠTĚPÁNSKÁ

NATIONAL MUSEUM

VINOHRADSKÁ

ŽOFÍN

MYSLÍKOVA

NAVRÁTILOVA

KRAKOVSKÁ

RÍMSKÁ

DITTRICHOVA

KARLOVO

ŘEZNICKÁ

ŽITNÁ

BALBÍNOVA

RAŠÍNOVO

Heydrich Assassination Museum

TOWN

HÁLKOVA

MEZIBRANSKÁ

LEGEROVA

ANGLICKÁ

RESSLOVA

Dancing House

Karlovo Náměstí

JEČNÁ

I.P. Pavlova

BĚLEHRADSKÁ

VINO-HRADY

Náměstí Míru

TROJANOVA

LIPOVÁ

RUMUNSKÁ

ŠAFAŘÍKOVA

NA MORÁNI

U NEMOCNICE

DVOŘÁK MUSEUM

TYRŠOVA

LUBLAŇSKÁ

LONDÝNSKÁ

BELGICKÁ

BRUSELSKÁ

ZÁHŘEBSKÁ

NÁBŘEŽÍ

VYŠEHRADSKÁ

KATEŘINSKÁ

VINIČNÁ

NA BOJIŠTI

KE KARLOVU

SOKOLSKÁ

LEGEROVA

KOUBKOVA

KLÁŠTER NA SLOVANECH

Botanická Zahrada

BENÁTSKÁ

APOLINÁŘSKÁ

WENZIGOVA

TROJICKÁ

PODSKALSKÁ

NA SLUPI

Univerzita Karlova V Praze

STUDNIČKOVA

ALBERTOV

FRIČOVA

BOTIČSKÁ

HLAVOVA

HORSKÁ

NUSELSKÝ MOST

SARAJEVSKÁ

SVOBODOVA

250 Meters

250 Yards

VNISLAVOVA

NEKLANOVA

HORSKÁ

KŘESOMYSLOVA

The New Town

Key	
❶ Grand Hotel Evropa	❺ Dvořák Museum
❷ Lucerna Gallery	❻ State Opera
❸ Franciscan Garden	❼ Grand Café Slavia
❹ Museum of Communism	

museum's columns fill holes where Soviet bullets hit during the crackdown against the 1968 Prague Spring uprising. Masons—defying their communist bosses, who wanted the damage to be forgotten—showed their Czech spirit by intentionally mismatching their patches (80 Kč, daily May–Sept 10:00–18:00, Oct–April 9:00–17:00, halls of Czech fossils and animals).

The nearby Metro stop (Muzeum) is the crossing point of two Metro lines built with Russian know-how in the 1970s.

• *To the left of the National Museum (as you face it) is an ugly...*

Communist-Era Building

This structure housed the rubber-stamp Parliament back when they voted with Moscow. A Social Realist statue showing triumphant workers still stands at its base. It's now home to Radio Free Europe. After communism fell, RFE lost its funding and could no longer afford its Munich headquarters. In gratitude for its broadcasts—which kept the people of Eastern Europe in touch with real news—the current Czech government now rents the building to  RFE for 1 Kč a year. (As RFE energetically beams its American message deep into Islam from here, it has been threatened recently by Al-Qaeda, and new headquarters are being completed at an easier-to-defend locale near Franz Kafka's grave, at the Želivského Metro station.)

• *In front of the National Museum is the equestrian...*

St. Wenceslas Statue

Wenceslas (Václav) is the "good king" of Christmas-carol fame. He was the wise and benevolent 10th-century Duke of Bohemia.

A rare example of a well-educated and literate ruler, King Wenceslas I was credited by his people for Christianizing his nation and lifting up the culture. He astutely allied the Czechs with Saxony, rather than Bavaria, giving the Czechs a vote when the Holy Roman Emperor was selected (and therefore more political clout).

After his murder in 929, Wenceslas was canonized as a saint. He became a symbol of Czech nationalism and statehood—and remains an icon of Czech unity whenever the nation has to rally. Supposedly, when the Czechs face their darkest hour, Wenceslas will come riding out of Blaník Mountain (east of Prague) with an army of knights to rescue the nation. In 1620, when Austria stripped the Czechs of their independence, many people went to Blaník Mountain to see whether it had opened up. They did the same at other critical points in their history (in 1938, 1948, and 1968)—but Wenceslas never emerged. Although the Czech Republic is now safely part of NATO and the EU, Czechs remain realistic: If Wenceslas hasn't come out yet, the worst times must still lie ahead...

Study the statue. Wenceslas, on the horse, is surrounded by the four other Czech patron saints. Notice the focus on books. A small nation without great military power, the Czech Republic chose national heroes who enriched the culture by thinking, rather than fighting. This statue is a popular meeting point. Locals say, "I'll see you under the tail."

• *Now begin walking down the square. Thirty yards below the big horse is a small garden with a low-key...*

Memorial

This commemorates victims of communism, such as Jan Palach. In 1969, a group of patriots decided that an act of self-immolation would stoke the fires of independence. Jan Palach, a philosophy student who loved life—but wanted to live in freedom—set himself on fire on the steps of the National Museum for the cause of Czech independence. He died a few days later in a hospital ward. Czechs are keen on anniversaries, and huge demonstrations swept

the city on the 20th anniversary of Palach's death. These protests led, 10 months later, to the overthrow of the Czech communist government in 1989.

This grand square is a gallery of modern architectural styles. As you wander downhill, notice the fun mix, all post-1850: Romantic Neo-Gothic, Neo-Renaissance, and Neo-Baroque from the 19th century; Art Nouveau from about 1900; ugly Functionalism from the mid-20th century (the "form follows function" and "ornamentation is a crime" answer to Art Nouveau); Stalin Gothic from the 1950s "communist epoch" (a good example is the Jalta building, halfway downhill on the right); and the glass-and-steel buildings of the 1970s.

• *Walk a couple of blocks downhill through the real people of Prague (not tourists) to* **Grand Hotel Evropa**, *with its hard-to-miss, dazzling Art Nouveau exterior and plush café interior full of tourists. Stop for a moment to consider the events of...*

November of 1989

This huge square was filled every evening with more than 300,000 ecstatic Czechs and Slovaks who believed freedom was at hand. Assembled on the balcony of the building opposite Grand Hotel Evropa (look for the *Marks & Spencer* sign) were a priest, a rock star (famous for his unconventional style, which constantly unnerved the regime), Alexander Dubček (hero of the 1968 revolt), and Václav Havel (the charismatic playwright, newly released from prison, who was every freedom-loving Czech's Nelson Mandela). Through a sound system provided by the rock star, Havel's voice boomed over the gathered masses, announcing the resignation of the Politburo and saying that the Republic of Czechoslovakia's freedom was imminent. Picture that cold November evening, with thousands of Czechs jingling their keychains in solidarity, chanting at the government, "It's time to go now!" (To quell this revolt, government tanks could have given it the Tiananmen Square treatment—which had spilled patriotic blood in China just six months earlier. Locals believe that the Soviet head of state, Mikhail Gorbachev, must have made a phone call recommending that blood not be shed.) For more on the events leading up to this climactic rally, see the sidebar on the following page.
• *Immediately opposite Grand Hotel Evropa is the Lucerna Gallery (use entry marked* Palác Rokoko *and walk straight in).*

Lucerna Gallery

This grand mall retains some of its Art Deco glamour from the 1930s, with shops, theaters, a ballroom in the basement, and the fine Lucerna Café upstairs. You'll see a sculpture—called *Wenceslas Riding an Upside-Down Horse*—hanging like a swing from a glass dome. David Černý, who created the statue in 1999, is the Czech Republic's most original contemporary artist. Always aspiring to provoke controversy, Černý has painted a menacing Russian tank pink, attached crawling babies to the rocket-like Žižkov TV tower, defecated inside the National Gallery to protest the policies of its director, and sunk a shark-like Saddam Hussein inside an aquarium for a 2005 exhibition. Inside are also a **Ticketpro box office** (with all available tickets, daily 9:30–18:00), a lavish 1930s Prague cinema (under the upside-down horse, shows artsy films in Czech with English subtitles, or vice versa, 110 Kč), and the popular **Lucerna Music Bar** in the basement (disco themes from the '70s, '80s, and '90s, 100 Kč, nightly from 21:00—see page 146).

The Velvet Revolution of 1989

On the afternoon of November 17, 1989, 30,000 students gathered in Prague's New Town to commemorate the 50th anniversary of the suppression of student protests by the Nazis, which had led to the closing of Czech universities through the end of World War II. The 1989 demonstration—initially planned by the Communist Youth as a celebration of the communist victory over fascism—spontaneously turned into a protest *against* the communist regime. "You are just like the Nazis!" shouted the students. The demonstration was planned to end in the National Cemetery at Vyšehrad (the hill just south of the New Town). But when the planned events concluded in Vyšehrad, the students decided to march on toward Wenceslas Square, making history.

As they worked their way north along the Vltava River toward the New Town's main square, the students were careful to keep their demonstration peaceful. Any hint of violence, the demonstrators knew, would incite brutal police retaliation. Instead, as the evening went on, the absence of police became conspicuous. (In the 1980s, the police never missed a chance to participate in any demonstration...preferably outnumbering the demonstrators). At about 20:00, as the students marched down this very stretch of street toward Wenceslas Square, three rows of policemen suddenly blocked the demonstration at the corner of Národní and Spálená streets. A few minutes later, military vehicles with fences on their bumpers (having crossed the bridge by the National Theatre) appeared behind the marching students. This new set of cops compressed the demonstrators into the stretch of Národní Třída between Voršilská and Spálená. The end of Mikulandská street was also blocked, and policemen were hiding inside every house entry. The students were trapped.

At 21:30, the "Red Hats" (a special anti-riot commando force known for its brutality) arrived. The Red Hats lined up on both sides of this corridor. To get out, the trapped students had to run through the passageway as they were beaten from the left and right. Police trucks ferried captured students around the corner to the police headquarters (on Bartolomějská) for interrogation.

The next day, university students throughout Czechoslovakia decided to strike. Actors from theaters in Prague and Bratislava joined the student protest. Two days later, the students' parents—shocked by the attacks on their children—marched into Wenceslas Square. Sparked by the events of November 17, 1989, the wave of peaceful demonstrations ended later that year on December 29, with the election of Václav Havel as the president of a free Czechoslovakia.

Directly across busy Vodičkova street (with a handy tram stop) is the Světozor mall. Inside, you'll find the **World of Fruit Bar Světozor;** it's every local's favorite ice-cream joint. True to its name, the bar tops its ice cream with every variety of fruit. They sell cakes and milkshakes, too. Ask at the counter for an English menu.

• *Farther down the mall on the left is the entrance to the peaceful...*

Franciscan Garden (Františkánská Zahrada)

Its white benches and spreading rosebushes are a universe away from the fast beat of the city, which throbs behind the buildings that surround the garden.

Back on Wenceslas Square, if you're in the mood for a mellow hippie teahouse, consider a break at **Dobrá Čajovna** ("Good Teahouse") near the bottom of the square (#14—see page 132). Or, if you'd like an old-time wine bar, pop into the plain **Šenk Vrbovec** (nearby at #10); it comes with a whiff of the communist days, embracing the faintest bits of genteel culture from an age when refinement was sacrificed for the good of the working class. They serve traditional drinks, Czech keg wine, Moravian wines (listed on blackboard outside), *becherovka* (the 13-herb liqueur), and—only in autumn—*burčák* (this young wine tastes like grape juice turned halfway into wine).

The bottom of Wenceslas Square is called **Můstek,** which means "Bridge"; a bridge used to cross a moat here, allowing entrance into the Old Town (you can still see the original Old Town entrance down in the Metro station).

• *Running to the right from the bottom of Wenceslas Square is the street called...*

Na Příkopě

Meaning "On the Moat," this busy boulevard follows the line of the Old Town wall, leading to one of the wall's former gates, the Powder Tower. Along the way, it passes the Museum of Communism (see page 81) and a couple of Art Nouveau sights (see next page). City tour buses (see page 46) leave from along this street, which offers plenty of shopping temptations (such as these malls: Slovanský Dům at Na Příkopě 22, and Černá Růže at Na Příkopě 12, next door to Mosers, which has a crystal showroom upstairs).

Na Příkopě: Art Nouveau Prague

Stroll up Na Příkopě to take in two of Prague's best Art Nouveau sights. The first one is on the street called Panská (turn right up the first street you reach as you walk up Na Příkopě from Wenceslas Square); the second is two blocks farther up Na Příkopě, next to the big, Gothic Powder Tower.

Art Nouveau

Prague is the best Art Nouveau town in Europe, with fun-loving facades gracing streets all over town. Art Nouveau, born in Paris, is "nouveau" because it wasn't inspired by Rome. It's neo-nothing...a fresh answer to all the revival styles of the later 19th century and an organic response to the Eiffel Tower

art of the Industrial Age. The style liberated the artist in each architect. Notice the unique curves and motifs expressing originality on each Art Nouveau facade. Artists such as Alfons Mucha believed that the style should include all facets of daily life. They designed everything from buildings and furniture to typefaces and cigarette packs.

Prague's three top Art Nouveau architects are Jan Koula, Josef Fanta, and Osvald Polivka (whose last name sounds like the Czech word for "soup"). Think "Cola, Fanta, and Soup"—easy to remember and impress your local friends.

Prague's Art Nouveau highlights include the facades lining the streets of the Jewish Quarter, the Mucha window in St. Vitus Cathedral, and Grand Hotel Evropa on Wenceslas Square. The top two sights for Art Nouveau fans are the Mucha Museum and the Municipal House.

▲▲Mucha Museum—This is one of Europe's most enjoyable little museums. I find the art of Alfons Mucha (MOO-kah, 1860–1939) insistently likeable. See the crucifixion scene he painted as an eight-year-old boy. Read how this popular Czech artist's posters, filled with Czech symbols and expressing his people's ideals and aspirations, were patriotic banners that aroused the national spirit. And check out the photographs of his models. With the help of an abundant supply of slinky models, Mucha was a founding father of the Art Nouveau movement. Partly overseen by Mucha's grandson, the museum is two blocks off Wenceslas Square and wonderfully displayed on one comfortable floor (120 Kč, daily 10:00–18:00, well-described in English, Panská 7, tel. 224-233-355, www.mucha .cz). The included 30-minute video is definitely worthwhile (in English, generally at :15 and :45 past the hour—ask for the starting time); it describes the main project of Mucha's life—the *Slav Epic*, currently on display in Moravský Krumlov (see page 221).

• *Coming back to Na Příkopě and continuing toward the Powder Tower, notice the Neo-Renaissance* **UniCredit Bank** *(formerly Živnostenská Banka, Prague's oldest banking institution) building on the corner of Nekázanka. It houses a modern bank with classy circa-1900 ambience (enter and peek into the main hall upstairs).*

At the end of Na Příkopě, you'll arrive at the...

▲▲**Municipal House (Obecní Dům)**—The Municipal House is the "pearl of Czech Art Nouveau." Financed by cultural and artis-

tic leaders, it was built (1905–1911) as a ceremonial palace to reinforce the self-awareness of the Czech nation. It features Prague's largest concert hall, a recommended Art Nouveau café (Kavárna Obecní Dům, see page 131), and two other restaurants. Pop in and wander around the lobby of the concert hall. Walk through to the ticket office on the ground floor. For the best look, including impressive halls and murals you won't see otherwise, take one of the regular hour-long **tours** (open daily 10:00–18:00; tours—150 Kč; generally at 10:15, 12:00, 14:00, and 16:00; in English 2/day, buy ticket from ground-floor shop where tour departs; tel. 222-002-101).

Standing in front of the Municipal House, you can survey four different styles of architecture. First, enjoy the pure Art Nouveau of the Municipal House itself. Featuring a goddess-like Praha presiding over a land of peace and high culture, the *Homage to Prague* mosaic on the building's striking facade stoked cultural pride and nationalist sentiment. Across the street, the classical fixer-upper from 1815 was the customs house, which has recently been turned into a giant stage for Broadway-style musicals. The stark national bank building (Česká Národní Banka) is textbook Functionalism from the 1930s. Farther away, across the square, former Neo-Romanesque barracks have been transformed into central Prague's biggest shopping mall and underground parking lot.

Powder Tower: The big, black Powder Tower (not worth touring inside) was the Gothic gate of the town wall, built to house the city's gunpowder. The decoration on the tower, portraying Czech kings, is the best 15th-century sculpture in town. If you go through the tower, you'll reach Celetná street, which leads past a few sights to the Old Town Square (see page 49).

Prague: Pre-1989

It's hard to imagine the gray and bleak Prague of the communist era. Before 1989, the city was a wistful jumble of possibility. Cobbled lanes were shadowed by decrepit, crusty buildings. Timbers—strung across the lanes like laundry lines—held crumbling buildings apart. Consumer goods were plain and uniform, stacked like Legos on thin shelves in shops where customers waited in line for a tin of pineapples or a bottle of ersatz Coke. The Charles Bridge and its statues were black with soot, and there was no commerce, except for a few shady characters trying to change money. Hotels had two price schedules: one for people of the Warsaw Pact nations, and another (6–8 times more expensive) for capitalists. This made the run-down, Soviet-style hotels as expensive as fine Western ones. At the train station, frightened but desperate characters would meet arriving foreigners to rent them a room in their flat, hoping to earn enough hard Western cash to buy batteries or Levi's at one of the hard-currency stores.

Národní Třída: Communist Prague

From Můstek at the bottom of Wenceslas Square, you can head west on Národní Třída (in the opposite direction from Na Příkopě and the Art Nouveau sights) for an interesting stroll through urban Prague to the National Theatre and the Vltava River. But first, consider dropping into the Museum of Communism, a few steps down Na Příkopě (on the right).

▲▲**Museum of Communism**—This museum traces the story of communism in Prague: the origins, dream, reality, and nightmare; the cult of personality; and finally, the Velvet Revolution (see sidebar on page 77). Along the way, it gives a fascinating review of the Czech Republic's 40-year stint with Soviet economics, "in all its dreariness and puffed-up glory." You'll find propaganda posters, busts of communist All-Stars (Marx, Lenin, Stalin), and a photograph of the massive stone Stalin that overlooked Prague until 1962. Slices of communist life are re-created here, from a bland store counter to a typical classroom (with textbooks using Russia's Cyrillic alphabet—no longer studied—and a poem on the chalkboard that extols the virtues of the tractor). Don't miss the Jan Palach exhibit and the 20-minute video (plays continuously, English subtitles) that shows how the Czech people chafed under the big Red yoke from the 1950s through 1989 (180 Kč, daily 9:00–21:00, Na Příkopě 10, above a McDonald's and next to a casino—Lenin is turning over in his grave, tel. 224-212-966, www .museumofcommunism.com).

• *Now head for the river (with your back to Wenceslas Square, go left*

The New Town

down 28 Října to Národní Třída). Along the way, Národní Třída has a story to tell.

Národní Třída and the Velvet Revolution—Národní Třída ("National Street") is where you feel the pulse of the modern

city. The street, which connects Wenceslas Square with the National Theatre and the river, is a busy thoroughfare running through the heart of urban Prague. In 1989, this unassuming boulevard played host to the first salvo of a Velvet Revolution that would topple the communist regime.

Make your way down Národní Třída until you hit the tram tracks (just beyond the Tesco department store). On the left, look for the photo of Bill Clinton playing saxophone, with Václav Havel on the side (this is the entrance to Reduta, Prague's best jazz club—see page 147; next door are two recommended eateries, Café Louvre and Le Patio—see pages 131 and 128). Just beyond that, you'll come to a short corridor with white arches. Inside this arcade is a simple memorial to the hundreds of students injured here by the police on November 17, 1989 (see sidebar on page 77).

Along the Vltava River

I've listed these sights from north to south, beginning at the grand, Neo-Renaissance National Theatre, which is five blocks south of Charles Bridge and stands along the riverbank at the end of Národní Třída.

National Theatre (Národní Divadlo)—Opened in 1883 with Smetana's opera *Libuše,* this theater was the first truly Czech venue in Prague. From the very start, it was nicknamed the "Cradle of Czech Culture." The building

is a key symbol of the Czech national revival that began in the late 18th century. In 1800, "Prag" was predominantly German. The Industrial Revolution brought Czechs from the countryside into the city, their new urban identity defined by patriotic teachers and priests. By 1883, most of the city spoke Czech, and the opening of this theater represented the birth of the modern Czech nation. It remains an important national icon: The state annually pours more subsidies into this theater than into all of Czech film production. It's the most beautiful venue in town for opera and ballet, often with world-class singers (see page 143).

Next door (just inland, on Národní Třída) is the boxy, glassy facade of the **Nová Scéna.** This "New National Theatre" building, dating from 1983 (the 100th anniversary of the original National Theatre building), reflects the bold and stark communist aesthetic.

Across the street from the National Theatre is the former haunt of Prague's intelligentsia, **Grand Café Slavia,** a Viennese-style coffeehouse that is fine for a meal or drink with a view of the river (see page 131).

•Just south of the National Theatre in the Vltava, you'll find...

Prague's Islands—From the National Theatre, the Legions' Bridge (Most Legií) leads across the island called **Střelecký Ostrov.** Covered with chestnut trees, this island boasts Prague's best beach (on the sandy tip that points north to Charles Bridge). You might see a fisherman pulling out trout from a river that's now much cleaner than it used to be. Bring a swimsuit and take a dip just a stone's throw from Europe's most beloved bridge. In summer, the island hosts open-air movies (most in English or with English subtitles, nightly mid-July–early Sept at about 21:00, www.strelak.cz).

In the mood for boating instead of swimming? On the next island up, on **Slovanský Ostrov,** you can rent a boat (40 Kč/hr for rowboats, 60 Kč/hr for paddleboats, bring a picture ID as deposit). A lazy hour paddling around Střelecký Ostrov—or just floating sleepily in the middle of the river surrounded by this great city's architectural splendor—is a delightful experience on a sunny day. It's cheap, easy, fun (and it's good for you).

• A 10-minute walk (or one stop on tram #17) from the National Theatre, beyond the islands, is Jirásek Bridge (Jiráskův Most), where you'll find the...

Dancing House (Tančící Dům)—If ever a building could get your toes tapping, it would be this one, nicknamed "Fred and Ginger" by American architecture buffs. This metallic samba is the work of Frank Gehry (who designed the equally striking Guggenheim Museum in Bilbao, Spain, and Seattle's Experience Music Project). Eight-legged Ginger's wispy dress and Fred's metal mesh head are easy to spot. The building's top-floor

restaurant, La Perle de Prague, is a fine place for a fancy French meal (VIPs often eat and drink here, reservation needed even to get into the elevator, tel. 221-984-160).

Of course, most Czechs have never heard of Fred and Ginger. Some prefer to think that the two "figures" represent the nation's greatest 20th-century heroes, the WWII paratroopers Gabčík and Kubiš. Their 1942 assassination of SS second-in-command Reinhard Heydrich, who controlled the Nazi-occupied Czech lands, was the most significant act of Czech resistance. German retaliation was violent. Hundreds of Czechs were executed, and two villages—Lidice and Ležáky—were summarily razed to the ground. In the weeks following the assassination, the two paratroopers hid along with other freedom fighters in the crypt of the **Greek Orthodox Church** on Resslova street, one block up from the Dancing House. One soldier betrayed the others. The Gestapo surrounded the church. To escape capture, each of the men inside the church saved his last bullet for himself. Today, the church crypt shelters a modest exhibition on the history of the Czech resistance movement.

• *Three blocks up Resslova street is...*

Charles Square (Karlovo Náměstí)—Prague's largest square is covered by lawns, trees, and statues of Czech writers. It's a quiet antidote to the bustling Wenceslas and Old Town squares. The Gothic New Town Hall at the top-left corner of the square has excellent views and labeled panoramic photographs that help you orient yourself to what you see. The little parlor across the street has some of the best Italian ice cream in town.

THE LITTLE QUARTER

Malá Strana

This charming neighborhood, huddled under the castle on the west bank of the river, is low on blockbuster sights but high on ambience. The most enjoyable approach from the Old Town is across Charles Bridge. From the end of the bridge (TI in tower), Mostecká street leads two blocks up to the Little Quarter Square (Malostranské Náměstí) and the huge Church of St. Nicholas. But before you head up there, consider a detour to Kampa Island (all described below).

Between Charles Bridge and Little Quarter Square

Kampa Island

One hundred yards before the castle end of the Charles Bridge, stairs on the left lead down to the main square of Kampa Island

(mostly created from the rubble of the Little Quarter, which was destroyed in a 1540 fire). The island features relaxing pubs, a breezy park, hippies, lovers, a fine contemporary art gallery, and river access. From the main square, Hroznová lane (on the right) leads to a bridge. Behind the old mill wheel, notice the high-water marks from the flood of 2002. The water wheel is the last survivor of many that once lined the canal here. Each mill once had its own protective water spirit *(vodník)*. Today, only one wheel—and one spirit (Mr. Kabourek)—remains.

• *Fifty yards beyond the bridge (on the right, under the trees) is the...*

Lennon Wall (Lennonova Zeď)

While Lenin's ideas hung like a water-soaked trench coat upon the Czech people, the rock singer John Lennon's ideas gave many locals hope and a vision. When Lennon was killed in 1980, a large wall was spontaneously covered with memorial graffiti. Night after night, the police would paint over the "All You Need Is Love" and "Imagine" graffiti. And day after day, it would reappear. Until independence came in 1989, travelers, freedom-lovers, and local hippies

gathered here. Silly as it might seem, this wall is remembered as a place that gave hope to locals craving freedom. Even today, while the tension and danger associated with this wall is gone, people come here to imagine. *"John žije"* is Czech for "John lives." In the left-hand corner of the wall, a small gate leads to a quiet courtyard with a recommended outdoor café dedicated to John and George.

• *From here, you can continue up to the Little Quarter Square.*

On or near Little Quarter Square

The focal point of this neighborhood, the Little Quarter Square (Malostranské Náměstí) is dominated by the huge Church of St. Nicholas. Note that there's a handy Via Musica ticket office across from the church.

Church of St. Nicholas (Kostel Sv. Mikuláše)—When the Jesuits came to Prague, they found the perfect piece of real estate for their church and its associated school—right on Little Quarter Square. The church (built 1703–1760) is the best example of High Baroque in town. It's giddy with curves and illusions. The altar features a lavish gold-plated Nicholas, flanked by the two top Jesuits: the founder, St. Ignatius Loyola and his missionary follower, St. Francis Xavier. Climb up the **gallery** through the staircase in the left transept for a close-up look at a collection of large canvases and illusionary frescoes by Karel Škréta, the greatest Czech Baroque painter. Notice that at first glance, the canvases are utterly dark. But as sunbeams shine through the window, various parts of the painting brighten up. Like a looking-glass, it reflects the light, creating a play of light and darkness. This painting technique reflects a central Baroque belief: The world is full of darkness, and the only hope that makes it come alive comes from God. The church walls seem to nearly fuse with the sky, suggesting that happenings on earth are closely connected to heaven. Find St. Nick with his bishop's miter in the center of the ceiling, on his way to heaven (60 Kč, church open daily 9:00–17:00, opens at 8:30 for prayer).

Little Quarter

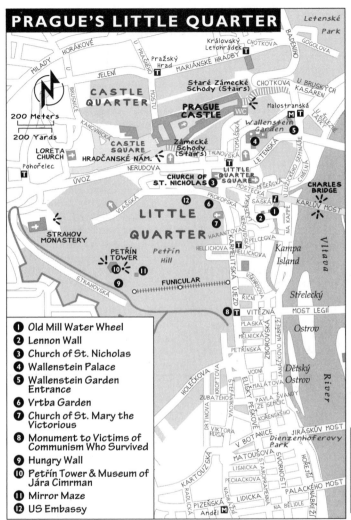

PRAGUE'S LITTLE QUARTER

① Old Mill Water Wheel
② Lennon Wall
③ Church of St. Nicholas
④ Wallenstein Palace
⑤ Wallenstein Garden Entrance
⑥ Vrtba Garden
⑦ Church of St. Mary the Victorious
⑧ Monument to Victims of Communism Who Survived
⑨ Hungry Wall
⑩ Petřín Tower & Museum of Jára Cimrman
⑪ Mirror Maze
⑫ US Embassy

Tower Climb: For a good look at the city and the church's 250-foot dome, climb 215 steps up the bell tower (50 Kč, April–Oct daily 10:00–18:00, closed Nov–March, tower entrance is outside the right transept).

Concerts: The church is also an evening concert venue; tickets are generally on sale at the door (450 Kč, generally nightly except Tue at 18:00, www.psalterium.cz).

• *From here, you can hike 10 minutes uphill to the castle (and five more minutes to the Strahov Monastery). For information on these sights, see the next chapter. If you're walking up to the castle, consider going via...*

Jára Cimrman:
When Optimists Should Be Shot

"I am such a complete atheist that I am afraid God will punish me." Such is the pithy wisdom of Jára Cimrman, the man overwhelmingly voted the "Greatest Czech of All Time" in a nationwide poll in 2005. Who is Jára Cimrman? A philosopher? An explorer? An inventor? He is all of these things, yes, and much more. Today, a museum celebrates his life (see page 92).

Born in the mid-19th century to a Czech tailor of Jewish descent and an Austrian actress, Cimrman studied in Vienna before starting off on his journeys around the world. He traversed the Atlantic by a steamboat he designed himself, taught drama to peasants in Peru, and drifted across the Arctic Sea on an iceberg. Other astounding feats soon followed. Cimrman was the first to come within 20 feet of the North Pole. He was the first to invent the light bulb (unfortunately, Edison beat him to the patent office by five minutes). It was he who suggested to the Americans the idea for a Panama Canal, though, as usual, he was never credited. Indeed, Cimrman surreptitiously advised many of the world's greats: Eiffel on his tower, Einstein on his theories of relativity, Chekhov on his plays. ("You can't just have *two* sisters," Cimrman told the playwright. "How about three?") In 1886, long before the world knew of Sartre or Camus, Cimrman was writing tracts such as *The Essence of the Existence,* which would become the foundation for his philosophy of "Cimrmanism," also known as "non-existentialism." (Its central premise: "Existence cannot not exist.")

This man of unmatched genius would have won the honor of "Greatest Czech of All Time" if not for the bureaucratic narrow-mindedness of the poll's sponsors, who had a single objection to Cimrman's candidacy: He's not real. Jára Cimrman is the brainchild of two Czech humorists—Zdeněk Svěrák and Jiří Šebánek—who brought their patriotic Renaissance man to life in 1967 in a satirical radio play. So, even though Cimrman handily won the initial balloting in January of 2005, Czech TV officials—blatantly biased against his non-existentialism—refused to let him into the final rounds of the competition.

How should we interpret the fact that the Czechs would

Little Quarter

Nerudova Street—This steep, cobbled street, leading from Little Quarter Square to the castle, is named for Jan Neruda, a gifted 19th-century journalist (and somewhat less talented fiction writer). It's lined with old buildings still sporting the characteristic doorway signs (e.g., the lion, three violinists, house of the golden suns) that once served as street addresses. The surviving signs are carefully restored and protected by law. They represent the family rather choose a fictional character as their greatest countryman over any of their flesh-and-blood national heroes—say, Charles IV (the 14th-century Holy Roman Emperor who established Prague as the cultural and intellectual capital of Europe), Jan Hus (the 15th-century religious reformer who challenged the legitimacy of the Catholic Church), Comenius (the 17th-century educator and writer, considered one of the fathers of modern education), or Martina Navrátilová (someone who plays a sport with bright green balls)? The more cynically inclined—many Czechs among them—might point out that the Czech people have largely stayed behind their mountains for the past millennia, with little interest in, or influence on, happenings elsewhere in the world. Perhaps Cimrman is so beloved because he embodies that most prickly of ironies: a Czech who was greater than all the world's greats, but who for some hiccup of chance has never been recognized for his achievements.

Personally, I like to think that the vote for Cimrman says something about the country's rousing enthusiasm for blowing raspberries in the face of authority. Throughout its history—from the times of the Czech kings who used crafty diplomacy to keep the German menace at bay, to the days of Jan Hus and his questioning of the very legitimacy of any ruler's power, to the flashes of anti-communist revolt that at last sparked the Velvet Revolution in 1989—the Czechs have maintained a healthy disrespect for those who would tell them what is best or how to live their lives. Other countries soberly choose their "Greatest" from musty tomes of history, but the Czechs won't play this silly game. Their vote for a fictional personage, says Cimrman's co-creator Svěrák, says two things about the Czech nation: "That it is skeptical about those who are major figures and those who are supposedly the 'Greatest.' And that the only certainty that has saved the nation many times throughout history is its humor."

Cimrman would agree. A man of greatness, he was always a bit skeptical of those who saw themselves as great, or who marched forward under the banner of greatness. As Cimrman liked to say, "There are moments when optimists should be shot."

name, the occupation, or the various passions of the people who once inhabited the houses. (If you were to replace your house number with a symbol, what would it be?) In 1777, in order to collect taxes more effectively, Hapsburg empress Maria Theresa decreed that numbers be used instead of these quaint house names. This neighborhood is filled with old noble palaces, now generally used as foreign embassies and offices of the Czech parliament.

North of Little Quarter Square, near Malostranská Metro Station

Twenty yards from the Malostranská Metro station (go left from the top of the escalator and turn right when you get outside), a few blocks north of Little Quarter Square, is a fine palace and garden. If you want to reach Little Quarter Square from here, follow Valdštejnská street.

Wallenstein Palace Garden (Valdštejnská Palac Zahrada)—Of the neighborhood's many impressive palace gardens, this is by far the largest and most beautiful. The complex—consisting of a palace (generally closed) and the surrounding garden (generally open)—was commissioned during the Thirty Years' War by the Hapsburg general and Czech nobleman Albrecht z Valdštejna (or, in German, Albrecht von Wallenstein). It's a testimony to how war can be such a great business for the unscrupulous. For 21 years (1618–1639), the mercenary Albrecht conspired with all sides involved in the war. He was the banker of the Czech Estates Uprising until he ran off to Vienna with the money to join the Hapsburgs. Plundering territories in the name of the Catholic faith, Albrecht followed his own simple rule: half for the emperor, half for me. When Hapsburg favors waned, Albrecht secretly negotiated with the Swedes. When desperate Hapsburgs put him in charge of their armies once again, he continued to play both sides. Finally, somebody had enough: Albrecht was murdered in his bedroom in 1639.

The inconspicuous entry to the palace's Wallenstein Garden is by the Malostranská Metro station. The garden, renovated in the late 1990s, features a large pool surrounded by peacocks. The statues that line the central walkway, inspired by Greek mythology, were done by the Danish artist Adrian de Vries—arguably the best Renaissance sculptor outside Italy. Notice the elegant classical shapes, a sharp contrast to the chubbiness of the Baroque figures on the Charles Bridge and elsewhere in the city. The original statues were stolen by invading Swedish armies in 1648, and are still in Sweden; the present replicas were cast in the early 1900s.

The Renaissance garden and the palace were built by Italian architects, just like most of the Little Quarter. The theatrical loggia—the *sala terena*—is a drama and music stage inspired by Greek amphitheaters. Notice the unusual pairing of columns—at the time, a trendy invention of the Italian architect Andrea Palladio. Inside, the gory depictions of the Trojan War tell you about the taste and character of the owner. (A handy, free WC is to the left of the amphitheater.) The bizarre grotto wall farther on the left was an expression of an uncertain age. It creates the illusion of caves and holes, stalagmites and stalactites, interspersed with partially hidden stone goblins, frogs, and snakes (count how many you can find). The wall continues into a cage with live owls that completes the transition from dead to living nature. The twisted cries of the owls deepen the surreal sensation of the place. Exit through the door in the right corner of the garden by the *sala terena*. You'll pass into a small courtyard surrounded by what once was the residential part of the palace. Today, the upper chamber of the Czech Parliament meets inside.

Cost and Hours: Garden—free, April–Oct daily 10:00–18:00, closed Nov–March; Palace—usually closed to the public.

Near the Garden: For a terraced Baroque garden to compare to this Renaissance one, visit the **Vrtba Garden** (Vrtbovská Zahrada, 100 Kč, daily 10:00–18:00; just south of Little Quarter Square, on Karmelitská before the Church of St. Mary the Victorious—see below).

South of Little Quarter Square, to Petřín Hill

Karmelitská street, leading south (along the tram tracks) from Little Quarter Square, is home to these sights.

Church of St. Mary the Victorious (Kostel Panny Marie Vítězné)—This otherwise ordinary Carmelite church displays Prague's most worshipped treasure, the Infant of Prague (Pražské Jezulátko). Kneel at the banister in front of the tiny, lost-in-gilded-Baroque altar, and find the prayer in your language (of the 13 in the folder). Brought to Czech lands during the Hapsburg era by a Spanish noblewoman who came to marry a Czech nobleman, the Infant has become a focus of worship and miracle tales in Prague and Spanish-speaking countries. South Americans come on pilgrimage to Prague just to see this one statue. An exhibit upstairs shows tiny embroidered robes given to the Infant, including ones from Hapsburg empress Maria Theresa of Austria (1754) and Vietnam (1958), as well as a video showing a nun lovingly dressing the doll-like sculpture (free, Mon–Sat 9:30–17:30, Sun 13:00–17:00, English-language Mass Sun at 12:00, Karmelitská 9, www.pragjesu.com).

• *Continue a few more blocks down Karmelitská to the south end of the Little Quarter (where the street is called Újezd, roughly across the Legions' Bridge from the National Theatre). Here you find yourself at the base of...*

Petřín Hill—This hill, topped by a replica of the Eiffel Tower, features several unusual sights.

The figures walking down the steps in the hillside make up the **Monument to Victims of Communism Who Survived.** The monument's figures are gradually atrophied by the totalitarian regime. They do not die, but slowly disappear, one limb at a time. The statistics say it all: In Czechoslovakia alone, 205,486 people were imprisoned, 248 were executed, 4,500 died in prison, 327 were shot attempting to cross the border, and 170,938 left the

Czechs After Communism

Many Czech survivors of communist prisons (honored by the Monument to Victims of Communism Who Survived, listed on page 91) feel a sense of injustice. Following World War II, many of the Czechs who collaborated with the Nazis were brought to justice. In contrast, after communism fell in 1989, few individuals responsible for the crimes committed by the communist regime faced retribution. In fact, when the country's industrial infrastructure was privatized in the early 1990s, the former Communist Party big shots used their connections to take control of some of the country's new capitalist enterprises. Many of the old Party leaders morphed into the bosses of the new Czech economy.

The Czech Republic was the first post-communist country to ban informants of the secret police from public office (a policy called *lustrace*, or "lustration"). They were also the first to outlaw the propagation of communism (and other totalitarian ideologies). Even so, efforts to enforce this legislation have been less than successful. Many former agents have destroyed evidence, while others contend that they were not aware of their own cooperation.

In the early 1990s, stalwart members of the Communist Party fended off attempts at reform and preserved a fossil of an institution that still draws about 15 percent of votes in national elections. Today's "vanguards of progress" no longer preach class warfare, but instead they blend empty rhetoric ("We have

country. To the left of the monument is the **Hungry Wall,** Charles IV's 14th-century equivalent of FDR's work-for-food projects. On the right (50 yards away) is the base of a handy **funicular**—hop on to reach Petřín Tower (uses 20-Kč tram/Metro ticket, runs daily, every 10–15 min from 8:00–22:00).

The summit of Petřín Hill is considered the best place in Prague to take your date for a romantic city view. Built for an exhibition in 1891, the 200-foot-tall **Petřín Tower** is a fifth the height of its Parisian big brother, which was built two years earlier. But, thanks to this hill, the top of the tower sits at the same elevation as the real Eiffel Tower. Climbing the 400 steps rewards you with amazing views over the city. Local wives drag their men to Petřín Hill each May Day to reaffirm their love with a kiss under a blooming sour-cherry tree.

In the tower's basement is the funniest sight in Prague, the **Museum of Jára Cimrman, Genius Who Did Not Become Famous.** The museum traces Cimrman's (fictional) life, including pictures and English descriptions of the thinker's overlooked inventions (50 Kč includes tower and Cimrman museum, daily a solution") with vague finger-pointing ("Who took away our hard-won securities?"). To become more palatable to a wider public and to hide their Stalinist roots, they altered their symbol, exchanging the unsavory red star for a far more innocuous pair of cherries (allegedly to recall the Paris Commune of 1871).

Their nostalgic-about-the-good-old-times message registers mainly with Czechs who find it difficult to adapt to a more complex and risk-prone society. Many of them (including members of the younger generation) find communism's ordered worldview—familiar since childhood—to be the most easily comprehensible. Today, they read the newspapers for reassurance that capitalism is responsible for many social ills, that the European Union is German imperialism in disguise, and—in some extreme cases—that China is pairing up with Russia to defend humanity.

The idealistic Velvet Revolutionaries of 19 years ago thought that communism would naturally disappear over time—but they failed to realize how deeply the years of authoritarian rule affected everyone, even its opponents. Today, the sight of familiar communist faces in Parliament is a reminder for the Czechs of how little they'd reflected on their recent past. And visitors surprised by the communist presence in a newly free Czech Republic can take it as a reminder that difficult experiences, individual as much as collective ones, take lifetimes to process—especially if kept buried inside.

10:00–22:00). For more on the mysterious Cimrman, see the sidebar on page 88.

The **mirror maze** next door is nothing special, but fun to quickly wander through since you're already here (50 Kč, daily 10:00–22:00).

Little Quarter

THE CASTLE QUARTER

Hradčany

Looming above Prague, dominating its skyline, is the Castle Quarter. Prague Castle and its surrounding sights are packed with Czech history, as well as with tourists. In addition to the castle itself, I enjoy visiting the nearby Strahov Monastery—which has a fascinating old library and beautiful views over all of Prague.

Castle Square (Hradčanské Náměstí)—right in front of the castle gates—is at the center of this neighborhood. Stretching along the promontory away from the castle is a regal neighborhood that ends at the Strahov Monastery. Above the castle are the Royal Gardens, and below the castle are more gardens and lanes leading down to the Little Quarter (see previous chapter).

Getting to Prague Castle

If you're not up for a hike, the tram offers a sweat-free ride up to the castle. Taxis are expensive, as they have to go the long way around (200 Kč).

By Foot: Begin in the Little Quarter (see page 85), just across Charles Bridge from the Old Town. Hikers can follow the main cobbled road (Mostecká) from Charles Bridge to Little Quarter Square, marked by the huge, green-domed Church of St. Nicholas. (The nearest Metro stop is Malostranská, from which Valdštejnská street leads down to Little Quarter Square.) From Little Quarter Square, hike uphill along Nerudova street (described on page 88). After about 10 minutes, a steep lane on the right leads to the castle. (If you continue straight, Nerudova becomes Úvoz and climbs to the Strahov Monastery.)

By Tram: Trams #22 and #23 take you up to the castle (see page 47 for my self-guided tram tour, which ends at the castle). While you can catch the tram in various places, these three stops are particularly convenient: at the Národní Třída Metro stop (between Wenceslas Square and the National Theatre in the New Town); in front of the National Theatre (Národní Divadlo, on the riverbank in the New Town); and at Malostranská (the Metro stop in the Little Quarter). After rattling up the hill, these trams make three stops near the castle: Get off at **Královský Letohrádek** for the scenic approach to the castle (through the Royal Gardens—see below); or stay on one more stop to get off at **Pražský Hrad** (most direct but least interesting—simply walk along U Prašného Mostu over the bridge into the castle); or go yet two more stops to **Pohořelec** to visit the Strahov Monastery before hiking down to the castle. To get to the monastery from this tram stop, follow the tram tracks uphill for 50 yards, enter the fancy gate on the left near the tall redbrick wall, and you'll see the twin spires of the monastery. The library entrance is in front of the church on the right.

Tram Tips: When you're choosing which of the castle's three tram stops to get off at, consider the time of day. The castle is plagued with crowds. If you're visiting in the morning, use the Pražský Hrad tram stop for the quickest commute to the castle. Be at the door of St. Vitus Cathedral when it opens at 9:00 (just 10–15 minutes later, it'll be swamped with tour groups). See the castle sights quickly, then move on to the Strahov Monastery. I'd avoid the castle entirely mid-morning, but by mid-afternoon, the tour groups are napping and the grounds are (relatively) uncrowded. If you're going in the afternoon, take the tram to the Pohořelec stop, see the Strahov Monastery, then wander down to the castle.

Sights Above the Castle, near the Královský Letohrádek Tram Stop

These sights, above Prague Castle, are only worth visiting if you get off tram #22 or #23 at Královský Letohrádek (the Royal Summer Palace is across the street from this stop, WC at gate).

Royal Summer Palace (Královský Letohrádek)—This gift of love is like a Czech Taj Mahal, presented by Emperor Ferdinand I to his beloved Queen Anne. It's the purest Renaissance building in town. You can't go inside, but the building's detailed reliefs are worth a close look. In good Renaissance style, they're based on classical, rather than Christian, stories. The one depicted here is Virgil's *Aeneid*. The fountain in front of the palace features the most elaborate bronze-work in the country. (For a trip to Tibet, stick your head under the bottom of the fountain. The audio rainbow you hear is the reason it's called the Singing Fountain.)

• *From here, set your sights on the cathedral's lacy, black spires—marking the castle's entrance—and stroll through the...*

Royal Gardens (Královská Zahrada)—Once the private grounds and residence (you'll see the building) of the communist presidents, these were opened to the public with the coming of freedom

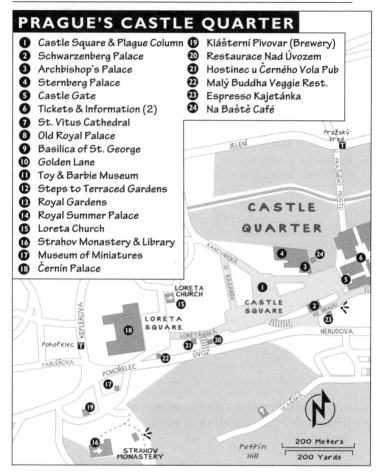

PRAGUE'S CASTLE QUARTER

- ❶ Castle Square & Plague Column
- ❷ Schwarzenberg Palace
- ❸ Archbishop's Palace
- ❹ Sternberg Palace
- ❺ Castle Gate
- ❻ Tickets & Information (2)
- ❼ St. Vitus Cathedral
- ❽ Old Royal Palace
- ❾ Basilica of St. George
- ❿ Golden Lane
- ⓫ Toy & Barbie Museum
- ⓬ Steps to Terraced Gardens
- ⓭ Royal Gardens
- ⓮ Royal Summer Palace
- ⓯ Loreta Church
- ⓰ Strahov Monastery & Library
- ⓱ Museum of Miniatures
- ⓲ Černín Palace
- ⓳ Klášterní Pivovar (Brewery)
- ⓴ Restaurace Nad Úvozem
- ㉑ Hostinec u Černého Vola Pub
- ㉒ Malý Buddha Veggie Rest.
- ㉓ Espresso Kajetánka
- ㉔ Na Baště Café

under Václav Havel (free, April–Oct daily 10:00–18:00, closed Nov–March). Walk through these gardens (with fine views of St. Vitus Cathedral) to the gate, which leads you over the moat and into Castle Square, the entrance to the vast castle complex.

▲Strahov Monastery and Library, near the Pohořelec Tram Stop

Twin Baroque domes high above the castle mark the Strahov Monastery. This complex is best reached from the Pohořelec stop on tram #22 or #23 (from the stop, go up the red-railed ramp and through the gate into the monastery grounds). If you're coming on foot from the Little Quarter, allow 15 minutes for the uphill hike. After seeing the monastery, hike down to the castle (a 5-min walk).

Monastery: The monastery (Strahovský Klášter Premonstrátů) had a booming economy of its own in its heyday, with vineyards,

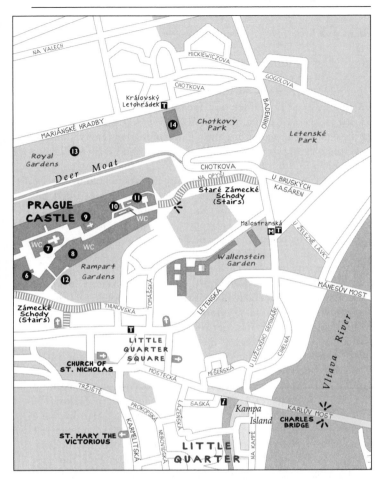

brewery, and a sizeable beer hall—all still open. Its main church, dedicated to the Assumption of St. Mary, is an originally Romanesque structure decorated by the monks in textbook Baroque (usually closed, but look through the window inside the front door to see its interior).

Library: The adjacent library (Strahovská Knihovna) offers a

peek at how enlightened thinkers in the 18th century influenced learning (80 Kč, daily 9:00–12:00 & 13:00–17:00). Cases in the library gift shop show off illuminated manuscripts (described in English). Some are in old Czech, but these are rare. Because the Enlightenment believed in the universality of knowledge, there was little place for vernaculars—therefore, few books here are in the Czech language. Two rooms (seen only from the door) are filled with 10th- to 17th-century books, shelved under elaborately painted ceilings. The theme of the first and bigger hall is philosophy, with the history of man's pursuit of knowledge painted on the ceiling. The other hall focuses on theology. Notice the gilded locked case containing the *libri prohibiti* (prohibited books) at the end of the room. Only the abbot had the key, and you had to have his blessing to read these books—by writers such as Nicolas Copernicus and Jan Hus, and even including the French encyclopedia. As the Age of Enlightenment began to take hold in Europe at the end of the 18th century, monasteries still controlled the books. The hallway connecting these two library rooms was filled with cases illustrating the new practical approach to natural sciences. Find the dried-up elephant trunks, baby dodo bird (which became extinct in the 17th century), and one of the earliest models of an electricity generator.

Nearby Views: Just downhill from the monastery, past the venerable linden trees (a symbol of the Czech people) and through the gate, the views from the **monastery garden** are among the best in Prague. From the public perch below the tables, you can see St. Vitus Cathedral (the heart of the castle complex), the green dome of the Church of St. Nicholas (marking the center of the Little Quarter), the two dark towers fortifying both ends of Charles Bridge, and the fanciful black spires of the Týn Church (marking the Old Town Square). On the horizon is the modern **Žižkov TV and radio tower** (conveniently marking the liveliest nightlife zone in town—see page 147). Begun in the 1980s, it was partly meant to jam Radio Free Europe's broadcast from Munich. By the time it was finished, communism was dead, and Radio Free Europe's headquarters had actually moved to Prague.

To reach the castle from Strahov Monastery, take Loretánská (the upper road, passing Loreta Square—see below); this is a more interesting route than the lower road, Úvoz, which takes you steeply downhill, below Castle Square (see map on page 96).

Or, for one more little sight, consider visiting the Museum of Miniatures. From the monastery garden viewpoint, backtrack through the gate to the big linden trees, and leave through a passage on your right. At the door is the miniscule...

Museum of Miniatures: You'll see 40 teeny exhibits, each under a microscope, crafted by an artist from St. Petersburg. Yes, you could fit the entire museum in a carry-on-size suitcase, but good things sometimes come in very, very small packages—it's fascinating to see minutiae such as a padlock on the leg of an ant. An English flier explains it all (entry-50 Kč, kids-20 Kč, daily 9:00–17:00).

On Loreta Square, Between Strahov Monastery and Castle Square

From the monastery, take Loretánská street to Loreta Square (Loretánské Náměstí). As you wander this road, you'll pass several mansions and palaces, and an important pilgrimage church.

Loreta Church—This church has been a hit with pilgrims for centuries, thanks to its dazzling bell tower, peaceful yet plush cloister, sparkling treasury, and much-venerated Holy House (110 Kč, Tue–Sun 9:00–12:15 & 13:00–16:30, closed Mon).

Once inside the entry, follow the one-way clockwise route. Strolling along the cloister, notice that the ceiling is painted with the many places Mary has miraculously appeared to the faithful in Europe.

In the garden-like center of the cloister stands the ornate **Santa Casa (Holy House),** considered by some pilgrims to be part of Mary's home in Nazareth. Because many pilgrims returning from the Holy Land docked at the Italian port of Loreto, it's called the Loreta Shrine. The Santa Casa is the "little Bethlehem" of Prague. It is the traditional departure point for Czech pilgrims setting out on the long, arduous journey to Europe's most important pilgrimage site, Santiago de Compostela, in northwest Spain. Inside, on the left wall, hangs what some consider to be an original beam from the house of Mary. It's overseen by a much-venerated statue of the Black Virgin. The Santa Casa itself might seem like a bit of a letdown, but consider that you're entering the holiest spot in the country for generations of believers.

The small Baroque church behind the Santa Casa is one of the most beautiful in Prague. The decor looks rich—but the marble and gold is all fake (tap the columns). From the window in the back, you can see a stucco relief on the Santa Casa that shows angels rescuing the house from a pagan attack in Nazareth and making a special delivery to Loreto in Italy.

Continue around the cloister. In the last corner is St. Bearded Woman (Svatá Starosta). This patron saint of unhappy marriages is a woman whose family arranged for her to marry a pagan man. She prayed for an escape, sprouted a beard...and the guy said, "No way." While she managed to avoid the marriage, it angered her father, who crucified her. The many candles here are from people suffering through unhappy marriages.

Take a left just before the exit and head upstairs, following signs to the treasury—a room full of jeweled worship aids (well-described in English). The highlight here is a monstrance

---

European Flags Fly in the Czech Republic

Today, the blue flag of the European Union flies alongside the Czech flag on the roof of government buildings, such as the Ministry of Foreign Affairs. The Czech Republic entered the EU along with nine other countries on May 1, 2004. Most Czechs are disappointed they weren't admitted much earlier.

The former president of the Czech Republic, Václav Havel, said the EU offers Europe the historic chance to finally get together and resolve issues over a table, rather than on the battlefield. But there are Euro-skeptics, including the right wing, the communists, and the current Czech president, Václav Klaus, who argues that the country is surrendering too much of its autonomy to Brussels. Still, most Czechs are optimistic about their future in the EU, and the majority of the government feels that membership will benefit the country. The year following Czech entry into the EU saw the largest GDP growth since 1989, as well as growing foreign investment. Japanese and Korean companies now find it advantageous to produce goods in the Czech Republic (or Slovakia), since assembling their final products within these member countries exempts them from EU tariffs.

(Communion wafer holder) from 1699, with more than 6,000 diamonds.

Enjoy the short carillon concert at the top of the hour; from the lawn in front of the main entrance, you can see the racks of bells being clanged. (At the exit, you'll see a schedule of English-language Masses and upcoming *pout'*—pilgrimages—departing from here.)

• *On the opposite side of the square is...*

Černín Palace—This palace once belonged to one of the most cosmopolitan Czech families, and so in 1918, it was turned into the Ministry of Foreign Affairs. In May of 2005, a memorial to the first secretary of state of Czechoslovakia, Edvard Beneš, was unveiled in front of the Ministry. This second president of Czechoslovakia, who led the country from exile in London during World War II, is highly controversial these days (see page 184). The tiny size of the statue expresses the nation's present uncertainty about the legacy of the man.

Beneš faces the bronze portrait bust of Hana Benešová, Edvard's wife, on the nearby house where she lived for a brief period. Hana has long been regarded as the force behind many of Edvard's crucial decisions. Czechs typically measure statesmen by their wives, since many Czechs regard men as pathologically ambitious and imprudent creatures, whose success and apparent political wisdom are due to the out-of-sight, sensible judgment of their better halves.

Castle Square (Hradčanské Náměstí)

This is the central square of the Castle Quarter. Enjoy the awesome city view and the two entertaining bands that play regularly at the gate. (If the Prague Castle Orchestra is playing, say hello

to friendly, mustachioed Josef, and consider getting the group's terrific CD.) A café with dramatic city views called Espresso Kajetánka hides a few steps down, immediately to the right as you face the castle (see page 134). From here, stairs lead into the Little Quarter.

Castle Square was a kind of medieval Pennsylvania Avenue—the king, the most powerful noblemen, and the archbishop lived here. Look uphill from the gate. The Renaissance **Schwarzenberg Palace** (on the left, with the big rectangles scratched on the wall, now under renovation) was where the Rožmberks "humbly" stayed when they were in town from their Český Krumlov estates. The Schwarzenberg family inherited the Krumlov estates and aristocratic prominence in Bohemia, and stayed in the palace until the 20th century.

The archbishop still lives in the yellow Rococo **palace** across the square (with the three white goose necks in the red field—the coat of arms of Prague's archbishops).

Through the portal on the left-hand side of the palace, a lane

leads to the **Sternberg Palace** (Šternberský Palác), filled with the National Gallery's skippable collection of European paintings—including minor works by Albrecht Dürer, Peter Paul Rubens, Rembrandt, and El Greco (100 Kč, Tue–Sun 10:00–18:00, closed Mon).

The black Baroque sculpture in the middle of the square is a **plague column,** erected as a token of gratitude to the saints who saved the population from the epidemic, and an integral part of the main square of many Hapsburg towns.

The statue marked *TGM* honors **Tomáš Garrigue Masaryk** (1850–1937), a university prof and a pal of Woodrow Wilson. At

Castle Quarter

Tomáš Garrigue Masaryk
(1850–1937)

Tomáš Masaryk was the George Washington of Czechoslovakia. He founded the first democracy in Eastern Europe at the end of World War I, uniting the Czechs and the Slovaks to create Czechoslovakia. Like Václav Havel 70 years later, Masaryk was a politician whose vision extended far beyond the mountains enclosing the Bohemian basin.

Masaryk was born into a poor servant family in southern Moravia. After finishing high school, the village boy set off to attend university in Vienna. Masaryk earned his Ph.D. in sociology just in time for the opening of the Czech-language university in Prague. By that time, he was already married to an American music student named Charlotta Garrigue, who came from a prominent New York family. (The progressive Tomáš actually took her family name as part of his own.) Charlotta opened the doors of America's high society to Masaryk. Among the American friends he made was a young Princeton professor named Woodrow Wilson.

Masaryk was greatly impressed with America, and his admiration for its democratic system became the core of his gradually evolving political creed. He traveled the world and went to Vienna to serve in the parliament. By the time World War I broke

the end of World War I, Masaryk united the Czechs and the Slovaks into one nation and became its first president (see sidebar above).

▲▲Prague Castle (Pražský Hrad)

For more than a thousand years, Czech leaders have ruled from Prague Castle. Today, Prague's Castle is, by some measures, the biggest on earth. Four stops matter, and all are explained here: St. Vitus Cathedral, Old Royal Palace, Basilica of St. George, and the Golden Lane.

Hours: Castle sights are open daily April–Oct 9:00–17:00, Nov–March 9:00–16:00, last entry 15 minutes before closing;

out in 1914, Masaryk was 64 years old and—his friends thought—ready for retirement. But while most other Czech politicians stayed in Prague and supported the Hapsburg Empire, Masaryk went abroad in protest and formed a highly original plan: to create an independent, democratic republic of Czechs and Slovaks. Masaryk and his supporters recruited an army of 100,000 Czechs and Slovak soldiers who were willing to fight with the Allies against the Hapsburgs...establishing a strong case to put on his friend Woodrow Wilson's Oval Office desk.

On the morning of October 28, 1918, news of the unofficial capitulation of the Hapsburgs reached Prague. Local supporters of Masaryk's idea quickly took control of the city and proclaimed the free republic. As the people of Prague tore down double-headed eagles (a symbol of the Hapsburgs), Czechoslovakia was born.

On November 11, 1918, four years after he had left the country as a political nobody, Masaryk arrived in Prague as the greatest Czech hero since the revolutionary priest Jan Hus. The dignified old man rode through the masses of cheering Czechs on a white horse. He told the jubilant crowd, "Now go home—the work has only started." Throughout the 1920s and 1930s, Masaryk was Europe's most vocal defender of democratic ideals against the rising tide of totalitarian ideologies.

In 2001, the US government honored Masaryk's dedication to democracy by erecting a monument to him in Washington, D.C.—he is one of only three foreign leaders (along with Gandhi and Churchill) to have a statue in the American capital.

grounds are open daily 5:00–23:00. St. Vitus Cathedral is closed Sunday mornings for Mass. Be warned that the cathedral can be unexpectedly closed due to special services—consider calling ahead to confirm (tel. 224-373-368 or 224-372-434). If you're not interested in entering the museums, you could try a nighttime visit—the castle grounds are safe, peaceful, floodlit, and open late.

Tickets: When you visit, the cathedral may have a new moderately priced 50-Kč fee (which was being discussed by the Church and the president at the time of publication). If this fee becomes official, cathedral tickets (which will get you past the main tower) will be sold in the TIs outside the cathedral, just like the castle combo-tickets described below. The front of the cathedral will remain free.

For the other castle sights, rather than buying the comprehensive long-tour ticket (350 Kč), I recommend getting the short-tour ticket (250 Kč, covers the Old Royal Palace, Basilica of St. George, and the Golden Lane at peak hours; buy in palace, Basilica, or the ticket offices on the two castle squares). If you want to save time, skip the packed Golden Lane during the day, and return at night for a romantic, crowd-free visit (free in the morning and evening).

Tours: Hour-long tours in English depart from the main ticket office about three times a day, but cover only the cathedral and Old Royal Palace (90 Kč plus ticket, tel. 224-373-368). You can rent an **audioguide** for 200 Kč (good all day) by picking it up at the main desk in the TI, located across from the cathedral entrance—show this book for this rate (promised through 2009 by the manager). The audioguide also entitles you to priority entrance into the cathedral—when the line in front of the entrance is long, walk to the exit door on the right and show the audioguide to the guard to be let in.

Crowd-Beating Tips: Huge throngs of tourists turn the castle grounds into a sea of people during peak times (9:30–12:30). St. Vitus Cathedral is the most crowded part of the castle complex. If you're visiting in the morning, be at the cathedral entrance promptly at 9:00, when the doors open. For 10 minutes, you'll have the sacred space for yourself (after about 9:15, tour guides jockeying unwieldy groups from tomb to tomb turn the church into a noisy human traffic jam). Late afternoon is least crowded.

Castle Gate and Courtyards—Begin at Castle Square. From here, survey the castle—the tip of a 1,500-foot-long series of courtyards,

churches, and palaces. The guard changes on the hour (5:00–23:00), with the most ceremony and music at noon.

Walk under the fighting giants, under an arch, through the passageway, and into the courtyard. The modern green awning with the golden-winged cat (just past the ticket office) marks the offices of the Czech president, who, according to the constitution, is more of a figurehead than a power broker. The most recent president—and at the time of this writing the favorite for the 2008 election—is Václav Klaus. He's popular with members of the older generation (who like consistency), but is bitterly resented by younger people, many of whom see him as incapable of considering points of view other than his own. Outside the Czech Republic, Klaus is known for his unconstructive criticism of the European Union, and more recently, for his denunciation of the campaign against global warming (the reality of which he denies). In the fall of 2007, Klaus—who in his most recent book argues that the "environmental hysteria" fundamentally endangers the freedom

The Battle Between Church and State for St. Vitus Cathedral

There's no question that St. Vitus Cathedral is close to the hearts of Czechs. But in recent years controversy has erupted over just what aspect of the national spirit the cathedral embodies.

The cathedral was nationalized in the 1950s, and was managed by the Czech government for the next several decades. But in 1993—after the fall of communism—the Church began vying with the state for property rights. Since this building holds such symbolic value for the Czechs, it's not just the keys to the country's most precious artwork at stake. Those who wanted the cathedral to remain state-owned pointed out that it was the king, not the Church, who commissioned the cathedral, and that its completion in the 19th century was inspired more by patriotism than by religious fervor. The Church, however, pointed out the cathedral's role as a pilgrimage site, arguing that it should be dedicated to prayer. In 2006, the court finally ruled in the Church's favor (and against public opinion).

The Church has been cash-strapped since the fall of communism. While the state returned thousands of deteriorating chapels throughout the country to the Church, it didn't return ownership of the lands that once provided the revenue for maintenance. So, perhaps understandably, once the keys changed hands, the Church saw an easy source of cash. Hoping that the throngs of cathedral visitors would help them bring new life to neglected rural chapels, they immediately imposed a 100-Kč entrance fee. Some accused them of greediness. But before the coins had enough time to fill a single coffer, the Highest Court overruled the decision, returned the cathedral to the state (which made the entrance free), and a new round of legal proceedings began again.

---

of the individual—became the face of the Exxon-sponsored campaign in the American media that preceded a UN conference on global warming.

As you walk through another passageway, you'll find yourself facing...

▲▲▲**St. Vitus Cathedral (Katedrála Sv. Víta)**—The Roman Catholic cathedral symbolizes the Czech spirit—it contains the tombs and relics of the most important local saints and kings, including the first three Hapsburg kings.

Cathedral Facade: Before entering, check out the facade. What's up with the guys in suits carved into the facade below the big round window? They're the architects and builders who finished the church. Started in 1344, construction was stalled by wars and plagues. But, fueled by the 19th-century rise of Czech nationalism, Prague's top church was finished in 1929 for the 1,000th anniversary of the death of St. Wenceslas. While it looks all Gothic, it's actually two distinct halves: the original 14th-century Gothic around the high altar, and the modern Neo-Gothic nave. For 400 years, a temporary wall sealed off the functional, yet unfinished, cathedral.

Mucha Stained-Glass Window: Go inside, buy your ticket, show your ticket at the fenced-off area, and find the third window on the left. This masterful 1931 Art Nouveau window is by Czech artist Alfons Mucha (if you like this, you'll love the Mucha Museum in the New Town—see page 79; also see Mucha's masterpiece, *Slav Epic*, described on page 221).

Notice Mucha's stirring nationalism: Methodius and Cyril, widely considered the fathers of Slavic-style Christianity, are top and center. Cyril—the monk in black holding the Bible—brought the word of God to the Slavs. They had no written language in the ninth century—so he designed the necessary alphabet (Glagolitic, which later developed into Cyrillic). Methodius, the bishop, is shown baptizing a mythic, lanky, long-haired Czech man—a reminder of how he brought Christianity to the Czech people. Scenes from the life of Cyril on the left and scenes from the life of Methodius on the right bookend the stirring and epic Slavic scene. In the center are a kneeling boy and a prophesying elder—that's

young St. Wenceslas and his grandmother, St. Ludmila. In addition to being specific historical figures, these characters are also symbolic: The old woman, with closed eyes, stands for the past and memory, while the young boy, with a penetrating stare, represents the hope and future of a nation. Notice how master designer Mucha draws your attention to these two figures through the use of colors—the dark blue on the outside gradually turns into green, then yellow, and finally the gold of the woman and the crimson of the boy in the center. In Mucha's color language, blue stands for the past, gold for the mythic, and red for the future. Besides all the meaning, Mucha's art is simply a joy to behold. (And on the bottom, the tasteful little ad for *Banka Slavie,* which paid for the work, is hardly noticeable.)

Hapsburg Emperor's Tomb: Continue circulating around the apse. The big royal tomb (within the black iron fence) is of the first Hapsburg emperor. It dates from 1590, when Prague was a major Hapsburg power.

Relief of Prague: As you walk around the high altar, study the fascinating carved-wood relief of Prague. It depicts the victorious Hapsburg armies entering the castle after the Battle of White Mountain, while the Protestant king Frederic escapes over the Charles Bridge (before it had any statues). Carved in 1630, 10 years after the famous event occurred, the relief also gives you a peek at Prague in 1620, stretching from the Týn Church to the cathedral (half-built at that time, up to where you are now). Notice that back then, the Týn Church was Hussite, so the centerpiece of its facade is not the Virgin Mary—but a chalice, symbol of Jan Hus' ideals. The old city walls—now replaced by the main streets of the city—stand strong. The Jewish Quarter (the slummy, muddy zone along the riverside below the bridge on the left) fills land no one else wanted.

Apse: Circling around the high altar, you pass graves of bishops, including the tomb of St. Vitus (behind the chair of the bishop). The stone sarcophagi contain kings from the Přemysl dynasty (12th to 14th centuries). Locals claim the gigantic, shiny tomb of St. John of Nepomuk has more than a ton of silver (for more on St. John of Nepomuk, see page 64). After the silver tomb, look up at the royal box from where the king would attend Mass in his jammies (an elevated corridor connected his private apartment with his own altar-side box pew).

Look for the finely carved wood panel that gives a Counter-Reformation spin on the Wars of Religion. It shows the "barbaric" Protestant nobles destroying the Catholic icons in the cathedral after their short-lived victory.

Wenceslas Chapel: A fancy roped-off chapel (right transept) houses the tomb of St. Wenceslas, surrounded by precious 14th-century murals showing scenes of his life (see description on page 74), and a locked door leading to the crown jewels. The Czech kings used to be crowned right here in front of the coffin, draped in red. The chapel is roped off because the wallpaper is encrusted with precious and semiprecious stones. (Lead us not into temptation.) You can view the chapel from either door (if the door facing the nave is crowded, duck around to the left to find a door that is most likely open).

Spire: You can climb 287 steps up the spire for one of the best views of the whole city (included in cathedral ticket, April–Oct daily 9:00–17:00 except Sun morning, last entry 45 minutes before

The Catholic Church in Prague

In stark contrast to Poland, the powerful Catholic Church—traditionally closely allied with the Hapsburgs and Austria—was never the favorite institution of the freedom-loving Czechs. The communists took advantage of this popular sentiment, and in their Marxist zeal did everything short of banning the Church to uproot the faith of the relatively few practicing Catholics. In the early 1950s, most monks and priests, including the archbishop, were arrested and sent to prisons, from which they were not released until the thawing that came with the Khrushchev era. A wise old priest remembers his 13 years in a labor camp as "a fascinating, well-spent time in the company of some truly great minds."

During the communist era, Church property was confiscated, churches quickly deteriorated, churchgoers were persecuted, and many priests had to become confidants of the secret police in order to continue their service. Ironically, by persecuting Catholics, the communists gave the Church the opportunity to improve its reputation with the Czechs. In the 1980s, the charismatic archbishop of Prague, Cardinal Tomášek, became a local hero  by frequently standing up to the regime. By 1989, Tomášek was a main symbol of anti-communist opposition (along with Václav Havel).

After 1989, many Czechs returned to the Catholic faith. The trend peaked in 1992 when Tomášek died (now buried under the Mucha window in St. Vitus Cathedral). Since then, the Church's hold has steadily declined, for various reasons. The media depict the Church as greedy; questions have arisen about the status of former Church property (see sidebar on page 105); and the new archbishop—named Vlk (Wolf), which his critics find fitting—is uninspiring.

These days, "new" and fashionable spiritual movements, such as Buddhism, are drawing Czechs in increasing numbers. The Dalai Lama is now one of Prague's most frequent visitors.

closing, closes at 16:00 Nov–March).

Back Outside the Cathedral: Leaving the cathedral, turn left (past the public WC). The **obelisk** was erected in 1928—a single piece of granite celebrating the 10th anniversary of the establishment of Czechoslovakia. It was originally much taller, but broke in transit—an inauspicious start for a nation destined to last only 70 years. Up in the fat, green tower of the cathedral is the Czech Republic's biggest bell, nicknamed "Zikmund." In June of 2002, it cracked—and two months later, the worst flood in recorded history hit the city—which the locals saw as a sign. As a nation sandwiched

between great powers, Czechs are deeply superstitious when it comes to the tides of history. Often feeling unable to influence the course of their own destiny, they helplessly look at events as we might look at the weather and other natural phenomena—trying to figure out what fate has in store for them next.

Find the 14th-century **mosaic** of the Last Judgment outside on the right transept. It was commissioned Italian-style by King Charles IV, who was modern, cosmopolitan, and ahead of his time. Jesus oversees the action, as some go to heaven and some go to hell. The Czech king and queen kneel directly below Jesus and the six patron saints. On coronation day, they would walk under this arch, which would remind them (and their subjects) that even those holding great power are not above God's judgment. The royal crown and national jewels are kept in a chamber (see the grilled windows) above this entryway, which was the cathedral's main entry for centuries while the church remained uncompleted.

Across the square and 20 yards to the right, a door leads into the Old Royal Palace (in the lobby, there's a WC with a window shared by the men's and women's sections—meet your partner to enjoy the view).

Old Royal Palace (Starý Královský Palác)—Starting in the

12th century, this was the seat of the Bohemian princes. While extensively rebuilt, the **large hall** is late Gothic, designed as a multipurpose hall for the old nobility. It's big enough for jousts—even the staircase was designed to let a mounted soldier gallop in. It was filled with market stalls, giving nobles a chance to shop without actually going into town. In the 1400s, the nobility met here to elect their king. This tradition survived until modern times, as the parliament crowded into this room until the late 1990s to elect the Czechoslovak (and later Czech) president. (The last three elections happened in another, far more lavish hall in the castle.) Look up at the flower-shaped, vaulted ceiling.

On your immediate right, enter the two small Renaissance rooms known as the **"Czech Office."** From these rooms (empty today except for their 17th-century porcelain heaters), two governors used to oversee the Czech lands for the Hapsburgs in Vienna. In 1618, angry Czech Protestant nobles poured into these rooms and threw the two Catholic governors out of the window. An old law actually permits defenestration—throwing people (usually bad politicians) out of windows when necessary. Old prints on the wall show the second of Prague's many defenestrations. The two governors landed—fittingly—in a pile of horse manure. Even though they suffered only broken arms and bruised egos, this event kicked off the huge and lengthy Thirty Years' War.

Look down on the chapel from the end, and go out on the balcony for a fine Prague view. Is that Paris' Eiffel Tower in the distance? No, it's Petřín Tower—a fine place for a relaxing day at the park, offering sweeping views over Prague (see page 92).

As you exit through the side door, pause at the door to consider the subtle yet racy little Renaissance knocker. Go ahead—play with it for a little sex in the palace (be gentle).

Across from the palace exit is the...

Basilica and Convent of St. George (Bazilika Sv. Jiří)—Step into the beautiful-in-its-simplicity Basilica of St. George to see Prague's best-preserved Romanesque church. Notice the char-

acteristic double windows on the gallery, as well as the walls made of limestone (the rock that Prague rests on). In those early years, the building techniques were not yet advanced, and the ceiling is made of wood, rather than arched with stone. St. Wenceslas' grandmother, St. Ludmila, who established this first Bohemian convent, was reburied here in 973. Look for Gothic frescoes depicting this cultured woman (to the right of the altar space). The Baroque front—which dates from much later—was added on the exterior at the same time as the St. John of Nepomuk chapel (through which you exit the church). The scary-looking bones under the chapel altar are replicas—neither St. John's nor real.

Today, the **convent** next door houses the National Gallery's

Collection of Old Masters, featuring the best Czech paintings from the Mannerist and Baroque periods (100 Kč, Tue–Sun 10:00–18:00, closed Mon).

Continue walking downhill through the castle grounds. Turn left on the first street, which leads into the...

Golden Lane (Zlatá Ulička)—This street of old buildings, which originally housed goldsmiths, is jammed with tourists during the day and lined with overpriced gift shops. Franz Kafka lived briefly at #22. There's a deli/bistro at the top. In the morning (before 9:00) and at night (after 17:00 in summer, 16:00 in winter), the tiny street is free, empty, and romantic. Exit the lane through a corridor at the last house (#12).

Toy and Barbie Museum (Muzeum Hraček)—At the bottom of the castle complex, just after leaving the Golden Lane, a long, wooden staircase leads to two entertaining floors of old toys and dolls thoughtfully described in English. You'll see a century of teddy bears, 19th-century model train sets, and an incredible Barbie collection (the entire top floor). Find the buxom 1959 first edition, and you'll understand why these capitalistic sirens of material discontent weren't allowed here until 1989 (60 Kč, 120 Kč per family, not included in any castle tickets, daily 9:30–17:30, WC next to entrance).

After Your Castle Visit: Tourists squirt slowly through a fortified door at the bottom end of the castle. From there, you can follow the steep lane directly back to the riverbank (and the Malostranská Metro station).

Or you can take a hard right and stroll through the long, delightful park. Along the way, notice the modernist design of the **Na Valech Garden,** which was carried out by the court architect of the 1920s, Jože Plečnik of Slovenia.

Halfway through the long park is a viewpoint overlooking **terraced gardens;** you can zigzag down through these gardens into the Little Quarter (80 Kč, April–Oct daily 10:00–18:00, closed Nov–March).

If you continue through the park all the way to Castle Square, you'll find two more options: a staircase leading down into the Little Quarter, or a cobbled street taking you to historic Nerudova street (described on page 88).

Congratulations. You've conquered the castle.

SLEEPING

Peak season for hotels in Prague is late April, May, June, September, and early October. Easter and Christmas are the most crowded times, when prices are jacked up a bit. I've listed peak-time prices—if you're traveling in July or August, you'll find rates generally 15 percent lower, and from November through March, about 30 percent lower.

Room-Booking Services
Prague is awash with fancy rooms on the push list; private, small-time operators with rooms to rent in their apartments; and roving agents eager to book you a bed and earn a commission. You can save about 30 percent by showing up in Prague without a reservation and finding accommodations upon arrival. However, it is a hustle, and you will not necessarily get your ideal choice. If you're coming in by train or car, you'll encounter booking agencies. They can almost always find you a reasonable room, and, if it's a private guest house, your host can even come and lead you to the place.

Athos Travel has a line on 200 properties (ranging from hostels to 5-star hotels), 90 percent of which are in the historical center. To book a room, call them or use their handy website, which allows you to search for a room, based on various criteria (best to arrange in advance during peak season, can also help with last-minute booking off-season, tel. 241-440-571, fax 241-441-697, www.a-prague.com, info@a-prague.com). Readers report that Athos is aggressive with its business policies—while there's no fee to cancel well in advance, they strictly enforce penalties on cancellations within 48 hours.

AVE, at the Main Train Station (Hlavní Nádraží), is another booking service (daily 6:00–23:00). With the tracks at your back, walk down to the orange ceiling and past the "Meeting Point"

Sleep Code

(20 Kč = about $1, country code: 420)
S = Single, **D** = Double/Twin, **T** = Triple, **Q** = Quad, **b** = bathroom, **s** = shower only. Unless otherwise noted, credit cards are accepted, and breakfast and tax are included. Everyone listed here speaks English.

To help you sort easily through these listings, I've divided the rooms into three categories based on the price for a standard double room with bath:

$$$ Higher Priced—Most rooms 4,000 Kč or more.
$$ Moderately Priced—Most rooms between 3,000–4,000 Kč.
$ Lower Priced—Most rooms 3,000 Kč or less.

(don't go downstairs)—their office is in the left corner by the exit to the rip-off taxis. Their display board shows discounted hotels, and they have a slew of hotels and small pensions available (2,000-Kč pension doubles in old center, 1,500-Kč doubles a Metro ride away). You can reserve by email, using your credit card as a deposit (tel. 251-551-011, fax 251-555-156, www.avetravel.cz, ave@avetravel .cz), or just show up at the office and request a room. Be clear on the location before you make your choice. They sell taxi vouchers for those who want the convenience of a ride from the train station's taxi stand, though they cost double the fair rate.

For a more personal touch, Lída Jánská's **Magic Praha** helps with accommodations (tel. 235-325-170, mobile 604-207-225, www.magicpraha.cz, magicpraha@magicpraha.cz; see "Helpful Hints," page 39). Lída rents a well-located apartment with a river view near the Jewish Quarter.

Web-booking services, such as Priceline.com and Biddingfortravel.com, enable budget travelers to snare fancy rooms on the push list for half the rack rate. It's not unusual to find a room in a four-star hotel for 1,300 Kč—but keep in mind that many of these international business-class hotels are far from the city center.

Old Town Hotels and Pensions

You'll pay higher prices to stay in the Old Town, but for many travelers, the convenience is worth the expense. These places are all within a 10-minute walk of the Old Town Square.

$$$ Hotel Maximilian is a sleek, mod, 70-room place with Art Deco black design; big, plush living rooms; and all the business services and comforts you'd expect in a four-star hotel. It

HOTELS IN PRAGUE'S OLD TOWN

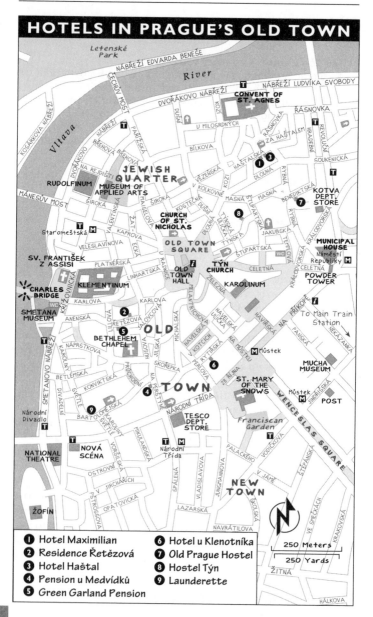

1 Hotel Maximilian
2 Residence Řetězová
3 Hotel Haštal
4 Pension u Medvídků
5 Green Garland Pension
6 Hotel u Klenotníka
7 Old Prague Hostel
8 Hostel Týn
9 Launderette

250 Meters
250 Yards

faces a church on a perfect little square just a short walk from the action (Db-4,500 Kč, extra bed-1,500 Kč, their "preferred rate" gives you a 14 percent discount if you lock in a reservation with no cancellation option, check online for lower rates, Haštalská 14, tel. 225-303-111, fax 225-303-110, www.maximilianhotel.com, reservation@maximilianhotel.com).

$$$ Residence Řetězová is on a central but delightfully quiet cobbled lane. Its medieval shell has been remodeled into nine elegant, plush, and spacious apartments—each one is unique. You can enjoy the mystery and ambience of old Prague with all the modern comforts (Db-4,100–5,600 Kč, large apartment-10,200 Kč for up to 6 people; 20 percent discount with advance reservation, this book, and cash; check online for lower, last-minute rates and to choose your room; free Internet access, Řetězová 9, tel. & fax 222-221-800, www.residenceretezova.com, info@residenceretezova.com).

$$ Hotel Haštal is next to Hotel Maximilian (listed above) on the same quiet, hidden square in the Old Town. A popular hotel back in the 1920s, it was tactfully renovated to complement the neighborhood's vibrant circa-1900 architecture. Its 24 rooms are comfortable, but the walls are a bit thin (Sb-2,900 Kč, Db-3,600 Kč, extra bed-550 Kč, 20 percent discount when booking online, air-con, Haštalská 16, tel. 222-314-335, www.hastal.com, info @hastal.com). The hotel's small restaurant is understandably popular with locals for its reasonably priced lunch specials and draft beer.

$$ Pension u Medvídků has 31 comfortably renovated rooms in a big, rustic, medieval shell with dark wood furniture. Upstairs, you'll find lots of beams—or, if you're not careful, they'll find you (Sb-2,300 Kč, Db-3,500 Kč, Tb-4,500 Kč, extra bed-500 Kč, "historical" rooms 10 percent more, apartment for 20 percent more, manager Vladimír promises readers of this book a 10 percent discount with cash if you book direct, Internet access, Na Perštýně 7, tel. 224-211-916, fax 224-220-930, www.umedvidku.cz, info @umedvidku.cz). The pension runs a popular beer-hall restaurant with live music most Fridays and Saturdays until 23:00—request an inside room for maximum peace.

$$ Green Garland Pension (U Zeleného Věnce), on the same quiet pedestrian street as Residence Řetězová, has a warm and personal feel rare in the Old Town. Located in a thick 14th-century building with open beams, it has a blond-hardwood charm decorated with a woman's touch. Its nine rooms are clean and simply furnished (big Sb-2,900 Kč, Db-3,400 Kč, bigger Db-3,700 Kč, Tb-4,400 Kč, 10 percent discount with cash, family suite, Řetězová 10, tel. 222-220-178, fax 224-248-791, www.uzv.cz, pension@uzv.cz).

$$ Hotel u Klenotníka (At the Jeweler), with 11 modern, comfortable rooms in a plain building, is three blocks off the Old

Town Square (Sb-2,500 Kč, small double-bed Db-3,300, bigger twin-bed Db-3,800 Kč, Tb-4,500 Kč, Marie and Helena promise 10 percent off when booking direct with this book, Rytířská 3, tel. 224-211-699, fax 224-221-025, www.uklenotnika.cz, info @uklenotnika.cz).

Under the Castle, in the Little Quarter

The first three listings are buried on quiet lanes deep in the Little Quarter, among cobbles, quaint restaurants, rummaging tourists, and embassy flags. The last is a 10-minute walk up the river on a quiet and stately street with none of the intense medieval cityscape of the others.

$$$ Hotel Sax reopened in 2008 after a designer-planned renovation of all 22 rooms in a 1950–60s fashion. With a fruity atrium and a distinctly modern, stark feel, this is a stylish, no-nonsense place (Sb-4,200 Kč, Db-4,900 Kč, Db suite-5,600 Kč, extra bed-1,000 Kč, 10 percent off with advance reservation and this book, elevator, Jánský Vršek 3, tel. 257-531-268, fax 257-534-101, www.sax.cz, hotel@sax.cz).

$$ Dům u Velké Boty (House at the Big Boot), on a quiet square in front of the German Embassy, is the rare quintessential family hotel in Prague: homey, comfy, and extremely friendly. Charlotta, Jan, and their two sons treat every guest as a (thirsty) friend, and the wellspring of their stories never runs dry. Each of their 12 rooms is uniquely decorated, most in tasteful 19th-century Biedermeier style (tiny S-2,100 Kč, two D rooms that share a bathroom-3,400 Kč each, Db-4,450 Kč, extra bed-725 Kč, 10 percent off with advance reservation and this book, prices can be soft when slow, cash only, free Internet access and Wi-Fi, Vlašská 30, tel. 257-532-088, www.bigboot.cz, info@bigboot.cz). While they don't include tax or breakfast in their rates, I've included them in the prices above for easy comparison. There's no hotel sign on the house—look for the splendid geraniums that Jan nurtures in the windows.

$$ Hotel Julián is an oasis of professional, predictable decency in an untouristy neighborhood. Its 32 spacious, fresh, well-furnished rooms and big, homey public spaces hide behind a noble Neoclassical facade. The staff is friendly and helpful (Sb-3,680 Kč, Db-3,980 Kč, Db suite-4,800 Kč, extra bed-900 Kč, discount for booking online, 15 percent discount off rack rate with this book, free tea and coffee in room, air-con, elevator, plush and inviting lobby, parking lot; Metro: Anděl, then an 8-min walk; or take tram #6, #9, #12, #20, or #58 for two stops; Elišky Peškové 11, Praha 5, reservation tel. 257-311-150, reception tel. 257-311-145, fax 257-311-149, www.julian.cz, casjul@vol.cz). Free lockers and a shower are available for those needing a place

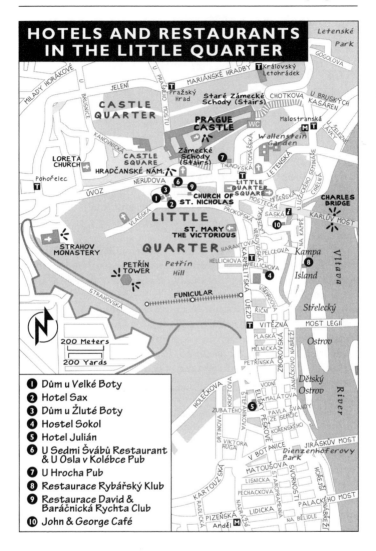

HOTELS AND RESTAURANTS IN THE LITTLE QUARTER

❶ Dům u Velké Boty
❷ Hotel Sax
❸ Dům u Žluté Boty
❹ Hostel Sokol
❺ Hotel Julián
❻ U Sedmi Švábů Restaurant & U Osla v Kolébce Pub
❼ U Hrocha Pub
❽ Restaurace Rybářský Klub
❾ Restaurace David & Baráčnická Rychta Club
❿ John & George Café

to stay after check out (for example, while waiting for an overnight train). Mike's Chauffeur Service, based here, is reliable and affordable (see page 151).

$$ Dům u Žluté Boty (House at the Yellow Boot) hides rustic wooden interiors behind colorful walls. Its seven rooms are each unique: Some preserve 16th-century wooden ceilings; some feel like mountain lodges; and others are a bit marred by an insensitive 1970s remodel. Top-floor rooms can get a bit stuffy during summer heat waves, although fans are provided (Sb-2,700 Kč, Db-3,300 Kč, Tb-3,800 Kč, extra bed-500 Kč, 15 percent discount with cash

Sleeping

and this book, some thin walls, Jánský Vršek 11, tel. 257-532-269, fax 257-534-134, www.zlutabota.cz, hotel@zlutabota.cz).

Away from the Center

Moving just outside central Prague saves you money—and gets you away from the tourists and into some more workaday residential neighborhoods. The following listings (great values compared to the downtown hotels listed previously) are all within a 5- to 15-minute tram or Metro ride from the center.

Beyond Wenceslas Square

These hotels are in urban neighborhoods on the outer fringe of the New Town, beyond Wenceslas Square. But they're still within several minutes' walk of the sightseeing zone, and are well-served by trams.

$$$ Sieber Hotel, with 20 rooms, is a quality, four-star, business-class hotel in an upscale residential neighborhood near the former royal vineyards (Vinohrady). They do a good job of being homey and welcoming (Sb-4,480 Kč, Db-4,780 Kč, extra bed-990 Kč, fourth night free, ask for discount when you book direct and pay with cash, 30 percent discount for last-minute reservations, air-con, elevator, Internet access, 3-min walk to Metro: Jiřího z Poděbrad, or tram #11, Slezská 55, Praha 3, tel. 224-250-025, fax 224-250-027, www.sieber.cz, reservations@sieber.cz).

$$ Hotel Anna, with 24 bright, pastel, and classically charming rooms, is a bit closer in—just 10 minutes by foot east of Wenceslas Square (Sb-2,350 Kč, Db-3,160 Kč, Tb-3,830 Kč, special online offers, non-smoking rooms, elevator, Budečská 17, Praha 2, Metro: Náměstí Míru, tel. 222-513-111, fax 222-515-158, www.hotelanna.cz, sales@hotelanna.cz). They run a similar hotel (same standards and prices) nearby.

$$ Hotel 16 is a sleek and modern business-class place with an intriguing Art Nouveau facade, polished cherry-wood elegance, high ceilings, and 14 fine rooms (Sb-2,800 Kč, Db-3,500 Kč, bigger Db-3,700 Kč, Tb-4,700 Kč, 10 percent discount with this book, triple-paned windows, back rooms facing the garden are quieter, air-con, elevator, Internet access, 10-min walk south of Wenceslas Square, Metro: I. P. Pavlova, Kateřinská 16, Praha 2, tel. 224-920-636, fax 224-920-626, www.hotel16.cz, hotel16@hotel16.cz).

The Best Values, Farther from the Center

These accommodations are a 10- to 20-minute tram ride from the center, but once you make the trip, you'll see it's no problem—and you'll feel pretty smug saving $50–100 a night per double by not sleeping in the Old Town. The Šemíka and Lída are within a stone's throw of peaceful Vyšehrad Park, with a legendary castle

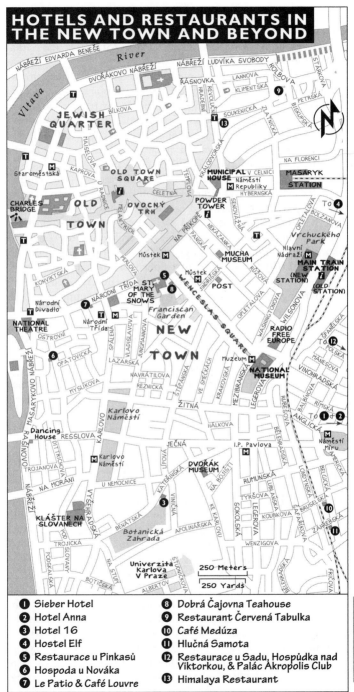

HOTELS AND RESTAURANTS IN THE NEW TOWN AND BEYOND

1. Sieber Hotel
2. Hotel Anna
3. Hotel 16
4. Hostel Elf
5. Restaurace u Pinkasů
6. Hospoda u Nováka
7. Le Patio & Café Louvre
8. Dobrá Čajovna Teahouse
9. Restaurant Červená Tabulka
10. Café Medúza
11. Hlučná Samota
12. Restaurace u Sadu, Hospůdka nad Viktorkou, & Palác Akropolis Club
13. Himalaya Restaurant

on a cliff overlooking the Vltava River. The Adalbert is on the grounds of an ancient monastery and the Větrník is adjacent, with two of Prague's best-preserved natural areas (Star Park and Šárka) just a short walk away.

$$ Hotel Adalbert occupies an 18th-century building in the Břevnov Monastery (one of the Czech Republic's oldest monastic institutions, founded in 993). Meticulously restored after the return of the Benedictine monks in the 1990s, the monastery complex is the ultimate retreat for those who come to Prague for soul-searching or just wanting a quiet place away from the bustle. Join the monks for morning (7:00) and evening (18:00) Mass in the St. Margaret Basilica, a large and elegant Baroque church executed with unusual simplicity. You can help yourself in the monastery fruit orchard, and eat in the atmospheric monastery pub (Klášterní Šenk). The hotel itself caters primarily to business clientele and takes ecology seriously: recycling, water conservation, and free tram tickets for guests (Sb-2,600 Kč, Db-3,600 Kč, extra bed-1,050 Kč, ask for a first-floor room as some of the attic rooms—room numbers in the 200s—feel a bit cramped, Wi-Fi, free parking, ask for 10 percent Rick Steves discount when you reserve, halfway between city and airport at Markétská 1, Praha 6, tram #22 to Břevnovský Klášter; 5 min by tram beyond the castle, 20 min from Old and New Towns; tel. 220-406-170, fax 220-406-190, www.hoteladalbert.cz, info@hoteladalbert.cz).

$ Pension Větrník fills an attractive, white-and-orange former 17th-century windmill in one of Prague's most popular residential areas, right next to the Břevnov Monastery and midway between the airport and the city. Owner Miloš Opatrný is a prize-winning Czech chef who sailed the world feeding cruise-ship passengers. On request, Miloš will prepare a feast you'll never forget. The six rooms here are the pride of the Opatrný family, who live on the upper floors. The garden has a good-hearted bear of a dog and a tennis court—rackets and balls are provided (Db-2,200 Kč, suite-3,300 Kč, extra bed-550 Kč, U Větrníku 4, Praha 6; airport bus #179 stops right in front of the house, tram #18 goes straight to Charles Bridge, both take 20 min; tel. 220-612-404, fax 235-361-406, www.pensionvetrnik.wz.cz).

$ Hotel u Šemíka, named for a heroic mythical horse, offers 25 rooms in a quiet residential neighborhood just below Vyšehrad Castle and the Slavín cemetery where Dvořák, Mucha, and Čapek are buried. It's a 10-minute tram ride south of the Old Town (Sb-2,000 Kč, Db-2,650 Kč, apartment-3,350–3,700 Kč for 2–4 people, extra bed-600 Kč, ask for the "direct booking" Rick Steves 10 percent discount; from the center, take tram #3, #17, or #21 to Výtoň, go under rail bridge, and walk 3 blocks uphill to Vratislavova 36; Praha 2, tel. 224-920-736, fax 224-911-602, www.usemika.cz, usemika@usemika.cz).

$ Guest House Lída, with 12 homey and spacious rooms, fills a big house in a quiet residential area farther inland, a 15-minute tram ride from the center. Jan, Jiří, and Jitka Prouza, who run the place, are a wealth of information and know how to make people feel at home (Sb-1,380 Kč, small Db-1,440 Kč, Db-1,760 Kč, Tb-2,110 Kč, Qb-2,530 Kč, cash only, family rooms, top-floor family suite with kitchenette, Internet access, parking garage-200 Kč/day, Metro: Pražského Povstání; exit Metro and turn left on Lomnického between the Metro station and big blue-glass ČSOB building, follow Lomnického for 500 yards, then turn left on Lopatecká, go uphill and ring bell at Lopatecká #26, no sign outside; Praha 4, tel. & fax 261-214-766, www.lidabb.eu, lidabb @seznam.cz). The Prouza brothers also rent four apartments across the river, an equal distance from the center (Db-1,600 Kč, Tb-1,900 Kč, Qb-2,100 Kč).

Hostels in the Center

It's tough to find a double for less than 3,000 Kč in the old center. But Prague has an abundance of fine hostels—each with a distinct personality, and each excellent in its own way for anyone wanting a 400-Kč dorm bed or an extremely simple, twin-bedded room for about 1,300 Kč.

$ Old Prague Hostel is a small and very friendly place with 70 beds on the second and third floors of an apartment building on a back alley near the Powder Tower. The spacious rooms were once apartment bedrooms, so it feels less institutional than most hostels. Hanging out in the comfy TV lounge/breakfast room, you'll feel like part of an international family. Older travelers would feel comfortable in this mellow place (six D-1,360 Kč, bunk in 3- to 8-person room-450–530 Kč; includes breakfast, sheets, towels, lockers, and free Internet access; in summer reserve one month ahead, Benediktská 2, see map on page 114 for location, tel. 224-829-058, fax 224-829-060, www.oldpraguehostel.com, oldpraguehostel @seznam.cz).

$ Hostel Týn is hidden in a silent courtyard two blocks from the Old Town Square. Because the management is aware of its value, they don't bother being too friendly (D-1,200 Kč, T-1,400 Kč, bunk in 4- to 5-bed co-ed room-400 Kč, lockers, reserve one week ahead, Týnská 19, located on map on page 114, tel. 224-828-519, mobile 776-122-057, www.hostel-tyn.web2001.cz, backpacker@razdva.cz).

$ Hostel Elf, a 10-minute walk from the Main Train Station or one bus stop from the Florenc Metro station, is fun-loving, ramshackle, covered with noisy, self-inflicted graffiti, and the wildest of these hostels. They offer cheap, basic beds, a helpful staff, and lots of creative services—kitchen, free luggage room, free Internet access, laundry, no lockout, free tea, cheap beer, a terrace, and lockers (120 beds, D-900 Kč, bunk in 6- to 11-person room-320 Kč, includes sheets and breakfast, cash only, reserve four days ahead, Husitská 11, Praha 3, take bus #133 or 207 from Florenc Metro station for one stop to U Památníku, tel. 222-540-963, www.hostelelf.com, info@hostelelf.com).

$ Hostel Sokol, plain and institutional with 100 beds, is peacefully located just off park-like Kampa Island in the Tyrš House buildings (the seat of the Czech Sokol Organization). Big WWI hospital–style rooms are lined with single beds and lockers (bunk in 8- to 14-person room-350 Kč, cash only, no breakfast, easy to reserve without deposit by phone or email, open 24/7, kitchen, Nosticova 2, located on map on page 117, tel. 257-007-397, fax 257-007-340, www.sokol-cos.cz/index_en.htm, hostel@sokol-cos.cz). From the Main Train Station, ride tram #9 to Újezd. From the Holešovice station, take tram #12 to Hellichova. From either tram stop, walk 200 yards to the hostel.

EATING

A big part of Prague's charm is found in wandering aimlessly through the city's winding old quarters, marveling at the architecture, watching the people, and sniffing out fun restaurants. You can eat well here for very little money. What you'd pay for a basic meal in Vienna or Munich will get you a feast in Prague. In addition to meat-and-potatoes Czech cuisine (see "Czech Food," page 16), you'll find trendy, student-oriented bars and lots of fine ethnic eateries. For ambience, the options include traditional, dark Czech beer halls; elegant Art Nouveau dining rooms; and hip and modern cafés.

Watch out for scams. Many restaurants put more care into ripping off green tourists (and even locals) than into their cooking. Tourists are routinely served cheaper meals than what they ordered, given a menu with a "personalized" price list, charged extra for things they didn't get, or shortchanged. Speak Czech. Even saying "Hello" in Czech (see phrases on page 269) will get you better service. Avoid any menu without clear and explicit prices. Be careful of waiters padding the tab. Carefully examine your itemized bill and understand each line (a 10 percent service charge is sometimes added—in that case, there's no need to tip extra). Tax is always included in the price, so it shouldn't be tacked on later. Part with very large bills only if necessary, and deliberately count your change. Never let your credit card out of your sight. Make it a habit to get cash from an ATM to pay for your meals. (Credit cards can cost merchants as much as 10 percent.) Remember, there are two parallel worlds in Prague: the tourist town and the real city. Generally, if you walk two minutes away from the tourist flow, you'll find better value, ambience, and service.

I've listed these eating and drinking establishments by neighborhood (see "Prague's Four Towns," page 36). The most options—and highest prices—are in the Old Town. If you want a memorable splurge, see "Dining with Style" on page 135. For a light meal, consider one of Prague's many cafés (see "Cafés" on page 131). Many of the places listed here are handy for an efficient lunch, but may not offer fine evening dining. Others make less sense for lunch, but are great for a slow, drawn-out dinner. Read the descriptions to judge which is which.

Fun, Touristy Neighborhoods: Several areas are pretty and well-situated for sightseeing, but lined only with touristy restaurants. While these places are not necessarily bad values, I've listed only a few of your many options—just survey the scene in these spots and choose whatever looks best. Kampa Square, just off the Charles Bridge, feels like a small-town square. Havelská Market is surrounded by colorful little eateries, any of which give a fine perch for viewing the market scene while you munch. The massive Old Town Square is *the* place to nurse a drink or enjoy a meal while watching the tide of people, both tourists and locals, sweep back and forth. There's often some event on the main square, and its many restaurants provide tasty and relaxing vantage points.

Dining with a View: For great views, consider these options: **U Prince Terrace** (rooftop dining above a fancy hotel, completely touristy but awesome views, recommended and described on page 130); the **Bellavista Restaurant** at Strahov Monastery; **Petřínské Terasy** and **Nebozízek** next to the funicular stop halfway up Petřín Hill; and the many overpriced but elegant places serving scenic meals along the riverbanks. For the best cheap riverside dinner, have a picnic on a paddleboat (see page 83). There's nothing like drifting down the middle of the Vltava River as the sun sets, while munching on a picnic meal and sipping a beer with your favorite travel partner.

In or near the Old Town

Characteristically Czech Places

With the inevitable closing of cheap student pubs (replaced by shops and hotels that make more money), it's getting difficult to find a truly Czech pub in the historic city center. Most Czechs no longer go to "traditional" eateries, preferring the cosmopolitan taste of the world to the mundane taste of sauerkraut. As a result, ancient institutions with "authentic" Czech ambience have become touristy—but they're still great fun, a good value, and respected by Czechs. Expect wonderfully rustic spaces, smoke, surly service, and reasonably good, inexpensive food. Understand every line on your bill.

Plzeňská Restaurace u Dvou Koček (By the Two Cats) is a typical Czech pub with cheap, no-nonsense, hearty Czech food and beer. Sandwiched between the two red-light-district streets,

Czech Beer

Czechs are among the world's most enthusiastic beer *(pivo)* drinkers—adults drink an average of 80 gallons a year. The pub is a place to have fun, complain, discuss art and politics, talk hockey, and chat with locals and visitors alike. The *pivo* that was drunk in the country before the Industrial Revolution was much thicker, providing the main source of nourishment for the peasant folk. Even today, it doesn't matter whether you're in a *restaurace* (restaurant), a *hostinec* (pub), or a *hospoda* (bar)—a beer will land on your table upon the slightest hint to the waiter, and a new pint will automatically appear when the old glass is almost empty. (You must tell the waiter *not* to bring more.) Order beer from the tap (*točené* means "draft," *sudové pivo* means "keg beer"). A *pivo* is large (.5 liter, or 17 oz); a *malé pivo* is small (.3 liter, or 10 oz). Men invariably order the large size. *Pivo* for lunch has me sightseeing for the rest of the day on Czech knees.

The Czechs invented lager in nearby Plzeň ("Pilsen" in German), and the result, Pilsner Urquell, is on tap in many local pubs. But be sure to venture beyond this famous beer. The Czechs produce plenty of other good beers, including Krušovice, Gambrinus, Staropramen, and Kozel. Budvar, from the town of Budějovice ("Budweis" in German), is popular with Anheuser-Busch's attorneys. (The Czech and the American breweries for years disputed the "Budweiser" brand name. The solution: The Czech Budweiser is sold under its own name in Europe, China, and Africa, while in America it markets itself as Czechvar.)

The big degree symbol on bottles does not indicate the percentage of alcohol content. Twelve degrees is about 4.2 percent alcohol, 10 degrees is about 3.5 percent alcohol, and 11 and 15 degrees are dark beers.

Each establishment has only one kind of beer on tap; to try a particular brand, look for its sign outside. A typical pub serves only one brand of 10-degree beer, one brand of 12-degree beer, and one brand of dark beer. Czechs do not mix beer with anything, and do not hop from pub to pub (in one night, it is said, you must stay loyal to one man—or woman—and to one beer). *Na zdraví* means "to your health" in Czech.

and now filled with tourists rather than Czechs, the restaurant somehow maintains its charm (200 Kč for three courses and beer, serving original Pilsner Urquell, piano or accordion music nightly until 23:00, under an arcade, facing a tiny square between Perlová and Skořepka streets).

Restaurace u Pinkasů, with a menu that reads like a 19th-century newspaper, is a Prague institution, founded in 1843. It's best in summer, when you sit in the garden behind the building, in the shade of the Gothic buttresses of the St. Mary of the Snows Church. But its waiters could win the award for the rudest service in town (daily 9:00–24:00, tucked in a courtyard near the bottom of Wenceslas Square, on the border between Old and New towns, located on map on page 119, Jungmannovo Náměstí 16, tel. 221-111-150).

Restaurace u Provaznice (By the Ropemaker's Wife) has all the Czech classics, peppered with the story of a once-upon-a-time-faithful wife. (Check the menu for details of the gory story.) It's less touristed and less expensive than the other restaurants in this area. Natives congregate here for their famously good "pig leg" with horseradish and Czech mustard (daily 11:00–24:00, a block into the Old Town from the bottom of Wenceslas Square at Provaznická 3, tel. 224-232-528).

U Medvídků (By the Bear Cubs), which started out as a brewery in 1466, is now a flagship beer hall of the Czech Budweiser. The one large room is bright, noisy, touristy, and a bit smoky (daily 11:30–23:00, a block toward Wenceslas Square from Bethlehem Square at Na Perštýnì 7, tel. 224-211-916). The small beer bar next to the restaurant (daily 16:00–3:00 in the morning) is used by university students during emergencies—such as after most other pubs have closed.

U Zlatého Tygra (By the Golden Tiger) has long embodied the proverbial Czech pub, where beer turns strangers into kindred spirits, who cross the fuzzy line between memory and imagination as they tell their hilarious life stories to each other. Today, "the Tiger" is a buzzing shrine to one of its longtime regulars, the writer Bohumil Hrabal (see page 275), whose fictions immortalize many of the colorful characters that once warmed the wooden benches here (daily 15:00–23:00, often jam-packed, just south of Karlova at Husova 17).

Hospoda u Nováka, behind the National Theatre (i.e., not so central), is emphatically Czech, with few tourists. It takes good care of its regulars (you'll see the old monthly beer tabs in a rack just inside the door). Nostalgic communist-era signs are everywhere. During that time, pubs like this were close-knit communities where regulars escaped from the depression of daily life. Today, the U Nováka is a bright and smoky hangout where you can still happily curse whatever regime you happen to live under. While the English menu lists the well-executed Czech classics, it doesn't list the cheap daily specials (daily 10:00–23:00, V Jirchářích 2, see "New Town" map on page 119, tel. 224-930-639).

Restaurace u Betlémské Kaple, behind Bethlehem Chapel, is not "ye olde" Czech. It has light wooden decor, cheap lunch deals, and fish specialties that attract natives and visitors in search of a good Czech bite for Czech prices (daily 11:00–23:00, Betlémské Náměstí 2, tel. 222-221-639).

Česká Kuchyně (Czech Kitchen) is a blue-collar cafeteria serving steamy old Czech cuisine to a local clientele. It's fast, practical, cheap, and traditional as can be. There's no English inside, so—if you want apple charlotte, but not tripe soup—be sure to review the small English menu in the window outside before entering. Note the numbers of your preferred dishes, because they correspond to the Czech menu that you'll see inside. Pick up your tally sheet as you enter, grab a tray, point liberally to whatever you'd like, and keep the paper to pay as you exit. It's extremely cheap...unless you lose your paper (daily 9:00–20:00, very central, across from Havelská Market at Havelská 23, tel. 224-235-574).

Restaurace Mlejnice (The Mill) is a fun little pub strewn with farm implements and happy eaters, located just out of the tourist crush two blocks from the Old Town Square. They serve hardy traditional and modern Czech plates for 150–180 Kč. Reservations are smart in the evening (daily 11:00–24:00, between Melantrichova and Železná at Kožná 14, tel. 224-228-635).

Hip Restaurants

Country Life Vegetarian Restaurant is a bright, easy, nonsmoking cafeteria with a well-displayed buffet of salads and hot veggie dishes. It's midway between the Old Town Square and the bottom of Wenceslas Square. They're serious about their vegetarianism, serving only plant-based, unprocessed, and unrefined food. Its dining area is quiet and elegantly woody for a cafeteria, with three tables and wicker chairs outside in the courtyard (Sun–Thu 9:00–20:30, Fri 9:00–17:00, closed Sat, through courtyard at Melantrichova 15/Michalská 18, tel. 224-213-366).

Lehká Hlava (Clear Head) Vegetarian Restaurant, tucked away on a cul-de-sac, has a mission to provide a "clear atmosphere for enjoying food." Sitting as if in an enchanted forest, diners enjoy dishes from around the world. Reserve in advance for evenings (100–150-Kč plates, two-course 90-Kč daily special, no eggs, no smoke, lots of vegan dishes, daily 11:30–23:30, between Bethlehem Chapel and the river at Boršov 2, tel. 222-220-665).

Klub Architektů, next to Bethlehem Chapel, is a modern hangout in a medieval cellar that serves excellent original dishes, hearty salads, Moravian wines, and Slovak beer (daily, Betlémské Náměstí 169, tel. 224-401-214).

At **Le Patio,** on the big and busy Národní Třída, the first thing you'll notice are the many lanterns suspended from the ceiling—and the big ship moored out back (okay, just its hulking bow). Le Patio has a hip, continental feel, but for a place that also sells furniture (head straight back, and down the stairs), it definitely needs comfier dining chairs. The atmosphere is as pleasant and carefully designed as the dishes, with international fare from India, France, and points in between. There's always a serious vegetarian option available (200–350-Kč plates, daily 8:00–23:00, Národní 22, see "New Town" map on page 119, tel. 224-934-375). Diners enjoy live music on Friday and Saturday nights (19:30–22:30).

Ethnic Eateries and Bars near Dlouhá Street

Dlouhá, the wide street leading away from the Old Town Square behind the Jan Hus monument (left of Týn Church), is lined with ethnic restaurants catering mostly to cosmopolitan locals. Within a couple of blocks, you can eat your way around the world. From Dlouhá, wander the Rámová/Haštalská area to survey a United Nations of eateries: You'll find Moroccan (**Dahab,** with some interesting hubbly-bubbly action at Dlouhá 33), French (**Chez Marcel** at Haštalská 12 is understandably popular—with a fun-loving waitstaff), Thai, Afghan, Italian, and these four, which deserve special consideration:

Indian: At **Himalaya,** Slovak waitresses dressed in *salwar kameez* serve their decidedly North Indian chef's vegetarian platters and tandoori meats with Pilsner beer to a Bollywood beat for Czech prices (Mon–Fri 11:00–23:00, Sat–Sun 12:00–23:00, Soukenická 2, at the end of Dlouhá across Revoluční, see map on page 119, tel. 233-353-594).

Irish: **Molly Malone's Irish Pub,** hidden in a forgotten corner of the Jewish Quarter, may seem a strange recommendation in Prague—home of some of the world's best beer—but it has the kind of ambience that locals (and few tourists) seek out. Molly Malone's has been the expat and local favorite for Guinness ever since the Velvet Revolution enabled the Celts to return to one of their homelands. Worn wooden floors, dingy walls, and the Irish manager transport you right into the heart of blue-collar Dublin—which is, after all, a popular place for young Czechs to find jobs in the high-tech industry (Sun–Thu 11:00–1:00 in the morning, Fri–Sat 11:00–2:00 in the morning, U Obecního Dvora 4, tel. 224-818-851).

Latin American: **La Casa Blů,** with cheap lunch specials, Mexican plates, Staropramen beer, and greenish *mojitos*, is your Spanish village in Prague and one of the last student bastions in the Old Town. Painted in warm orange-and-red and guarded by

RESTAURANTS IN THE OLD TOWN

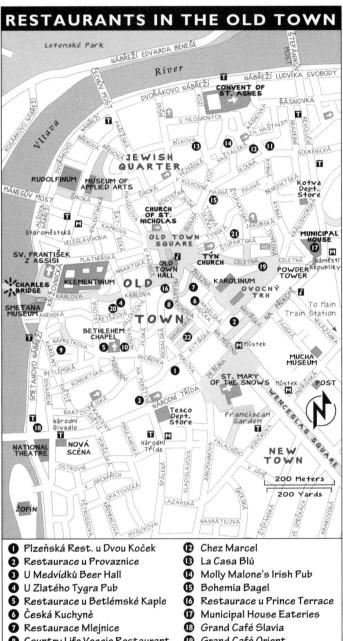

1. Plzeňská Rest. u Dvou Koček
2. Restaurace u Provaznice
3. U Medvídků Beer Hall
4. U Zlatého Tygra Pub
5. Restaurace u Betlémské Kaple
6. Česká Kuchyně
7. Restaurace Mlejnice
8. Country Life Veggie Restaurant
9. Lehká Hlava Veggie Restaurant
10. Klub Architektů
11. Dahab
12. Chez Marcel
13. La Casa Blů
14. Molly Malone's Irish Pub
15. Bohemia Bagel
16. Restaurace u Prince Terrace
17. Municipal House Eateries
18. Grand Café Slavia
19. Grand Café Orient
20. Café Montmartre
21. Ebel Coffee House
22. Havelská Market

creatures from Mayan mythology, La Casa Blů is packed nightly with smoke, guitar music, and a fusion of Czechs and Chileans (Mon–Sat 11:00–23:00, Sun 14:00–23:00, on the corner of Kozí and Bílkova, tel. 224-818-270).

North American: **Bohemia Bagel** is hardly authentic— exasperated Czechs insist that bagels have nothing to do with Bohemia. Owned by an American, this practical café caters mostly to youthful tourists, with good sandwiches (100–125 Kč), a little garden out back, and Internet access (1.50 Kč/min). If homesick, you'll love the menu, with everything from Philly cheesesteak to bacon and eggs (daily 7:00–24:00, Masná 2, tel. 224-812-560).

In the Jewish Quarter

These four eateries are well-located to break up a demanding tour of the Jewish Quarter—all within two blocks of each other on or near Široká (see map on page 66). Also consider the nearby ethnic eateries listed above.

Kolkovna, flagship of a franchise owned by Pilsner Urquell, is big and woody, yet modern, serving a fun mix of Czech and international cuisine—ribs, salads, cheese plates, and good beer (a bit overpriced but good energy, daily 11:00–24:00, across from Spanish Synagogue at V Kolkovně 8, tel. 224-819-701).

Franz Kafka Café, with a cool, dark, and woody interior strewn with historic photos of the ghetto and a few good side- walk tables, is great for a relaxing salad, sandwich, snack, or drink (150-Kč salads, daily 10:00–21:00, a block from the cemetery at Široká 12).

Pekařství ("Bakery") is a little deli with fresh sandwiches, greasy microwavable meat pies, tempting cakes, yogurt, and a cooler full of drinks. It's self-serve and dirt-cheap, with plain circa- 1960 linoleum loft seating upstairs (daily 7:00–22:30, Široká 10, near the Pinkas Synagogue). Head upstairs to see the insane direc- tor of the National Gallery throwing paint on a nude woman.

Restaurace U Knihovny (By the Library), situated steps away from the City and National Libraries as well as the Pinkas Synagogue, is a favorite lunch spot for Czechs who work nearby. Their cheap daily lunch specials consist of seven imaginative varia- tions on traditional Czech themes, the service is friendly, and the stylish red-brick interior is warm. Smoking is not permitted dur- ing lunch (daily 11:00–23:00, on the corner of Veleslavínova and Valentinská, mobile 732-835-876).

Dining with an Old Town Square View

Restaurant u Prince Terrace, in the five-star U Prince Hotel facing the Astronomical Clock, is designed for foreign tourists. A sleek elevator takes you to its rooftop, where every possible inch is used to serve good food (international with plenty of fish) from their open-air grill. The view is arguably the best in town—especially at sunset. The menu is a fun but overpriced mix, with photos that make ordering easy. Being in such a touristy spot, waiters are experts at nicking you with confusing menu charges; don't be afraid to confirm exact prices before ordering. This place is also great for just a drink at sunset or late at night (fine salads, 240–300-Kč plates, daily until 24:00, brusque staff, outdoor heaters when necessary, Staroměstské Náměstí 29, tel. 224-213-807—but no reservations possible).

Art Nouveau Splendor in the Municipal House

The Municipal House (Obecní Dům), the sumptuous Art Nouveau concert hall, has three restaurants: a café, a French restaurant,

and a beer cellar (all at Náměstí Republiky 5). The dressy café, Kavárna Obecní Dům, is drenched in chandeliered, Art Nouveau elegance and offers the best value and experience here (light, pricey meals and drinks with great atmosphere and bad service, 250-Kč three-course special daily for lunch or dinner, open daily 7:30–23:00, live piano or jazz trio 16:00–20:00, tel. 222-002-763). The fine and formal French restaurant in the next wing oozes Mucha elegance (700–1,000-Kč meals, daily 12:00–16:00 & 18:00–23:00, tel. 222-002-777). The overpriced, touristy beer cellar is open daily 11:30–23:00.

Cafés

Dripping with history, these places are as much about the ambience as they are about the coffee. Most cafés also serve sweets and light meals.

Grand Café Slavia, across from the National Theatre (facing the Legií Bridge on Národní street), is a fixture in Prague, famous as a hangout for its literary elite. Today, it's tired and clearly past its prime, with an Art Deco interior, lousy piano entertainment, and celebrity photos on the wall. But its iconic status makes it a fun stop for a coffee—skip the food (daily 8:00–23:00, sit as near the river as possible). Notice the *Drinker of Absinthe* painting on the wall (and on the menu for 55 Kč)—with the iconic Czech writer struggling with reality.

Café Louvre is a longtime elegant favorite (opened in 1902) that still draws an energetic young crowd. From the big and busy Národní street, you walk upstairs into a venerable world of newspapers on sticks (including English) and waiters in vests and aprons. The back room has long been the place for billiard tables (100 Kč/hr). An English flier tells its history (200-Kč plates, 120-Kč two-course lunch offered 11:00–15:00, open daily 8:00–23:30, Národní 22, see "New Town" map on page 119, tel. 224-930-949).

Grand Café Orient is just two flights up off busy Celetná street, yet a world away from the crush of tourism below. Located in the Black Madonna House, the café is upstairs from the Museum of Czech Cubism (see page 57) and fittingly decorated with a Cubist flair. With its stylish old circa-1910 decor toned to dark green, this space is full of air and light—and a good value as well (salads, sandwiches, great balcony seating, Mon–Fri 9:00–22:00, Sat–Sun 10:00–22:00, Ovocný Trh 19, at the corner of Celetná near the Powder Tower, tel. 224-224-240).

Café Montmartre, on a small street parallel to Karlova, combines Parisian ambience with unbeatable Czech prices. Dreamy Czech minds found their asylum here after Grand Café Slavia (see above) and other long-time favorites either closed down or become stuck in their past. The main room is perfect for discussing art and politics, while the intimate room behind the courtyard is where you recite poetry to your date (Mon–Fri 9:00–23:00, Sat–Sun 12:00–23:00, Řetězová 7, tel. 222-221-244).

Ebel Coffee House, in the Ungelt courtyard behind the Týn Church, is the local Starbucks—priding itself on its wide assortment of fresh coffee from every coffee-growing country in the world, inviting cakes, and a colorful setting that delights the mind as much as the caffeine (daily 9:00–22:00, Týn 1, tel. 224-895-788).

John & George Café, in the courtyard on the other side of the Lennon Wall, is a secluded spot serving raspberry drinks, fresh sandwiches, and Italian coffee next to a flower garden, an English lawn, and one of the oldest trees in Prague (daily 11:00–22:00, Velkopřevorské Náměstí 4, look for small gate at left end of Lennon Wall, entrance to indoor seating area is another 20 yards to the left, see "Little Quarter" map on page 117, tel. 257-217-736).

Teahouses

Many Czech people are bohemian philosophers at heart and prefer the mellow, smoke-free environs of a teahouse to the smoky, traditional beer hall. Young Czechs are much more interested in traveling to exotic destinations like Southeast Asia, Africa, or Peru than to Western Europe, so the Oriental teahouses set their minds in vacation mode.

While there are teahouses all over town, a fine example in a handy locale is Prague's original one, established in 1991. **Dobrá Čajovna** (Good Teahouse), just a few steps off the bustle of

Wenceslas Square, takes you into a very peaceful world that elevates tea to an almost religious ritual. At the desk, you'll be given an English menu and a bell. Grab a seat and study the menu, which lovingly describes each tea. The menu lists a world of tea (very fresh, prices by the small pot), "accompaniments" (such as Exotic Miscellany), and light meals "for hungry tea drinkers." When you're ready to order, ring your bell to beckon a tea monk—likely a member of the Lovers of Tea Society (Mon–Sat 10:00–21:30, Sun 14:00–21:30, near the base of Wenceslas Square, opposite McDonald's at Václavské Náměstí 14, www.cajovna.com).

In the Little Quarter

These characteristic eateries are handy for a bite before or after your Prague Castle visit. For locations, see the map on page 117.

U Sedmi Švábů (By the Seven Roaches) is a touristy den where even the cuisine is medieval. Since America had not yet been discovered in the Middle Ages, you won't find any corn, potatoes, or tomatoes on the menu. The salty yellow things that come with the Krušovice beer are chickpeas. Carnivores thrive here: Try the skewered meats *(špíz u Sedmi Švábů)*, flaming beef *(flambák)*, or pork knuckle (daily 11:00–23:00, Janský Vršek 14, tel. 257-531-455).

U Osla v Kolébce (By the Donkey in the Cradle) fills a peaceful courtyard just a minute off the touristy hubbub of Nerudova. The laid-back scene consists of two restaurants with nearly identical simple menus, dominated by tasty sausages and salads (daily 10:00–22:00, Jánský Vršek 8, below Nerudova, next door to U Sedmi Švábů, tel. 731-407-036).

U Hrocha (By the Hippo), a very authentic little pub packed with beer-drinkers and smoke, serves simple, traditional meals—basically meat starters with bread. Just below the castle near Little Quarter Square (Malostranské Náměstí), it's actually the haunt of many members of Parliament, which is located just around the corner (daily 12:00–23:00, chalkboard lists daily meals in English, Thunovská 10).

Restaurace Rybářský Klub, on Kampa Island overlooking the river, is run by the Society of Czech Fishermen and serves one of the widest and tastiest selections of freshwater fish in Prague, at reasonable prices. Dine on fish-cream soup, pike, trout, carp, or catfish under the imaginative artwork of Little Quarter painter Mr. Kuba. On warm evenings, late May through October, the Society fills its dock with tables and offers my choice for the best riverside dining in town (three-course meal for around 400 Kč, riverside menu not as extensive as indoor restaurant menu, daily 12:00–23:00, U Sovových Mlýnů 1, tel. 257-534-200).

In the Castle Quarter

To locate the following restaurants, see the map on page 96.

Klášterní Pivovar (Monastery Brewery), founded by an abbot in 1628 and re-opened in 2004, has two large rooms and a pleasant courtyard. This is the place to enjoy rare unpasteurized yeast beer, brewed on the premises. The wooden decor and circa-1900 newspaper clippings (including Hapsburg Emperor Franz Josef's "Proclamation to My Nations," announcing the beginning of the First World War) evoke the era when Vienna was Europe's artistic capital, Prague was building its Eiffel Tower, and life moved much slower than today. To accompany the beer, try the beer-flavored cheese served on toasted black-yeast bread (daily 10:00–22:00, Strahovské Nádvoří 301, tel. 233-353-155, www.klasterni-pivovar .cz). It's directly across from the entrance to the Strahov Library (not to be confused with the enormous, group-oriented Klášterní Restaurace next door, to the right).

Restaurace Nad Úvozem is hidden in the middle of a staircase that connects Loretánská and Úvoz streets. This secret spot, which boasts super views of Prague, offers excellent food for surprisingly low prices, given its location. Try the roast beef in plum sauce (170 Kč). The service is slower when the restaurant is full, as the kitchen has limited space (daily 12:00–21:00; as you go down Loretánská watch for pans, scoops, and spoons hanging on chains on your right at #15; tel. 220-511-532). To discourage pub-goers from mingling with diners, the beer here is terribly overpriced (69 Kč).

Hostinec u Černého Vola (By the Black Ox) is a smoky, dingy old-time pub—its survival in the midst of all the castle splendor and tourism is a marvel. It feels like a kegger on the banks of the river Styx, with classic bartenders serving up Kozel beer (traditional "goat" brand with excellent darks) and beer-friendly light meals. The pub is located on Loretánská (no sign outside, sniff for cigarette smoke and look for the only house on the block without an arcade—or see map on page 96, daily 10:00–22:00, English menu on request).

Malý Buddha (Little Buddha) serves delightful food— especially vegetarian—and takes its theme seriously. You'll step into a mellow, low-lit escape of bamboo and peace to be served by people with perfect complexions and almost no pulse (Tue–Sun 13:00–22:30, closed Mon, non-smoking, between the castle and Strahov Monastery at Úvoz 46, tel. 220-513-894).

Espresso Kajetánka, just off Castle Square, has magnificent city views. It's a good-if-overpriced place for a drink or snack as you start or end your castle visit (daily 10:00–20:00, Ke Hradu, tel. 257-533-735).

Na Baště, more convenient but not as scenic, is in a garden through the gate to the left of the main castle entry. The outdoor seating, among Jože Plečnik's ramparts and obelisks, is the castle at its most peaceful (Sun–Thu 11:00–23:00, Fri–Sat 11:00–24:00, tel. 281-933-010).

Dining with Style

In Prague, a fancy candlelit dinner with fine wines and connoisseur-approved dishes costs more than most locals can afford—but it's still a bargain in comparison to similar restaurants in Paris or Dallas. I list only two such splurges: one aristocratic, Old World, and under the castle; one more modern, untouristy, and near the Old Town Square.

Restaurace David, with two little 18th-century rooms hiding on a small cobblestone street opposite the American Embassy in the Little Quarter, is my choice for a romantic splurge. The exquisite cuisine, a modern incarnation of traditional Czech with French and European influences, ranges from game to roasted duck and liver. Your meal comes with the gourmet quotient of knives and fancy glasses, and graceful waiters serve you like an aristocrat—appropriate, considering the neighborhood. Reservations are recommended (most meals 600–1,000 Kč, open daily, Tržiště 21, see "Little Quarter" map on page 117, tel. 257-533-109).

Restaurant Červená Tabulka (Red Chalkboard) is in a low, nondescript townhouse in a quiet neighborhood outside of the tourist circus. Sit in the dressy candlelit interior or on the quiet and breezy cobbled courtyard. Either way, there's not a dumpling in sight. The menu features modern international dishes with a focus on fish (fine 300-Kč plates and gourmet presentation). The wines are excellent and a great value (daily 11:30–23:00, Lodecká 4, tel. 224-810-401). To get to the restaurant from the Municipal House, cross Náměstí Republiky and turn right onto Truhlářská; it's 200 yards down the street on the corner of quiet Petrské Náměstí square (see "New Town" map on page 119).

Rubbing Elbows with Hip Locals
Away from the Center, in Vinohrady and Žižkov

For the next four listings, see the "New Town" map on page 119 of the Sleeping chapter.

Café Medúza (Café Jellyfish), an authentic between-the-World-Wars café with plush sofas and pictures of 1930s movie stars, draws a crowd of dreamy young Czechs enjoying coffee, cigarettes, dark Svijany beer, and cheap lunch specials (daily 11:00–24:00, Belgická 17, Metro: Náměstí Míru; from Metro stop, walk down the street a bit and look for Belgická on your left; tel. 222-515-107).

At **Hlučná Samota** (Loud Solitude), the wooden floor and brick walls are dedicated to the great Czech writer, Bohumil Hrabal. Though he never visited here, Hrabal would surely be inspired by the rich mix of Czech and Italian cuisine (including honey duck, spinach salmon, and Prague's own Staropramen beer). On a nice day, the good sidewalk seating is a pleasure (daily 11:00–23:00, Záhřebská 14, tel. 222-522-839).

Restaurace u Sadu, dark and dingy, is decorated with old typewriters, radios, meat grinders, skis, and sledges. It serves cheap beer and decent food indoors on aged green tablecloths or outside on wooden tables. The way that Czechs of all generations drink beer in this classic blue-collar pub hasn't changed a beat since the 1920s (daily 10:00–4:00 in the morning, on Škroupa Square below TV tower at Škroupovo Náměstí 5, tel. 222-727-072). The restaurant up in the TV tower itself is expensive, but comes with a Sputnik's-eye view.

Hospůdka nad Viktorkou, named for this neighborhood's soccer team, is around the corner on Bořivojova street. This quintessential Žižkov pub features occasional live performances by local bands, a warm glass terrace in the winter, and a little courtyard with a shady canopy of chestnut trees in the summer (Mon–Fri 15:00–1:00, Sat–Sun 17:00–1:00, English menu available, Bořivojova 79, tel. 222-722-557).

SHOPPING

Prague's entire Old Town seems designed to bring out the shopper in visitors. Puppets, glass, and ceramics are traditional. For information on VAT refunds (for purchases of more than 2,000 Kč—about $100) and customs regulations, see page 278 in the appendix.

Shopping Streets

Shop your way from the Old Town Square up Celetná street to the Powder Tower, then along Na Příkopě to the bottom of Wenceslas Square (Václavské Náměstí). The city center is tourist-oriented—most locals do their serious shopping in the suburbs.

Celetná is lined with big stores selling all the traditional Czech goodies. Tourists wander endlessly here, mesmerized by the window displays. Celetná Crystal, about midway down the street, offers the largest selection of affordable crystal. You can have the glass safely shipped home directly from the shop.

Na Příkopě has a couple of good modern malls. The best is Slovanský Dům (daily 10:00–20:00, Na Příkopě 22), where you wander deep past a 10-screen multiplex into a world of classy restaurants and designer shops surrounding a peaceful, park-like inner courtyard. Another modern mall is Černá Růže (daily 10:00–20:00, Na Příkopě 12). Next door is Moser, which has a museum-like crystal showroom upstairs.

Národní Třída (National Street) is less touristy and lined with some inviting stores. The big Tesco department store in the middle sells anything you might need, from a pin for a broken watchband to a swimsuit (generally daily 9:00–21:00, Národní Třída 26).

Czech Puppets

The first puppets were born on the Indian subcontinent, and soon found their way to Europe and Southeast Asia. Czechs have treasured the art of puppets for centuries; at times of heavy German influence in the 18th century, traveling troupes of puppeteers kept the Czech language and humor alive in the countryside. While the language of "legitimate theater" had to be German, Czech was tolerated if it came out of a puppet's mouth.

Until recently, most grandfathers felt obliged to bequeath to their grandsons an assembly of their own linden-wood carved designs. The power of puppets peaked between 1938 and 1989, when the Czechs were ruled by a series of puppet governments. Today, Špejbl and Hurvínek, who have their own permanent stage in Prague, are the greatest Czechs for kids from Japan to Patagonia. Filmmaker Jan Švankmajer (see page 276) is turning wooden characters into Oscar-winning film stars.

Most marionettes sold in the tourist shops in Prague and Český Krumlov are meant as souvenirs. It takes a rare artist to turn pieces of wood into nimble puppets, and prices for these can reach into the thousands of dollars. But given that puppets have a glorious past and vibrant present in the Czech Republic, even a simple jester, witch, or Pinocchio can make a thoughtful memento of your Czech adventure.

Crystal and Garnets

Crystal: Along with shops on Celetná and Na Příkopě, a small square just off the Old Town Square, Malé Náměstí, is ringed by three major crystal retailers (generally open daily 10:00–20:00): Moser, Rott Crystal, and Crystalex (which claims to have "factory-direct" prices, at #6 on the square).

Czech Garnets: This extraordinary stone of fiery red color, which has unique refractive—some claim even curative—properties, is found only in Bohemia. The characteristic design of garnet jewelry, with the jewels overwhelming the metal setting, became popular in the 1890s and remains so today. Although garnet jewelry is sold in most crystal shops, the **Turnov Granát Co-op** has the largest selection (with shops at Dlouhá 30 and Panská 1, www.granat.eu). It oversees its own mining and represents over 300 traditional goldsmiths and jewelers. Make sure to ask your vendor for a certificate of authenticity as many shops sell glass imitations.

Bookstores

Anagram Bookshop, in the Ungelt courtyard behind the Týn Church, professes that of all the ways of acquiring books, writing them yourself is the most praiseworthy. While you won't be asked to leave a bit of yourself here, you will find books in English on a wide range of topics (Mon–Sat 10:00–20:00, Sun 10:00–19:00, Týn 4, tel. 224-895-737).

V Ráji, next to Maisel Synagogue in the Jewish Quarter, is the flagship store of a small publishing house dedicated to books about Prague. They offer an assortment of photo publications, fairy tales, and maps (Maiselova 12, tel. 222-326-925).

Kiwi Map Store, near Wenceslas Square, is one of Prague's best sources for maps (Mon–Fri 9:00–19:00, Sat 9:00–14:00, closed Sun, Jungmanova 23, tel. 224-948-455).

For CDs and DVDs, see the next chapter, "Entertainment."

ENTERTAINMENT

Prague booms with live and inexpensive theater, classical music, jazz, and pop entertainment. Everything is listed in several monthly cultural events programs (free at TIs) and in the *Prague Post* newspaper (60 Kč at newsstands).

You'll be tempted to gather fliers as you wander through the town. Don't bother. To really understand all your options (the street Mozarts are pushing only their concerts), drop by a **Via Musica** box office. There are two: One is next to Týn Church on the Old Town Square (daily 10:30–19:30, tel. 224-826-969), and the other is in the Little Quarter across from the Church of St.

Nicholas (daily 10:30–18:00, tel. 257-535-568). The event schedule posted on the wall clearly shows everything that's playing today and tomorrow, including tourist concerts, Black Light Theater, and marionette shows, with photos of each venue and a map locating everything (www.viamusica.cz).

Ticketpro sells tickets for the serious concert venues and most music clubs (daily 8:00–12:00 & 12:30–16:30, Rytířská 31, between Havelská Market and Estates Theatre; also has a booth in Tourist Center at Rytířská 12, daily 9:00–20:00; English-language reservations tel. 296-329-999).

Consider buying concert tickets directly from the actual venues. You won't save money, but more of your money will go to the musicians.

Locals dress up for the more "serious" concerts, opera, and ballet, but many tourists wear casual clothes—as long as you don't show up in shorts, sneakers, or sandals you'll be fine.

Black Light Theater

A kind of mime/modern dance variety show, Black Light Theater has no language barrier and is, for many, more entertaining than a classical concert. Unique to Prague (though somewhat comparable to a very low-budget Cirque du Soleil), Black Light Theater originated in the 1960s as a playful and mystifying theater of the absurd. These days, some aficionados lament that it's becoming a cheesy variety show, while others are uncomfortable with the sexual flavor of some acts. Still, it's an unusual theater experience that most enjoy. Shows last about 90 minutes. Avoid the first four rows, which get you so close that it ruins the illusion. Each theater has its own personality:

Ta Fantastika is traditional and poetic, with puppets and a little artistic nudity (*Aspects of Alice* nightly at 21:30, 620 Kč, reserved seating, near east end of Charles Bridge at Karlova 8, tel. 222-221-366, www.tafantastika.cz).

Image Theatre has more mime and elements of the absurd, with shows including *Clonarium, Fiction,* and *The Best of Image:* "It's precisely the fact that we are all so different that unites us" (shows nightly at 18:00 and 20:00, 480 Kč, open seating—arrive early to grab a good spot, just off Old Town Square at Pařížská 4, tel. 222-314-448, www.imagetheatre.cz).

Laterna Magica, in the big, glassy building next to the National Theatre, mixes Black Light techniques with film projection into a multimedia performance that draws Czech audiences (*Wonderful Circus, Rendezvous, Graffiti,* shows Mon–Sat at 20:00, no shows on Sun, 680 Kč, tel. 224-931-482, www.laterna.cz).

The other Black Light theaters advertised around town aren't as good.

Concerts

Each day, six to eight classical concerts designed for tourists fill delightful Old World halls and churches with music of the crowd-pleasing sort: Vivaldi, Best of Mozart, Most Famous Arias, and works by the famous Czech composer Antonín Dvořák. Concerts typically cost 400–1,000 Kč, start anywhere from 13:00 to 21:00, and last about an hour. Common venues are two buildings on the Little Quarter Square (the Church of St. Nicholas and the Prague Academy of Music in Liechtenstein Palace); in the Klementinum's Chapel of Mirrors; at the Old Town Square (in a different Church of St. Nicholas); and in the stunning Smetana Hall in the Municipal House (see page 143). The artists vary from excellent to amateurish.

A sure bet is the jam session held every Monday at 17:00 at **St. Martin in the Wall,** where some of Prague's best musicians gather to tune in and chat with each other (400 Kč, Martinská street, just

Entertainment

Entertainment

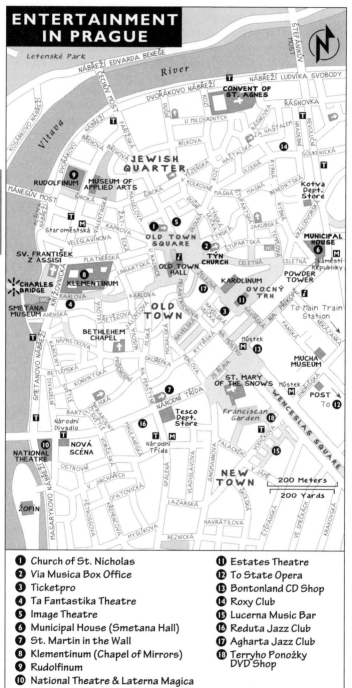

ENTERTAINMENT IN PRAGUE

1. Church of St. Nicholas
2. Via Musica Box Office
3. Ticketpro
4. Ta Fantastika Theatre
5. Image Theatre
6. Municipal House (Smetana Hall)
7. St. Martin in the Wall
8. Klementinum (Chapel of Mirrors)
9. Rudolfinum
10. National Theatre & Laterna Magica
11. Estates Theatre
12. To State Opera
13. Bontonland CD Shop
14. Roxy Club
15. Lucerna Music Bar
16. Reduta Jazz Club
17. Agharta Jazz Club
18. Terryho Ponožky DVD Shop

north of the Tesco department store in the Old Town).

The **Prague Castle Orchestra,** one of Prague's most entertaining acts, performs regularly on Castle Square. This trio—Josef on flute, Radek on accordion, and Zdeněk on bass—plays a lively Czech mélange of Smetana, swing, old folk tunes, and 1920s cabaret songs. Look for them if you're visiting the castle (see page 102) and consider picking up their fun CD. They're also available for private functions (mobile 603-552-448, josekocurek@volny.cz).

Serious music-lovers should consider Prague's two top ensembles: The **Czech Philharmonic,** which performs in the classical Neo-Renaissance Rudolfinum (on Palachovo Náměstí, in the Jewish Quarter on the Old Town side of Mánes Bridge), and the **Prague Symphony Orchestra,** based in the gorgeous Art Nouveau Municipal House.

Both orchestras perform in their home venues about five nights a month from September through June. Most other nights these spaces are rented to agencies that organize tourist concerts of varying quality for double the price (see the top of this section). Check first whether your visit coincides with either ensemble's performance.

One advantage of a tourist concert is that it allows you to experience music in one of Prague's best venues on the night of your choice. This is especially worth considering if you want to enjoy classical music in the Municipal House when the Symphony Orchestra isn't in town—but make sure your concert takes place in the building's Smetana Hall rather than in the much smaller Grégr Hall.

The Czech Philharmonic ticket office is at the Rudolfinum, on the right side under the stairs (250–1,000 Kč, open Mon–Fri 10:00–18:00, and until just before the show starts on concert days, tel. 227-059-352, www.ceskafilharmonie.cz, info@cfmail.cz).

The Prague Symphony Orchestra ticket office is on the right side of the **Municipal House,** on U Obecního Domu street opposite Hotel Paris (Mon–Fri 10:00–18:00, tel. 222-002-336, www .fok.cz, pokladna@fok.cz). A smaller selection of tickets is also available in the information office inside the Municipal House.

You'll find tickets for tourist concerts advertised and sold on the street in front of these buildings. Both the Rudolfinum and the Municipal House also act as chief venues for the Prague Spring, Prague Autumn, and Prague Proms music festivals (see "Festivals," page 145).

Opera and Ballet

The **National Theatre** (Národní Divadlo, on the New Town side of Legií Bridge)—with a must-see Neo-Renaissance interior (see page 81)—is best for opera and ballet (shows from 19:00, 300–1,000 Kč,

Mozart, Smetana, Dvořák, and More

The three major composers connected with Prague—Mozart, Smetana, and Dvořák—all have museums dedicated to their lives and work in the city.

During his frequent visits to Prague, Austrian **Wolfgang Amadeus Mozart** (1756–1791) stayed with his friends in the beautiful, small, Neoclassical Villa Bertramka, now the Mozart Museum. Surrounded by a peaceful garden, the villa preserves the time when the Salzburg prodigy felt more appreciated in Prague than in Austria. Intimate concerts are held some afternoons and evenings, either in the garden or in the small concert hall (110 Kč, daily April–Oct 9:30–18:00, Nov–March 9:30–17:00, Mozartova 169, Praha 5; from Metro: Anděl, it's a 10-min walk—head to Hotel Mövenpick and then go up alley behind hotel; tel. 257-317-465, www.bertramka.cz).

A statue of **Bedřich Smetana** (1824–1884), the father of Czech classical music, is seated in front of his museum, listening intently to the rapids of the Vltava River near the Charles Bridge (50 Kč, Wed–Mon 10:00–17:00, closed Tue, Novotného Lávka, Praha 1, tel. 224-229-075). Like Richard Wagner in Germany, Smetana aimed to stir the Romantic nationalist spirit of the Czechs. His finest work, the cycle of symphonic poems called *My Country (Má Vlast)*, was inspired by places and myths important to the Czech people. *Vltava*, the most beautiful of the poems, is played to get your attention as trains arrive in stations.

tel. 224-912-673, www.nationaltheatre.cz). The **Estates Theatre** (Stavovské Divadlo) is where Mozart premiered and personally directed many of his most beloved works (see above). *Don Giovanni*, *The Marriage of Figaro*, and *The Magic Flute* are on the program a couple of times each month (shows from 20:00, 800–1,400 Kč, between the Old Town Square and the New Town on a square called Ovocný Trh, tel. 224-214-339, www.estatestheatre.cz). A handy ticket office for both of these theaters is in the little square (Ovocný Trh) behind the Estates Theatre, next to a pizzeria.

The **State Opera** (Státní Opera) operates on a smaller budget and is also not as architecturally rewarding as the National Theatre (shows at 19:00 or 20:00, 400–1,200 Kč, buy tickets at the theater, on 5 Května—the busy street between the Main Train Station and Wenceslas Square, see map on page 73, tel. 224-227-693, www .opera.cz).

Antonín Dvořák (1841–1904) is the Czech Republic's best-known composer. For three years, Dvořák directed the National Conservatory in New York, during which time he composed his most famous work, the *New World Symphony (Z Nového Světa)*. Dvořák's advice to his students was to look for inspiration in America's own authentic melodies (African American spirituals and Native American music) rather than in European models. Dvořák's gentle opera of a water nymph, *Rusalka*, is considered by many to be the best Czech opera and is often performed in Prague's National Theatre. The Dvořák Museum is located in Villa America, which was once the composer's home (50 Kč, Tue–Sun 10:00–17:00, closed Mon, Ke Karlovu 20, Praha 2, located on map on page 73, tel. 224-923-363).

Two other important composers from Czech lands are the moderns Mahler and Janáček. **Gustav Mahler** (1860–1911), a Jew from Jihlava (see page 210), was a pioneer of atonal music. His best works are *Symphony No. 1: Titan* and *The Song of the Earth*, both inspired by the sounds of the Moravian woods and fields.

Leoš Janáček (1854–1928), the most original and least accessible Czech composer, was stimulated by language—its flow and abrupt pauses. He's known for his *Symphonietta* and *Lachian Dances (Lašské Tance)*, as well as the opera *Cunning Little Vixen (Příhody Lišky Bystroušky)*, another perennial in the National Theatre's repertoire.

Festivals

World-class musicians are in town during these musical festivals: **Prague Spring** (last three weeks of May, www.festival.cz), **Prague Autumn** (last half of Sept, www.pragueautumn.cz), and the newer **Prague Proms** (July–Aug, www.pragueproms.cz).

Music Clubs

Young locals keep Prague's many music clubs in business. Most clubs are neighborhood institutions with decades of tradition, generally holding only 100–200 people. Live rock and Bob Dylan–style folk are what younger generations go for. A number of good jazz clubs attract a diverse audience, from ages 18 to 80. In the last decade, ethnic music has also become hugely popular: Roma (Gypsy) bands, Moravian poets, African drummers, Cuban boleros, and Moroccan divas often sell out even the largest venues. You can buy tickets at the club, or, for most places, at the Ticketpro offices (see page 140). If you like jazz, I've listed some fine options; avoid the Jazzboat (advertised by commission-hungry hotels), which has mediocre musicians and high prices.

Buying Czech CDs and DVDs

While the most convenient places to get CDs of classical music are the shops in the **Via Musica** and **Rudolfinum** ticket offices (described previously), you'll find a larger selection and other genres at the huge **Bontonland** music and video store, at the bottom of Wenceslas Square (enter from the mall with the big *Kenvelo* sign on the outside). In the classical music section, you'll find many interpretations of Czech works. For the best Czech renditions, look for music performed by the Czech Philharmonic.

For contemporary, lighter music, get a CD by Čechomor (*Metamorphosis* is their best). This band, which began by playing traditional Czech music at weddings and funerals, synthesized the sound of folk ballads and has since become one of the most popular groups in the country. Jiří Pavlica and Hradišťan keep the music of Moravia alive, while Věra Bíla and Ida Kellarová capture the lively spirit of the Roma (Gypsies). Some cool Czech contemporary groups are Psí Vojáci, Neočekávaný Dýchánek, and Už Jsme Doma.

A handy place to get DVDs of Czech and European films is the tiny **Terryho Ponožky** shop in the Světozor mall just off Wenceslas Square (Mon–Sat 10:00–20:00, closed Sun; enter from Vodičkova 41, the store is on the right next to the Světozor Cinema; tel. 224-946-829, www.terryhoponozky.cz). Be warned that many European DVDs don't work on American DVD players (though they usually play on computers just fine).

In the Old Town

Roxy, a few blocks from the Old Town Square, features live bands from outside the country twice a week—anything from Irish punk to Balkan brass. On other nights, the floor is taken over by experimental DJs who will give you a healthy dose of Japanese pop (concerts start at 20:00, disco at 22:00, cover from 100 Kč, Mon free, easy to book online and pick up tickets at the door, Dlouhá 33, tel. 224-826-296, www.roxy.cz).

Agharta Jazz Club, which showcases some of the best Czech and Eastern European jazz, is just steps off the Old Town Square in a cool, Gothic cellar. Inside they also sell a wide selection of Czech jazz CDs (shows start nightly at 21:00, 200 Kč cover, Železná 16, tel. 222-211-275, www.agharta.cz).

In the New Town

Lucerna Music Bar, at the bottom of Wenceslas Square, is popular for disco nights. Friday and Saturdays are the "1980s Party," featuring the silly pop songs of the last years under communism, when spineless Czech pop stars took the easy route to success instead of coming up with thoughtful lyrics that could have furthered the cause of freedom. The scene is a big, noisy dance hall with a giant video screen. Young and trendy, the Lucerna has cheap prices, and even older tourists mix in easily (music nightly from 21:00, about 100-Kč cover, in the basement of Lucerna Gallery, Vodičkova 36, tel. 224-217-108).

The small **Reduta Jazz Club,** with cushioned brown sofas stretching along mirrored walls, will launch you straight into the 1960s classic jazz scene. The top Czech jazzmen—Stivín and Koubková—regularly perform. Even Bill Clinton played the sax here (live jazz every night from 21:00, on Národní street next to Café Louvre, tel. 224-933-486, www.redutajazzclub.cz).

In the Little Quarter

Baráčnická Rychta, with a gymnasium-like hall, saw many great polka parties in the 1920s. Since then, rock has replaced waltz, but the place still feels like a village dancehall, complete with flags of bakers' and butchers' guilds and black-and-white photos of the proud Austro-Hungarian landlords. It's a great scene if the hall is full, but less popular bands look a bit lost in the large space. Try the yeasty and strong Svijany beer here (three shows weekly starting at 20:00 or 21:00, arrive earlier to get a seat at a table, 150-Kč cover, on Tržiště, tucked away from tourists and out-of-town Czechs in a small courtyard directly across from the US Embassy, see map on page 87, tel. 257-532-461, www.baracnickarychta.cz).

In Žižkov

This hip neighborhood, below the Žižkov TV tower (Metro: Jiřího z Poděbrad), has Prague's highest concentration of cool pubs.

Palác Akropolis is *the* home of Czech independent music. Originally a 1920s movie theater, in the 1990s it was turned into a chill-out lounge, a literary café, and two halls that offer a mix of concerts, disco, and theater (advance ticket sales at café, Mon–Fri 10:00–24:00, Sat–Sun 16:00–24:00, corner of Kubelíkova and Fibichova, under TV tower, Metro: Jiřího z Poděbrad, see map on page 119, tel. 296-330-913, www.palacakropolis.cz).

Sports

Prague's top sports are soccer (that's "football" here) and hockey. Surprisingly, the Czechs are a world power in both. You'll find the latest schedules for games in the *Prague Post* newspaper (soccer—usually late Sat, Sun, or Mon afternoons Feb–May and Aug–Nov; hockey—Tue, Fri, Sun nights Sept–April). Both soccer and hockey games are rarely sold out—just show up at the stadium 15 minutes before the game starts.

Soccer

The Czech soccer team reached the finals of the 1996 European Cup, and the semifinals of the 2004 European Cup. They were eliminated in the first round of the 2006 World Cup, defeating the USA before suffering back-to-back losses to Ghana and Italy.

Within the Czech Republic, the two oldest and by far most successful soccer clubs are the bitter Prague rivals, Sparta and Slavia. In 2007, Slavia qualified for Europe's top club competition—the Champions' League—by beating Ajax Amsterdam and the Slovak champion Žilina, while Sparta was eliminated in the qualifying round by London's Arsenal. Sparta's 1970s-era stadium is at Letná (behind the metronome ticking above the river). Slavia's brand-new stadium opens in March 2008 in Vršovice (12 stops on tram #22 or #23 from the National Theatre).

The other two Prague teams in the top Czech league are the Bohemians and Viktoria Žižkov. Although both clubs operate on a fraction of the budget of the two big Ss, their fans make up for the lack of skill on the pitch with a die-hard attitude in the stands.

Hockey

The Czech national hockey team won four out of the last eight world championships. In 2006, the Czech team lost to Sweden in the final. Currently, more than 60 Czech players take the ice in America's NHL. Think Jaromír Jágr, one of the NHL's all-time leading scorers.

Sparta and Slavia, the traditional soccer powers, also have hockey teams, but the rivalry is less intense, as the teams from smaller towns are more than their equals. Slavia plays in the state-of-the-art Sazka Arena built for the 2004 world hockey championships (right at the Českomoravská Metro stop).

Back in the old days, ice hockey was the only battleground on which Czechoslovaks could seek revenge on their Russian oppressors (ice hockey is also the most popular sport in Slovakia). To this day, the hockey rink is where Czechs are proudest about their nationality. If you are in town in May during the hockey championships, join locals cheering their team in front of a giant screen on  the Old Town Square, as well as on other main squares around the country.

Sports on the Old Town and Wenceslas Squares

When there are sporting events of great interest (such as hockey and soccer championships), the Old Town Square plays host to huge TV screens, beer and bratwurst stands, and thousands of Czechs. The warm and friendly scene is like a big family gathering. Some fans lie on the cobblestones up front and focus on the game, while others mill around in the back and just enjoy the party.

Major running and biking events (such as the Prague International Marathon in mid-May) finish in the Old Town Square. The two biggest sporting events on Wenceslas Square are the Prague Pole Vault and a cycling competition that uses the square as a lap. The bottom of Wenceslas Square is also often set up for soccer, basketball, and beach volleyball tournaments. Both squares are also used for pop and folk concerts and for political rallies. These events are fine opportunities to feel the pulse of the Czech capital.

Entertainment

TRANSPORTATION CONNECTIONS

Centrally located Prague is a logical gateway between Western and Eastern Europe. Direct overnight trains connect Prague to Munich, and frequent day trains leave from Berlin and Vienna. From the East, Prague is connected by convenient night trains with Budapest, Kraków, and Warsaw (see below). For information on Prague's airport, see page 38.

If you're using a Eurailpass, keep in mind that it doesn't cover the Czech Republic. You need to buy a ticket for the Czech portion of the trip (if you're coming from Vienna, however, it's cheaper to buy a ticket for the whole route and not use up a travel day of a flexipass). You can either buy that in the station before leaving a Eurailpass-covered country, or save about €5 by buying it directly from the Czech conductor (German stations, for example, charge twice what Czechs do for Czech tickets; note that you can only buy tickets on board on long-distance trains—if you go to Prague indirectly via a milk-run train, you can be fined heavily for boarding without a ticket).

You'll find handy Czech train and bus schedules at www.vlak-bus.cz (train info tel. 221-111-122, little English spoken).

For rail travel tips, see page 284. Remember that for all train connections, it's important to confirm which of Prague's stations to use.

From Prague by Train to: Benešov (10-min walk to **Konopiště Castle;** hourly, 60 min), **Karlštejn** (2/hr, 40 min, then a 20-min walk to castle), **Křivoklát** (hourly, 90 min, transfer in Beroun), **Kutná Hora** (7/day, 1 hr, more with change in Kolín), **Český Krumlov** (8/day, 1/day direct, 4 hrs—bus is faster, cheaper, and easier), **České Budějovice** (nearly hourly, 2.5 hrs), **Třeboň** (7/day, 2.5 hrs, transfer at Veselí nad Lužnicí), **Telč** (3/day, 4–5 hrs, requires 2 changes; bus is better—see next page),

Třebíč (nearly hourly, 4–5 hrs, transfer in Brno; bus is better—see below), **Slavonice** (bus to Telč—see below—then 1-hr train to Slavonice, 4 hrs total), **Olomouc** (SC Pendolino train leaves 7/day from Holešovice station, 2 hrs; use Olomouc for connections to **Wallachia**), **Valtice** (hourly, 4 hrs, 1 transfer), **Břeclav** (with connections on to **Mikulov Wine Region**—see page 250; 9/day direct, 3 hrs, most from Holešovice station), **Brno** (every 2 hrs direct, 2.5 hrs), **Moravský Krumlov** (go to Brno, then take hourly 45-min train; bus from Prague to Brno is faster), **Berlin** (7/day, 4.5–5 hrs), **Munich** (2/day direct, 6 more with changes, 6–7.5 hrs, 1/night, 10 hrs), **Frankfurt** (8/day, 7–8 hrs, 1 change in Dresden or Nürnberg), **Vienna** (5/day direct, 4.5 hrs, 5 more with 1 change, 5–6 hrs), **Budapest** (3/day, 7 hrs; 2 overnight trains, 9 hrs), **Kraków** (1 direct train/day, 7 hrs; 2 more with 1–2 changes, 8 hrs), **Warsaw** (2/day direct including 1 night train, 8.5–9.5 hrs).

By Bus to: Terezín (hourly, 1 hr, from Florenc station), **Český Krumlov** (7/day, 3.5 hrs, from Florenc station; an easy direct 3-hr bus leaves at about 9:00), **Třeboň** (2/day, 2.5 hrs), **Telč** (5/day Mon–Fri, 3/day Sat–Sun, 2–3 hrs; more with a transfer in Jihlava, 3 hrs total), **Třebíč** (7/day, 2.5 hrs), **Lány** (1/day, 40 min), **Brno** (2/hr from Florenc station, 2.5 hrs). Note that some buses from Prague to Telč and Třebíč go from the Roztyly station (on the red Metro line), not the main bus station, Florenc.

By Car with a Driver: Mike's Chauffeur Service is a reliable family-run company with fair and fixed rates around town and beyond. Friendly Mike's motto is, "We go the extra mile for you" (round-trip fares with waiting time included, guaranteed through 2009 with this book: Český Krumlov-3,800 Kč, Terezín-1,900 Kč, Karlštejn-1,700 Kč, these prices for up to 4 people, minivan for up to 6 and brand-new minibus for 7 also available, tel. 241-768-231, mobile 602-224-893, www.mike-chauffeur.cz, mike.chauffeur @cmail.cz). On the way to Krumlov, Mike will stop at no extra charge at Hluboká Castle or České Budějovice, where the original Bud beer is made. Mike offers a "Panoramic Transfer to Vienna" for 7,000 Kč (depart Prague at 8:00, arrive Český Krumlov at 10:00, stay up to 6 hrs, 1-hr scenic Czech riverside-and-village drive, then a 2-hr autobahn ride to your Vienna hotel, maximum 4 people). Mike also offers a similar "Panoramic Transfer to Budapest" for 10,000 Kč (2 hrs to Český Krumlov, then 1-hr scenic drive to Linz, followed by 5–6 hrs on expressway to Budapest).

BEYOND PRAGUE

DAY TRIPS

Prague has plenty to keep a traveler busy, but don't overlook the enjoyable day trips in the nearby Bohemian countryside. Within an hour of Prague (in different directions), you'll find a rich medieval town, a sobering concentration camp, and three grand castles.

Down-to-earth Kutná Hora was once home to the world's largest silver mine; it's now known for its opulent cathedral, built with riches from the mining bonanza. Terezín, a walled town, served as a containment camp for Jews during World War II. The charming nearby town of Litoměřice offers an opportunity to reflect on the camp. Two of the country's most popular castles—Konopiště (better interior) and Karlštejn (better exterior)—give you a good look at the Czech version of this European medieval architectural form. Křivoklát Castle is one of the purest Gothic structures in the country, and a less touristy alternative to the other two castles. The village of Lány is a pilgrimage site for Czech patriots.

Kutná Hora

Kutná Hora (KOOT-nah HO-rah) is a refreshingly authentic town of 20,000, on top of what was once Europe's largest silver mine. In its heyday, the mine was so productive that Kutná Hora was Bohemia's "second city" after Prague. The standard coinage of much of Europe was minted here. By about 1700, the mining and minting petered out, and the city slumbered. Once rich, then ignored, Kutná Hora is now newly appreciated by tourists looking for a handy side-trip from Prague. Visitors are charmed by the wonderfully preserved town and its interesting sights: the fine St. Barbara's Cathedral, the fascinating silver mine, and the eerie Sedlec Bone Church. Start your visit

DAY TRIPS

To Berlin

GERMANY

Bautzen   Görlitz   Zgorzelec

POLAND

Dresden

Elbe

Bad Schandau

Zinnwald   Děčín

Cínovec

Teplice   Ústí nad Labem

Litoměřice

Terezín

CZECH   REPUBLIC

Mělník

To Karlovy Vary   Slaný

Lidice   AIRPORT

Rakovník   Lány

Křivoklát Castle

Beroun   Karlštejn Castle

Berounka River

Řevnice

To Plzeň

Konopiště Castle   Beneš ov

To Tábor & Český Krumlov

Vltava River

Labe River

Prague

Kolín

Kutná Hora

To Brno

To Brno

50 Kilometers

50 Miles

N

Kutná Hora

at Hrádek (the Czech Museum of Silver), make an appointment for a tour, and then build your day around it.

Kutná Hora, unlike dolled-up Český Krumlov, is a typical Czech town. The shops on the main square cater to locals, and the factory between the Sedlec Bone Church and the train station—since the 1930s, the biggest tobacco processor in the country—is now Philip Morris' headquarters for Central Europe. After touristy Prague, Kutná Hora is about as close to quintessential Czech life as you can get.

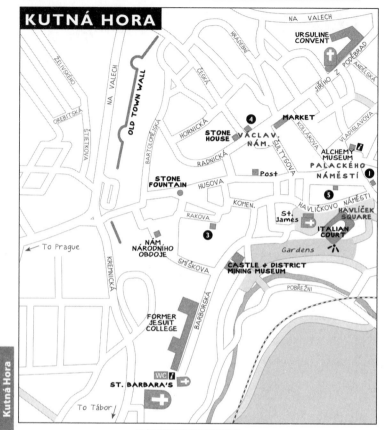

KUTNÁ HORA

ORIENTATION

Tourist Information

The main TI is on Palackého Náměstí, housed in the same building as the Alchemy Museum (Mon–Fri 9:00–18:00, Sat–Sun 10:00–16:00, tel. 327-512-378, www.kutnahora.cz). It offers Internet access and also rents bicycles (220 Kč/day, mobile 605-802-874).

A small TI kiosk, with handy WCs, is in front of the cathedral; you can hire a **local guide** here. Ideally, reserve ahead (500 Kč/hr Tue–Sun, no tours Mon, tel. 327-516-710, mobile 736-485-408, infocentrum@kh.cz).

SIGHTS

In Kutná Hora

St. Barbara's Cathedral (Chrám Sv. Barbory)—The cathedral was founded in 1388 by miners, who dedicated it to their patron. The dazzling interior celebrates the town's sources of wealth, with

To Train Station & Bone Church

A NE S K É NÁMĚSTÍ

VOCELOVA

NA LÁVKÁCH

LIBUŠINA

NA NÁMĚTI

ŠTEFÁNIKOVA

UHELNÁ

TYLOVA

RUDNÍ

ROHÁČOVA

SOKOLSKÁ

K BĚLIDLU

POTOČNÍ

ŽIŽKOVA BRÁNA

MĚSTSKÉ SADY

ZA OCTÁRNOU

ZAHRADNÍ

ČÁSLAVSKÁ

U LAZARA

MACHÁČKOVO NÁBŘEŽÍ

POBŘEŽNÍ

Creek

Vrchlice

N

200 Meters

200 Yards

❶ Hotel u Vlašského Dvora, Hotel Garni & Restaurace Donna
❷ Pension & Rest. u Kata
❸ Pivnice Dačický Restaurant
❹ New Peking Restaurant
❺ Piazza Navona Restaurant
❻ Dobrá Čajovna Teahouse

Kutná Hora

frescoes featuring mining and minting. Even the Renaissance vault—a stunning feat of the two Gothic geniuses of Prague, Matyáš Rejsek and Benedict Ried—is decorated with miners' coats of arms. The artistic highlight is the Smíšek Chapel to the right of the altar. The late-Gothic frescoes—*The Arrival of the Queen of Sheba, The Trial of Trajan,* and especially the fresco under the chapel's window depicting two men with candles—are the only works of a Dutch-trained master in Gothic Bohemia (30 Kč, daily 9:00–18:00 in summer, shorter hours off-season).

As you exit the cathedral, you'll see the Baroque Jesuit college on your left (currently being converted into a gallery). Jesuits arrived here in 1626 with a mission: to make the Protestant population Catholic again. The statues of saints on the artificial terrace in front of the college were inspired by the statues on Charles Bridge.

Hrádek and the Czech Museum of Silver—At this museum, located in Kutná Hora's 15th-century castle, you'll see an exhibit on mining and an intriguing horse-powered winch that hoisted

2,000 pounds of rock at a time out of the mine. Then you'll don a miner's coat and helmet and climb deep into the mine for a wet, dark, and claustrophobic 45-minute tour of the medieval shafts that honeycomb the land under the town (April–Oct Tue–Sun 10:00–18:00, closed Mon and Nov–March, tours generally every half hour, tel. 327-512-159). When you arrive in Kutná Hora, find out when the next English-language tour will run and reserve a spot; ask for Mr. Matuška, a charming retired miner.

Stone Fountain (Kamenná Kašna)—Because of the intensive mining under the town, Kutná Hora always struggled with the problem of obtaining drinking water. Water was brought to town by a sophisticated system of water pipes and stored in large tanks. At the end of the 15th century, the architect Rejsek built a 12-sided, richly decorated Gothic structure over one of these tanks. While no longer functioning, the fountain survives unchanged, the only structure of its kind in Bohemia (on the square called Rejskovo Náměstí).

Stone House (Kamenný Dům)—Notice the meticulous detail in the grape leaves, branches, and animals on the facade and up in the gable. Talented Polish craftsmen delicately carved the brittle stone into what was considered a marvel of its time. Skip the boring museum of local arts and crafts inside (40 Kč, daily 10:00–17:00, Radnická 183).

Alchemy Museum—The only one of its kind in the Czech Republic, it's run by a gracious, eccentric Englishman who (upon request) will personally guide you into the surprisingly deep medieval cellars of this otherwise unassuming house. There you'll find a laboratory dedicated to the pursuit of *prima materia* (primal matter). The English descriptions do a good job explaining the goals and methods of alchemy, and the fate of its failed practitioners. The rare Gothic tower in the rear of the house is set up as an alchemist's study (complete with ancient books), looking much as it did when a prince used this vaulted space in his quest to purify matter and spirit (50 Kč, daily April–Sept 10:00–17:00, Oct–March 10:00–16:00, on the main square in the same building as the TI, tel. 327-511-259, mobile 603-308-024, www.alchemy.cz).

Italian Court (Vlašský Dvůr)—This palace building, located on the site where Czech currency was once made, became Europe's most important mint and the main residence of Czech kings in the 1400s. Today, it hosts a museum on minting and local history. The 70-Kč entry gets you into the main Gothic hall (now a wedding chamber) and the Art Nouveau–decorated St. Wenceslas Chapel (April–Sept daily 9:00–18:00, shorter hours Oct–March, Havlíčkovo Náměstí). But neither the museum nor the building itself—largely a 19th-century imitation of the former palace—is particularly interesting. The flower-filled square in front of it, on the other hand, is worth a look...

Havlíček Square (Havlíčkovo Náměstí)—The monuments on this square are a *Who's Who* of important Czech patriots.

The statue in the middle of the square (and the square's namesake) is **Karel Havlíček** (1821–1856), the founder of Czech political journalism. From Kutná Hora, Havlíček ran an influential magazine highly critical of the Hapsburg government. In 1851, he was forced into exile and detained for five years in the Tirolean Alps under police surveillance. His integrity is illustrated with the inscription on the statue: "You can try to bribe me with favors, you can threaten me, you can torture me, yet I will never turn a traitor." His motto became an inspiration for generations of Czech intellectuals, most of whom faced a similar combination of threats and temptations. Havlíček (whose name means "little Havel") was much revered in the 1970s and 1980s, when the *other* Havel (Václav) was similarly imprisoned for his dissent.

The bronze statue in front of the Italian Court commemorates the founder of Czechoslovakia, **Tomáš Garrigue Masaryk** (1850–1937; see sidebar on page 102). The brief inscription on the back of the pedestal illustrates the statue's history, paralleling the country's troubled 20th-century history: erected by Kutná Hora townsmen on October 27, 1938 (the eve of the 20th anniversary of Czech independence); torn down in 1942 (by occupying Nazis, who disliked Masaryk as a symbol of Czech independence); erected again on October 27, 1948 (by freedom-loving locals, a few months after the communist coup); torn down again in 1957 (by the communists, who considered Masaryk an enemy of the working class); and erected once again on October 27, 1991. But notice that the Czechs, ever realistic, have left a blank space below the last entry....

On the wall to the left of the gate, you'll find the small, bronze tablet covered with barbed wire. This is an unassuming little **memorial** to the victims of communist misrule and torture.

Walk down the steps into a little park, and then turn right to reach a great viewpoint. It overlooks the tent-shaped roof of the cathedral and the scenic valley below. Nearby benches under the shade of linden trees invite you to sit back and think about those to whom the memorial is dedicated.

Market (Tržiště)—This double row of stalls selling fake Nike shoes and cheap jeans is as integral a part of today's Czech town as farmers' markets were in the past. The bazaars are run by Vietnamese immigrants, the largest minority in the Czech Republic. Many came in the 1970s, as part of a communist solidarity program that sent Vietnamese workers to Czech textile factories. They learned the language, adapted to the environment, and, after 1989, set off on a road to entrepreneurial success that allowed them to bring over friends and relatives (Mon–Fri 7:30–16:45, shorter hours Sat, closed Sun, near Stone House and New Peking Restaurant).

Near Kutná Hora

Sedlec Bone Church (Kostnice u Sedlci)—Located a mile away from the center of town, in Sedlec, this little church looks normal on the outside. Inside, the bones of 40,000 people decorate the walls and ceilings. Fourteenth-century plagues and 15th-century wars provided all the raw material necessary for the creepily creative monks who made these designs. Those who first placed these bones 400 years ago wanted viewers to remember that the earthly church is a community of both the living and the dead, a countless multitude that will one day stand before God. Later bone-stackers were more interested in design than theology...as evidenced by

the chandelier that includes every bone in the human body (40 Kč, July–Aug daily 8:00–18:00, April–June and Sept–Oct daily 9:00–17:00, Nov–March Tue–Sun 9:00–16:00, closed Mon). To get to the Bone Church, you can walk, catch a taxi (less than 100 Kč), or ride the city bus (leaves from Masarykova street, buy ticket at a newsstand).

SLEEPING

Although one day is enough for Kutná Hora, staying overnight saves you money (hotels are much cheaper here than in Prague) and allows you to better savor the atmosphere of a small Czech town.

Hotel u Vlašského Dvora and **Hotel Garni** are two newly renovated townhouses run by the same management. Furnished in a mix of 1930s and modern style, the hotels come with access to a fitness center and sauna. Hotel Garni is slightly nicer (Db-1,350 Kč, a few steps off main square at Havlíčkovo Náměstí 513, tel. 327-515-773, www.vlasskydvur.cz).

Pension U Kata, on a quiet street below the square, has 31 tastefully furnished rooms in pastel colors (Db-700 Kč, runs recommended restaurant at same address, Uhelná 596, tel. 327-515-096, www.ukata.cz, hotel@ukata.cz).

EATING

Pivnice Dačický has made a theme of its namesake, a popular 17th-century author who once lived in the house. Solid wooden tables rest under perky illustrations of medieval town life, and a local brew, also named after Dačický, flows from the tap. They serve standard Czech fare, as well as excellent game and fish, to an increasingly international crowd (daily 11:00–23:00, Rakova 8, tel. 327-512-248, mobile 603-434-367).

Restaurant U Kata (By the Executioner), inspired by the success of Dačický (above), is the alternative medieval space in town, with few tourists and equally good food and service (daily 10:30–23:00, Uhelná 596; run by Pension U Kata, above).

Dobrá Čajovna Teahouse also offers the chance to escape— not to medieval times, but to a Thai paradise. Filled with tea cases, water pipes, and character, this place is an ideal spot to dawdle away the time that this ageless town has reclaimed for you from rushed modern life (daily 14:00–22:00, Jungmannovo Náměstí 16, mobile 777-028-481).

Restaurace Donna features the fastest and tastiest ready-to-serve Czech dishes in town. If the weather's nice, sit in the court-yard behind the restaurant, shaded by chestnut trees (open daily, lunch specials until 15:00, on Havlíčkovo Náměstí, right above Hotel Garni).

Cuisines evolve. Today, the chicken roasted in paprika at the **New Peking** restaurant (next to the Stone House) and the spaghetti swimming in a sea of Czech ketchup and *klobasa* at **Piazza Navona** (daily, on the main square) are as Czech as the pork and sauerkraut.

TRANSPORTATION CONNECTIONS

Getting to Kutná Hora: The town is 40 miles east of Prague. Trains from Prague's Main Station (7/day, 1 hr, more with change in Kolín) stop near Kutná Hora, two miles from the town center. From there, local trains shuttle visitors to the central Kutná Hora Město station.

Terezín Concentration Camp

Terezín (TEH-reh-zeen), an hour by bus from Prague, was a fortified town named after Hapsburg empress Maria Theresa (it's called "Theresienstadt" in German). It was built in the 1780s with state-of-the-art star-shaped walls designed to keep out the Prussians. In 1941, the Nazis removed its 7,000 inhabitants and brought in 60,000 Jews, creating Terezín Concentration Camp. Ironically, the town's medieval walls, originally meant to keep Germans out, were later used by German conquerors to keep the Jews in.

This was the Nazis' model "Jewish town," a concentration camp dolled up for propaganda purposes. Here in this "self-governed Jewish resettlement area," Jewish culture seemed to thrive, as "citizens" put on plays and concerts, published a magazine, and raised their families. But it was all a carefully planned deception, intended to convince Red Cross inspectors that the Jews  were being treated well. Virtually all of Terezín's Jews (155,000 over the course of the war) ultimately ended up dying either here (35,000) or in extermination camps farther east.

One of the notable individuals held at Terezín was the Viennese artist Friedl Dicker-Brandeis. This daring woman, a leader in the Bauhaus art movement, found her life's calling in teaching children freedom of expression. She taught the children in the camp to distinguish between the central things—trees, flowers, lines—and peripheral things, such as the conditions of the camp. Of the 15,000 children who passed through Terezín from 1942–1944, fewer than 100 survived. (In 1944, Dicker-Brandeis volunteered to be sent to Auschwitz after her husband was sent there; she was killed a month later.)

The art of the children of Terezín is a striking testimony to the cruel horror of the Holocaust. In 1994, Hana Volavková, a Terezín survivor and the director of the Jewish Museum in Prague, collected the artwork and poems in the book *I Never Saw Another Butterfly*. Selections of the Terezín drawings are also displayed and well-described in English in Prague's Pinkas Synagogue (see page 67). And in 2003, a copy of 13-year-old Petr Ginz's drawing *Moon Country* was carried into space by an Israeli astronaut (see sidebar).

Most well-known of the cultural activities that took place at Terezín is the children's opera *Brundibár*. Written just before the war, the anti-Fascist opera premiered secretly in Prague at a time when Jewish activities were no longer permitted. From 1943–1944 the play, performed in Czech, ran 55 times in the camp. After the war it was staged internationally (including a successful run on Broadway) and was recently rewritten in the US as a successful children's book.

Petr Ginz, Young Artist and Writer

Born in 1928 to a Jewish father and non-Jewish mother, Prague teenager Petr Ginz excelled at art and was a talented writer who penned numerous articles, short stories, and even a science-fiction novel. Petr was sent to the concentration camp at Terezín in 1942, where he edited the secret boys' publication *Vedem (We Are Ahead)*, writing poetry and drawing illustrations, and paying contributors with food rations he received from home.

Some of Petr's artwork and writings were preserved by Terezín survivors and archived by the Jewish Museum in Prague. In 2003, Ilan Ramon, the first Israeli astronaut and the son of a Holocaust survivor, took one of Petr's drawings—titled *Moon Country*—into space aboard the final, doomed mission of the space shuttle Columbia.

The publicity over the Columbia's explosion and Petr's drawing spurred a Prague resident to come forward with a diary he'd found in his attic. It was Petr's diary from 1941–1942, hidden decades earlier by Petr's parents, and chronicling the year before the teen's deportation to Terezín. *The Diary of Petr Ginz* has since been published in more than 10 languages. Petr's journalistic talent is evident in the diary, in which he matter-of-factly documents the increasing restrictions on Jewish life in occupied Prague, interspersing the terse account with dry humor.

In the entry for September 19, 1941, Petr wrote, "They just introduced a special sign for Jews" and drew the Star of David. He continued, "On the way to school I counted 69 'sheriffs,'" referring to people wearing the star.

Petr spent two years at Terezín before being sent to Auschwitz, where he died in a gas chamber. He was 16.

Today, Terezín is an unforgettable day trip from Prague for those interested in touring a concentration camp memorial and museum. Allow three to six hours to see the entire camp thoroughly. With more time, visit the nearby, attractive town of Litoměřice (see below) for lunch before returning to Prague.

Cost, Hours, Information: The 200-Kč combo-ticket includes all parts of the camp. The Museum of the Ghetto, Magdeburg Barracks, Columbarium, and Hidden Synagogue are open daily April–Oct 9:00–18:00, Nov–March 9:00–17:30. The Small Fortress is open daily April–Oct 8:00–18:00, Nov–March 8:00–16:30. The Crematorium is open Sun–Fri April–Oct 10:00–18:00, Nov–March 10:00–16:00, closed Sat. Tel. 416-782-225, mobile 606-632-914, www.pamatnik-terezin.cz.

Eateries: In Terezín town, the Parkhotel Restaurant is the most elegant place for lunch (daily 10:00–22:00, around the block

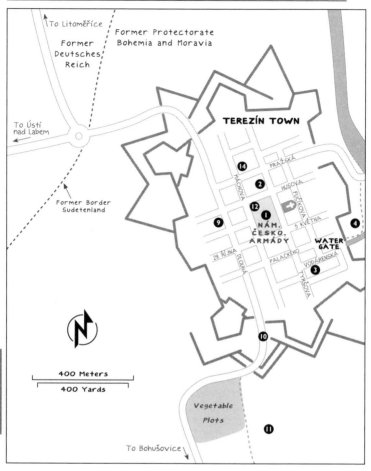

from the Museum of the Ghetto at Máchova 163, tel. 416-782-260). Avoid the stale sandwiches in the Museum of the Ghetto's dingy basement cafeteria, where most tour guides inexplicably shove their clients. The Small Fortress has a cafeteria.

Touring the Camp: There are two parts to a visit to Terezín: Terezín town and the Small Fortress, a half-mile to the east across the river. The bus from Prague drops you off at Terezín town's spacious ❶ **main square** (Náměstí Československé Armády). Picture the giant circus tent and barbed wire fence that stood on this square for two years during the war. Inside, Jewish workers boxed special motors for German vehicles being used on the frigid Soviet front. As part of year-long preparations for the famous Red Cross visit (which lasted all of six hours on June 23, 1944), the tent and fence were replaced by flower beds (which you still see on the square today) and a pavilion for outdoor music performances.

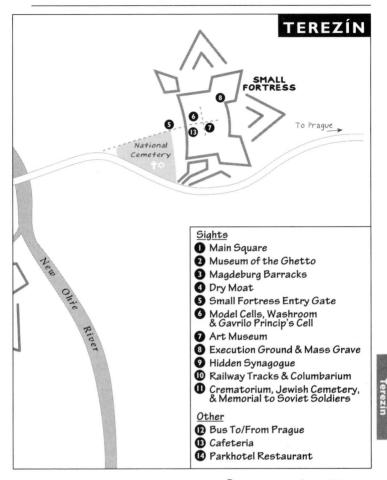

TEREZÍN

SMALL FORTRESS

To Prague →

National Cemetery

New Ohře River

Sights
1. Main Square
2. Museum of the Ghetto
3. Magdeburg Barracks
4. Dry Moat
5. Small Fortress Entry Gate
6. Model Cells, Washroom & Gavrilo Princip's Cell
7. Art Museum
8. Execution Ground & Mass Grave
9. Hidden Synagogue
10. Railway Tracks & Columbarium
11. Crematorium, Jewish Cemetery, & Memorial to Soviet Soldiers

Other
12. Bus To/From Prague
13. Cafeteria
14. Parkhotel Restaurant

Terezín

Walk around the corner to the ❷ **Museum of the Ghetto,** where you buy the Terezín combo-ticket (note show times for movies). You'll find two floors of exhibits about the development of the Nazi's "Final Solution" and a theater showing four excellent films. One film documents the history of the ghetto, and two focus on children's art in the camp. The fourth is made up of clips

from *Der Führer schenkt den Juden eine Stadt (The Führer Gives a City to the Jews)* by Kurt Gerron. Gerron, a Berlin Jew, was a 1920s movie star who appeared with Marlene Dietrich in *Blue Angel*. Deported to Terezín, Gerron in 1944 was asked by the Nazis to produce a propaganda film. Although in the resulting film, healthy (i.e., recently arrived) "Jewish settlers" are seen in Terezín happily viewing concerts, playing soccer, and sewing in their rooms, an unmistakable, deadly desperation radiates from their pallid faces. The only moment of genuine emotion comes towards the end, when a packed room of children applauds the final lines of the popular anti-Nazi opera *Brundibár*, "We did not let ourselves down, we chased the nasty Brundibár away. With a happy song, we won it all." Even the Nazis were not fooled: Gerron and his wife were shipped to Auschwitz and the film was never shown in public.

To learn more about living conditions in the camp, walk over to the ❸ **Magdeburg Barracks.** Peek inside the large courtyard (you'll recognize it as the "soccer stadium" in Gerron's film), then continue upstairs. On the right are rooms reproducing the camp cabaret stage and exhibits documenting the prisoners' literary, musical, and theatrical activities. On the left is a meticulously restored camp dormitory, complete with three-tiered beds, eyeglasses, dolls, chess boards, and sewing kits.

As you exit from the barracks (notice the high-water marks from the 2002 flood on the house opposite), turn right around the corner and walk 100 yards to a brick gate. As you cross a bridge over a ❹ **dry moat,** imagine the moat filled with plots of vegetables grown by starving Jews for well-fed SS officers.

Then turn left and walk along the moat. The top of the fortification walls on the other side were once equipped with benches and pathways. When you reach the main road, turn right across the New Ohře River (the original course of the river was diverted here when Terezín was built) and walk past the vast cemetery to the ❺ **Small Fortress**—you'll see its black-and-white-striped gate. From 1940–1945 this fortress functioned as a Gestapo prison, through which 32,000 inmates passed (of whom nearly 10 percent died here), chiefly members of the Czech resistance and communists. The 1,500 Jews interned here were treated with particular severity.

Inside the gate, turn left towards the notorious *Arbeit Macht Frei* sign (a postwar replica), painted above an arched gate. In the courtyard behind you will first find ❻ **model prison cells.** The **washroom** in the left corner was built solely for the purpose of fooling Red Cross inspectors. Turn the faucets: No pipes were ever installed to bring in water. The **shower room** farther to the left, on the other hand, was used to fool the Jews. Here they got used to the idea of communal bathing—so they wouldn't be

Terezín

suspicious when they were later taken to similar-looking installations at Auschwitz. (There were no gas chambers at Terezín—most of the deaths were caused by malnutrition and disease, and to a lesser extent, executions.)

Before the Nazis, the Small Fortress was used as a prison by the Austrian Monarchy. The little courtyard preserves the cell of the most famous prisoner from that time, the Bosnian Serb **Gavrilo Princip,** whose assassination of Archiduke Franz Ferdinand and his wife Žofie in 1914 sparked World War I. Princip died here in 1918 of tuberculosis.

Return through the *Arbeit Macht Frei* gate, then turn left into a large courtyard. On your right is an ❼ **art museum** with two floors of paintings by prominent Czech artists, with themes of camp life and the Spanish Civil War. Farther to the left is a path leading to the ❽ **execution ground** and a **mass grave** of the victims.

To take a break or finish your tour at this point, you could head to the handy cafeteria by the entry gate to the Small Fortress. The wood-and-metal chandeliers inside were produced by Jewish workers for the SS officers who once dined in these two rooms.

With more time, consider continuing your tour in Terezín town with the less-frequented sights, described below, that lie along or just off a main road called Dlouhá. At Dlouhá 17 look for the unique ❾ **hidden synagogue,** the only one of the camp's eight synagogues that survived. Although entry is included with your combo-ticket, you may need to ring the bell for the guard to open the door. Inside you'll find a courtyard; the bakery that used to be here hid the synagogue behind it. Today the atmospheric space is still inscribed with two Hebrew captions, which are translated as: "May my eyes behold, how You in compassion return to Sinai," and "If I forget Jerusalem, may my tongue rot and my right arm fall off." These words indicate that the prayer room belonged to a congregation of Zionists (advocates of a Jewish state), who, one would expect, were specifically targeted by the Nazis.

Continue down Dlouhá to the Bohušovice gate. On the ground you will see the remnants of ❿ **railway tracks.** In the early years

of the camp, Jews arrived at the train station in the nearby town of Bohušovice and then had to walk the remaining two miles to Terezín. This was too public a display for the Nazis, who didn't want locals to observe the transports and become suspicious. So the Jewish prisoners at Terezín were forced to construct a railway line that led right to Terezín...and back out again to Auschwitz.

As you exit the walled-in area, on the right you will find Jewish and Christian ceremonial halls and the main morgue, while on the left is a **Columbarium,** or storage space for urns. The Germans originally promised that the urns would be properly reburied after the war, but in 1945, to erase evidence, the ashes of Terezín victims (stored mainly in cardboard boxes) were dumped into the New Ohře River.

Continue along the road, then turn left past bucolic vegetable plots and fruit gardens to reach the ⓫ **Crematorium, Jewish Cemetery,** and a **Memorial to Soviet Soldiers.** Days before Terezín was liberated (on May 8, 1945) an epidemic of typhus spread through the camp. In the weeks after the war ended, scores of Soviet soldiers and medical workers who tried to contain the epidemic died, along with hundreds of former prisoners.

Our tour ends here. As you ponder Terezín, remember the message of all such memorials: Never again.

TRANSPORTATION CONNECTIONS

Getting to Terezín: The camp is about 40 miles northwest of Prague. Buses leave almost hourly from stands 16 and 17 at Prague's Florenc station (at the intersection of Metro lines B and C), and arrive in Terezín about one hour later at the public bus stop on the main square, around the corner from the Museum of the Ghetto. For schedules see www.vlak-bus.cz; you want "Terezín LT." Make sure to check the return departures, too. On the trip back to Prague, the bus drops you off at the Holešovice train station, on Metro line C.

Near Terezín: Litoměřice

With a bustling, beautifully restored Renaissance square, Litoměřice (lee-TOH-myer-zheet-seh, pop. 26,000)—located three miles north of Terezín—is a perfect lunch spot to lift your spirits after the bleakness of the camp. During the communist era, Litoměřice had the only seminary in the country. Today, there are still two huge Baroque churches here. Linger on the main square, Mírové Náměstí, and experience the life of this friendly, untouristy Czech town.

If arriving by bus from Terezín, get off at the first stop after the bridge; from here, it's a two-minute walk (slightly uphill) to the main square. From the square, several small streets filled with bakeries and convenience shops radiate outwards. The onion-shaped tower is south, and the higher part of the square is due west. Stroll around and get lunch on the square (see "Eating," below). After lunch, climb up the onion-shaped tower of the **Town**

Hall (the guide in the tower loves to talk), but skip the uninteresting museum on the square.

The short street next to the Town Hall leads onto the city walls, with good views. The statue at the viewpoint depicts the

Romantic poet **Karel Hynek Mácha** (1810–1836), who wrote the most famous Czech poem, "Máj." He died in Litoměřice. In 1939, his body was ceremonially exhumed and transferred to the Slavín cemetery atop Prague's Vyšehrad hill. Mácha became a symbol of the irrepressible Czech spirit, stirring Czech nationalism during the occupations of the Nazis first, then the communists after. In November 1989, demonstrating students were headed for the grave of Mácha, when they suddenly decided that they were tired of the communists...and thus started the Velvet Revolution.

EATING

The most convenient spot is the Czech fast-food joint **Joka,** which serves standard ready-to-eat meals and good soups daily (at the top, or northwest, corner of the square). You can get a sandwich, sit on the benches under trees by the fountain, and enjoy the view of the Renaissance-era townhouses. **Salva Guarda** is a bit stuffy and service is slow, but it's a decent sit-down option (daily 11:00–23:00, under the arches at the bottom, or southeast, corner of the square).

TRANSPORTATION CONNECTIONS

Between Terezín and Litoměřice: Buses from Prague to Terezín continue three miles to Litoměřice; buses returning to Prague stop first in Litoměřice, then Terezín. Easier yet, it's a five-minute

taxi trip between the camp and Litoměřice (about 150 Kč). The museum's ticket office will be happy to call a cabbie for you (such as Mr. Poláček, based in Terezín, tel. 606-833-480).

Returning to Prague: To reach Litoměřice's bus station, walk east on the main street (Dlouhá) down from the square to an intersection, cross it, and continue in the same direction along Na Kocandě street (an easy 10-min walk). The train station is nearby (though buses to Prague are preferable, as the train requires a transfer).

Konopiště Castle

Konopiště (KOH-noh-peesh-tyeh), the huge, Neo-Gothic residence of the Archduke Franz Ferdinand d'Este, is 30 miles south of Prague.

Construction of the castle began in the 14th century, but today's exterior and furnishings date from about 1900, when the heir to the Hapsburg throne, Archduke Franz Ferdinand, renovated his new home. As one of the first castles in Europe to have an elevator, a WC, and running water, Konopiště shows "modern" living at the turn of the 20th century.  Touring the castle gives you a good sense of who this powerful Hapsburg was, as well as a glimpse at one of the best medieval arms collections in the world (and lots of hunting trophies).

While the stretch between the parking lot and the castle entrance is overrun by tour groups, the **gardens** and the **park** are surprisingly empty. In the summer, the flowers and goldfish in the rose garden are a big hit with visitors. The peaceful 30-minute walk through the woods around the lake (wooden bridge at the far end) offers gorgeous castle views.

Tucked away in the bushes behind the pond is a pavilion coated with tree bark, a perfect picnic spot. This simple structure, nicknamed the **Kaiser's Pavilion,** was the site of a meeting between the German Kaiser Wilhelm and the Archduke Franz Ferdinand (for more information, see the sidebar).

Cost and Tours: Entrance to the castle is by one-hour guided tour only. Choose from three different routes: Route I (190 Kč, includes public and guest rooms, hunting hall, and shooting range), Route II (190 Kč, includes the oldest part of the castle, armory, elevator, and chapel), and Route III (300 Kč, includes private top-floor rooms of Franz Ferdinand and his family). All tickets are 30

Konopiště Cas.

Archduke Franz Ferdinand
(1863–1914)

Archduke Franz Ferdinand was the nephew of the Hapsburg Emperor Franz Josef, who ruled from 1848–1916 (longer than Queen Victoria). Ferdinand was the impatient successor to the Austro-Hungarian throne. Local legends (whose veracity historians categorically deny) say that Franz Ferdinand even built a chapel at Konopiště for the sole purpose of praying that his old, hated uncle might soon die...but the emperor went on to outlive the young archduke.

Franz Ferdinand fell out of his uncle's favor when he married a beautiful Czech countess (Žofie Chotková) from too low a background for the other Hapsburgs to accept—she was "only" aristocratic, not royal. To get out of sight of his relatives, Franz Ferdinand bought Konopiště and moved here.

Obsessed with hunting, Franz Ferdinand traveled around the world twice, shooting at anything in sight: deer, bears, tigers, elephants, and crocodiles. He eventually killed 300,000 animals, many of whom stare morbidly at you as hunting trophies covering the walls at Konopiště.

In the Kaiser's Pavilion on the grounds of Konopiště, Franz Ferdinand met with German Kaiser Wilhelm and tried to talk him out of plotting a war against Russia. Wilhelm argued that a war would work to the mutual benefit of Germany and Austria: Germans wanted colonies, and Austria—crippled by the aspirations of its many nationalities—could use a war to divert attention from its domestic problems. But Franz Ferdinand foresaw that war would be suicidal for Austria's overstretched monarchy.

Soon after, Franz Ferdinand went to Sarajevo, in the Hapsburg-annexed territories of Bosnia and Herzegovina. On that trip, young Gavrilo Princip, a Bosnian Serb, shot the Hapsburg archduke who so loved shooting. Franz Ferdinand's assassination ironically gave the Germans (and their pro-war allies in the Austro-Hungarian administration) the pretext for starting the war against Serbia (and their ally, Russia). The Great War soon broke out. The event Franz Ferdinand had tried to avoid was in fact sparked by his death.

Konopiště Cas.

percent cheaper if you join a Czech-speaking tour. While Route II gives you the most comprehensive look into the castle, its history, and celebrated collections, Route III—recently reopened after the rooms were meticulously restored to match 1907 photographs—launches you right into a turn-of-the-century time capsule.

Hours and Information: Castle open May–Aug Tue–Sun 9:00–12:30 & 13:00–17:00; April and Oct Tue–Fri 9:00–15:00

Sat–Sun 9:00–16:00; Sept Tue–Fri 9:00–16:00, Sat–Sun 9:00–17:00; closed Nov–March and Mon year-round. Tel. 317-721-366, www .zamek-konopiste.cz.

EATING

There are three touristy restaurants under the castle, but I'd bring picnic supplies from Prague (or buy them at the grocery store by the Benešov train station). While the crowds wait to pay too much for lousy food in the restaurants, you'll enjoy the peace and thought-provoking ambience of a **picnic** in the shaded Kaiser's Pavilion. Or eat cheaply with locals on Benešov's main square (try **U Zlaté Hvězdy**—"The Golden Star").

TRANSPORTATION CONNECTIONS

Getting to Konopiště: Trains from Prague's Main Station drop you in Benešov (hourly, 60 min). From the Benešov train station, the yellow-marked trail goes directly to the castle (1.25 miles), bypassing the enormous parking lot clogged with souvenir shops and bus fumes.

Karlštejn Castle

One of the Czech Republic's top attractions, Karlštejn Castle (KARL-shtayn) was built by Charles IV in about 1350 to house the crown jewels of the Holy Roman Empire. While a striking, fairy-tale castle from a distance, it's not much inside. The highlight of the castle's interior—the much venerated and sumptuous Chapel of the Holy Cross (built to house the crown jewels)—can be seen only with an advance reservation.

Cost and Tours: The Chapel of the Holy Cross—basically the only thing inside Karlštejn worth seeing—is part of tour route II (300 Kč). You can only visit this route with a group (15 people maximum per group, 1 group per hour), and reservations are required (30-Kč reservation fee per person, tel. 274-008-154 or 274-008-155, rezervace@stc.npu.cz). Route I is nowhere near as interesting (220 Kč, no reservation required, bigger groups, shorter tour).

Hours and Information: May–Sept Tue–Sun 9:00–12:00 & 13:00–18:00; April and Oct Tue–Sun 9:00–12:00 & 13:00–15:00; closed Nov–March and Mon year-round; tel. 274-008-154, www.hradkarlstejn.cz.

From Karlštejn Castle, an easy one-hour **hike** along the red-marked trail leads away from the tourists through a quiet forest to Srbsko. There, you'll find two good Czech **restaurants** and a **train station** (the Karlštejn–Prague train stops in Srbsko).

TRANSPORTATION CONNECTIONS

Getting to Karlštejn: The castle, 20 miles southwest of Prague, is accessible by train (2/hr, 40 min, then a 20-min walk; depart from Prague's Smíchov Station) or by car (30 min, direction Plzeň).

Křivoklát Castle

Křivoklát (KREE-vohk-laht), an original 14th-century castle, is beautiful for its simplicity and setting, amid hills and deep woods near the lovely Berounka River valley. Originally a hunting residence of Czech kings, it was later transformed into a royal prison that "entertained" a number of distinguished guests, among them the most notorious alchemist of the 1500s, the Englishman Edward Kelly.

In summer, Křivoklát comes alive with craftspeople—woodcarvers, blacksmiths, and basket-weavers—who work as if it were the 15th century. The absence of tacky souvenir shops, the plain Gothic appearance, and the background noise of hammers and wood chisels give Křivoklát an engaging character.

The tour of the interior lasts a sensible half hour. The highlight is the king's audience hall, with its delicately arched ceiling.

Cost, Hours, Information: 150 Kč with an English-speaking guide; 100 Kč if you go with a Czech group (pick up an explanation sheet in English, and you'll be fine with the Czechs). Open June–Aug Tue–Sun 9:00–12:00 & 13:00–17:00, closed Mon; May and Sept Tue–Sun 9:00–16:00, closed Mon; April and Oct Tue–Sun 9:00–15:00, closed Mon; Nov–Dec Sat–Sun 9:00–15:00, closed Mon–Fri; closed Jan–March, tel. 313-558-440, www.krivoklat.cz.

SLEEPING AND EATING

Hotel and Restaurant Sýkora, below the castle near the train station, has been a favorite among Czech hikers since the 1930s. If you want to stay for an evening concert in the castle courtyard or for a hike in the nearby woods, sleep in one of the hotel's 11 beautifully renovated rooms (Db-600 Kč, tel. 313-558-114, www.hotel-sykora.krivoklatsko.com, hotel.sykora@krivoklatsko.com).

TRANSPORTATION CONNECTIONS

Getting to Křivoklát: Trains leave Prague's Main Station for Beroun (hourly, 40 min), running through the delightful valley of the dreamy Berounka River. In Beroun, transfer to the cute little motor train to Křivoklát (dubbed by Czech hikers the "Berounka Pacific"; allow 90 min total for trip from Prague). From Křivoklát's train station, it's a 10-minute walk uphill to the castle. At the train station, confirm the schedule back—one train leaves just before noon, and three others depart during the afternoon.

Near Křivoklát: Lány

The village of Lány, about 15 miles from Křivoklát Castle, is close to patriotic Czech hearts. The castle in Lány served as the Czech "Camp David" for both Tomáš Garrigue Masaryk (the first president of Czechoslovakia, between the World Wars) and Václav Havel (the contemporary "father of the Czech Republic" and first post-communist president of the nation).

Masaryk and his family are buried in Lány's simple village cemetery. Masaryk's humble grave on a hill in the middle of the fields is a pilgrimage place for freedom-loving Czechs. The communists, wanting to erase Masaryk from the nation's memory, destroyed all of Masaryk's statues (see page 159) and barely mentioned his name in history textbooks. During the communist era, Czechs risked their careers by coming here on the Czech Independence Day to put candles on Masaryk's grave. Imagine: Every year on October 28, the police sealed off all roads to the village of Lány, and anyone who wanted access had to show an ID card. When you arrived at work the next morning, the boss would be waiting at the door, asking, "Where were you yesterday—and why?"

After 1989, Václav Havel—the symbol of the new Czech freedom—strove to restore dignity to the presidency. He went back to the tradition of the first Czech president, making Lány his home away from home. Havel's weekend sojourns here symbolized a return to Czech self-governance.

Hike to Křivoklát Castle: Consider making the 15-mile hike to Křivoklát Castle from Lány. From the cemetery, it's a five-minute walk to the trailhead on the main square where you will also find two grocery stores for replenishing your supplies. There are no restaurants or stores until Křivoklát. Follow the red-marked trail through woods and meadows with the help of a good map. This is one of the most beautiful hikes in the whole country, as it takes you through all the varieties of woods in Eastern Europe (beech, birch, poplar, oak, pine, spruce, fir), a hidden 1950s dam, and some stunning vistas. The *Praha-Západ* or *Křivoklátsko* hiking maps are excellent (sold in most Prague bookstores).

TRANSPORTATION CONNECTIONS

Getting to Lány: The bus leaves Prague Hradčanská Metro station at 7:05 on weekdays for Lány (direction Rakovník, 40 min). The bus first stops on the main square of the town, then at the cemetery. There is no public transportation between Křivoklát Castle and Lány.

ČESKÝ KRUMLOV

Lassoed by its river and dominated by its castle, this enchanting town feels lost in a time warp. While Český Krumlov is the Czech Republic's answer to Germany's Rothenburg, it has yet to be turned into a medieval theme park. When you see its awe-inspiring castle, delightful Old Town of shops and cobbled lanes, characteristic little restaurants, and easy canoeing options, you'll understand why having fun is a slam-dunk here.

Český Krumlov (CHESS-key KROOM-loff) means, roughly, "Czech Bend in the River." Calling it "Český" for short sounds silly to Czech-speakers (since dozens of Czech town names begin with "Český"). "Krumlov" for short is okay.

Since Krumlov is the second-most-visited town (1.5 million visits annually) in the Czech Republic, there's enough tourism to make things colorful and easy—but not so much that it tramples the place's charm. This town of 15,000 attracts a young, bohemian crowd, drawn here for its simple beauty, cheap living, and fanciful bars.

Planning Your Time

Because the castle and theater can be visited only with a guide (and English-language tours are offered just a few times a day), serious sightseers should reserve both tours first thing in the morning in person at the castle and theater (or call the castle), and then build their day around the tour times. Those who hate planning ahead on vacation can join a Czech tour anytime with an English information sheet.

A paddle down the river to Zlatá Koruna Abbey is a highlight (three hours, see "Canoeing and Rafting the Vltava," page 191), and a 20-minute walk up to the Křížový Vrch (Hill of the Cross) rewards you with a fine view of the town and its unforgettable riverside setting (see "Hiking," page 192). Other sights are quick visits and worthwhile only if you have a particular interest (Egon Schiele, puppets, torture, and so on).

The town itself is the major attraction. Evenings are for atmospheric dining and drinking. Sights are generally open 10:00–17:00 and closed on Monday.

ORIENTATION

Český Krumlov is extremely easy to navigate. The twisty Vltava River, which makes a perfect S through the town, ropes the Old Town into a tight peninsula. Above the Old Town is the Castle Town. Český Krumlov's one main street starts at the isthmus and heads through the peninsula. It winds through town and continues across a bridge before snaking through the Castle Town, the castle complex (a long series of courtyards), and the castle gardens high above. The main square, Náměstí Svornosti—with the TI, ATMs, and taxis—dominates the Old Town and marks the center of the peninsula. All recommended restaurants and hotels are within a few minutes' walk of this square. No sight in town is more than a five-minute stroll away.

Tourist Information

The helpful TI is on the main square (daily 9:00–19:00, July–Aug until 20:00, shorter hours in winter, tel. 380-704-622, www .ckrumlov.cz). Pick up the free city map. The 129-Kč *City Guide* book explains everything in town and includes a fine town and castle map in the back. The TI can check train, bus, and flight schedules. Ask about concerts, city walking tours in English, and canoe trips on the river. A second, less-crowded TI—actually a private business—is just below the castle (daily 9:00–19:00, tel. 380-725-110).

Arrival in Český Krumlov

By Train: The train station is a 20-minute walk from town (turn right out of the station, then walk downhill onto a steep cobbled path leading to an overpass into the town center). Taxis are standing by to zip you to your hotel (about 100 Kč), or call 602-113-113 to summon one.

By Bus: The bus station is just three blocks away from the Old Town (from the bus station lot, drop down to main road and turn left, then turn right at Potraviny grocery store to reach the center). Figure on 60 Kč for a taxi from the station to your hotel.

Český Krumlov's History

With the natural moat provided by the sharp bend in the Vltava, it's no wonder this has been a choice spot for eons. Celtic tribes first settled here a century before Christ. Then came German tribes. The Slavic tribes arrived in the ninth century. The Rožmberks—Bohemia's top noble family—ran the city from 1302 to 1602. You'll see their rose symbol all over town. In many ways, the 16th century was the town's Golden Age, when Český Krumlov hosted artists, scientists, and alchemists from all over Europe. In 1588, the town became home to an important Jesuit college. The Hapsburgs bought the region in 1602, ushering in a more Germanic period. (After that, as many as 75 percent of the town's people were German—until 1945, when most Germans were expelled.)

The rich mix of Gothic, Renaissance, and Baroque buildings is easy to under-appreciate. As you wander, look up...notice the surviving details in the stonework. Step into shops. Snoop into back lanes and tiny squares. Gothic buildings curve with the winding streets. Many precious Gothic and Renaissance frescoes were whitewashed in Baroque times (when the colorful trimmings of earlier periods were way out of style). Today, these precious frescoes are being rediscovered and restored.

With its rich German heritage, it was easy for Hitler to claim that this region—the Sudetenland—was rightfully part of Germany, and in 1938, the infamous Munich Agreement made it his. Americans liberated the town in 1945. Due to Potsdam Treaty–

Helpful Hints

Internet Access: Fine Internet cafés are all over town and in many of the accommodations. The TI on the main square has several fast, cheap, stand-up stations. Perhaps the best cybercafé is behind the TI by the castle (tel. 380-725-117). **Pension Teddy** has Internet access in its bar (1 Kč/min, open long hours daily, Rooseveltova street).

Bookstore: Shakespeare and Sons is a good little English-language bookstore (daily 11:00–20:00, a block below the main square at Soukenická 44, tel. 380-711-203).

Laundry: Pension Lobo runs a self-service launderette under the castle. Since there are only a few machines, you may have to wait (200 Kč to wash and dry, includes soap, daily 9:00–20:00, Latrán 73).

Festivals: Locals drink oceans of beer and celebrate their medieval roots at big events such as the Celebration of the Rose (Slavnosti Růže), where blacksmiths mint ancient coins, jugglers swallow fire, mead flows generously, and pigs are roasted approved ethnic cleansing, three million Germans in Czech lands were sent west to Germany. Emptied of its German citizenry, Český Krumlov turned into a ghost town, partially inhabited by Roma (Gypsies—see sidebar on page 188).

In the post-WWII world planned by Stalin and FDR, the border of the Soviet and American spheres of influence fell about here. While the communist government established order, the period from 1945 to 1989 was a smelly time capsule, as the town was infamously polluted. Its now-pristine river was foamy with pollutants from the paper mill just upstream, while the hills around the town were marred with blocks of prefabricated concrete. The people who moved in never fully identified with the town—in Europe, a place without ancestors is without life-giving roots. But the bleak years of communism paradoxically provided a cocoon to preserve the town. There was no money, so little changed, apart from a build-up of grime.

In the early 1990s, tourists discovered Český Krumlov, and the influx of money saved the buildings from ruin. Color returned to the facades, waiters again dressed in coarse linen shirts, and the main drag was flooded with souvenir shops.

With its new prosperity, today's Český Krumlov looks like a fairy-tale town. In fact, movie producers consider it ideal for films. *The Adventures of Pinocchio* was filmed here in 1995, as was the opening sequence for the 2006 film *The Illusionist*.

on open fires (June 19–21 in 2008, June 18–22 in 2009). The summer also brings a top-notch international jazz and alternative music festival to town, performed in pubs, cafés, and the castle gardens (July 18–Aug 23 in 2008, July 17–Aug 22 in 2009). During the St. Wenceslas celebrations, the square becomes a medieval market and the streets come alive with theater and music (Sept 26–28 in 2008, Sept 25–28 in 2009). Reserve a hotel well in advance if you'll be in town for these events (for more details, see www.ckrumlov.cz).

TOURS

Walking Tours—Since the town itself, rather than its sights, is what it's all about here, taking a guided walk is key for a meaningful visit. The TI sponsors three different guided walks. They are cheap, in English, and time well-spent. All meet in front of the TI on the main square. No reservations are necessary—just drop in and pay the guide. The **Historic Town Walk** offers the best general town introduction and is most likely to run (225 Kč, daily at 10:00, 90 min). The **Rose Tour** covers the Renaissance and town architecture (160 Kč, daily at 14:00, 60 min). The **Brewing History Tour,** which is the most intimate of the many brewery tours in this land that so loves its beer, takes you through the Eggenberg Brewery (150 Kč, daily at 12:30, 90 min). For a self-guided town walk, consider renting an **audioguide** from the TI (60 Kč/hr).

Private Guides—**Oldřiška Baloušková** is a hardworking, excellent, young English-speaking guide who can show you around her hometown (400 Kč/hr, mobile 737-920-901, krumlovguide @hotmail.com). **Jiří (George) Václavíček,** a gentle and caring man who perfectly fits mellow Český Krumlov, is a joy to share this town with (350 Kč/hr, tel. 380-726-813, mobile 603-927-995, jiri.vaclavicek@seznam.cz). **Karolína Kortušová** is an enthusiastic woman with great organizational skills. Her company, Krumlov Tours, can set you up with a good local tour guide, palace and theater admissions, river trips, and more (guides-400 Kč/hr, mobile 723-069-561, www.krumlovtours.com, info @krumlovtours.com).

SELF-GUIDED WALK

▲▲▲Welcome to Český Krumlov

The town's best sight is its cobbled cityscape, surrounded by its babbling river and capped by a dramatic castle. All of Český Krumlov's meager sights are laced together in this charming walk from the top of the Old Town, down its spine, across the river, and up to the castle.

• *Start at the bridge over the isthmus, once the fortified grand entry gate to the town.*

Horní Bridge: From this "Upper Bridge," note the natural fortification provided by the tight bend in the river. The last building in town (just over the river) is the Eggenberg Brewery (with daily tours—see "Tours," above). Behind that, on the horizon, is a pile of white apartment high-rises—built in the last decade of the communist era and considered the worst places in town to call home. Left of the brewery stands the huge monastery (not generally open to the public). Behind that on Kleť, the highest hilltop, stands a TV tower that locals say was built to jam Voice of America broadcasts. Facing the town, on your left, rafters take to the river for the sloppy half-hour float around town to the take-out spot just on your right.

• *A block downhill on Horní (Upper) street is the...*

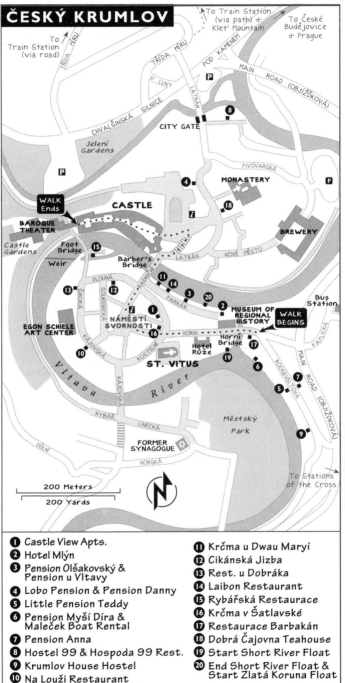

ČESKÝ KRUMLOV

To Train Station (via road)

To Train Station (via path) & Kleť Mountain

To České Budějovice & Prague

TŘÍDA MÍRU

TŘÍDA MÍRU

POD KAMENEM

MAIN ROAD (OBJÍŽĎKOVÁ)

U LUNY

CHVALŠINSKÁ SILNICE

LATRÁN

CITY GATE

Jelení Gardens

PIVOVARSKÁ

MONASTERY

CASTLE

WALK Ends

BAROQUE THEATER

BREWERY

Castle Gardens

Foot Bridge

NOVÉ MĚSTO

Weir

Barber's Bridge

LATRÁN

DLOUHÁ

RADNIČNÍ

Bus Station

ŠIROKÁ

SOUKENICKÁ

PARKÁN

WALK BEGINS

MUSEUM OF REGIONAL HISTORY

NÁMĚSTÍ SVORNOSTI

EGON SCHIELE ART CENTER

KÁJOVSKÁ

HORNÍ

Horní Bridge

MAIN ROAD (OBJÍŽĎKOVÁ)

KAPLICKÁ

ROOSEVELTOVA

KOSTELNÍ

Hotel Růže

ST. VITUS

KÁJOVSKÁ

Vltava River

RYBÁŘ.

LINECKÁ

Městský Park

DLOUHÁ

FORMER SYNAGOGUE

HORSKÁ

To Stations of the Cross

200 Meters

200 Yards

N

Český Krumlov

❶ Castle View Apts.
❷ Hotel Mlýn
❸ Pension Olšakovský & Pension u Vltavy
❹ Lobo Pension & Pension Danny
❺ Little Pension Teddy
❻ Pension Myší Díra & Maleček Boat Rental
❼ Pension Anna
❽ Hostel 99 & Hospoda 99 Rest.
❾ Krumlov House Hostel
❿ Na Louži Restaurant
⓫ Krčma u Dwau Maryí
⓬ Cikánská Jizba
⓭ Rest. u Dobráka
⓮ Laibon Restaurant
⓯ Rybářská Restaurace
⓰ Krčma v Šatlavské
⓱ Restaurace Barbakán
⓲ Dobrá Čajovna Teahouse
⓳ Start Short River Float
⓴ End Short River Float & Start Zlatá Koruna Float

Parting of the Roses

A five-petal rose is not just the distinctive mark of Český Krumlov and the Rožmberk rulers (literally, "Lords from the Rose Mountain"). You'll find it, in five-color combinations, all over South Bohemia.

A medieval legend, depicted inside Český Krumlov's castle, explains the division of the roses in the following way: A respected nobleman named Vítek split the property he had accumulated during his lifetime among five sons. Each son was also assigned his own coat of arms, all of which shared the motif of a five-petal rose. The oldest son, Jindřich, received a golden rose in a blue field, along with the lands of Hradec and Telč. Vilém received a silver rose in a red field, with the lands of Landštejn and Třeboň. Smil was given the lands of Stráž and Bystřice, and a blue rose in a golden field. Vok kept his father's coat of arms, a red rose in a white field, and became the lord in Rožmberk and Český Krumlov. Finally, the out-of-wedlock Sezima had to make do with a black rose and the tiny land of Ústí.

Over generations, the legend—which is corroborated by historical sources—served as a constant warning to the ambitious Rožmberks not to further split up their land. The Lords from the Rose Mountain were the rare Czech noble family that, for 300 years, strictly adhered to the principle of primogeniture (the oldest son gets all, and younger sons are subservient to him). Unlike Vítek, the patriarch, each successive ruler of the Rožmberk estates made sure to consolidate his possessions, handing more to his eldest son than he had received. As a result, the enterprising Rožmberks grew into the most powerful family in Bohemia. In 1501, their position as "first in the country after the king" became law.

Museum of Regional History: This small museum gives you a quick look at regional costumes, tools, and traditions. When you pay, pick up the English translation of the displays (it also includes a lengthy history of Krumlov). Start on the top floor, where you'll see a Bronze Age exhibit, old paintings, a glimpse of noble life, and a look at how the locals rafted lumber from Krumlov all the way to Vienna. Don't miss the fun-to-study ceramic model of Český Krumlov in 1800 (note the extravagant gardens high above the town). The lower floor comes with fine folk costumes and domestic art (50 Kč, daily 10:00–17:00, until 18:00 in July–Aug, Horní 152, tel. 380-711-674).

• *Below the museum, a little garden overlook affords a fine castle view. Immediately across the street, notice the Renaissance facade of...*

Hotel Růže: This former Jesuit college hides a beautiful courtyard. Pop inside to see a couple of bronze busts that stand like a shrine to the founders of Czechoslovakia. The one on the right, dedicated by the Czech freedom fighters, commemorates the first Czechoslovak president, Tomáš Garrigue Masaryk (in office 1918–1934; see sidebar on page 102). The bust on the left recalls Masaryk's successor, Edvard Beneš (in office 1934–1948; see sidebar on page 184).

• *Walk another block down the main drag, until you reach steps on the left leading to the...*

Church of St. Vitus: Český Krumlov's main church was built as a bastion of Catholicism in the 15th century, when the Roman Catholic Church was fighting the Hussites. The 17th-century Baroque high altar shows a totem of religious figures: the Virgin Mary (crowned in heaven), St. Vitus (above Mary), and way up on top, St. Wenceslas, the patron saint of the Czech people—long considered their ambassador in heaven. The canopy in the back, while empty today, once supported a grand statue of a Rožmberk atop a horse. The statue originally stood at the high altar. Too egotistical for Jesuits, it was later moved to the rear of the nave, and then lost for good. As you listen to the river, notice the empty organ case. While the main organ is out for restoration, the cute little circa-1716 Baroque beauty is getting plenty of use (see photos of the restoration work on the far wall, church open daily 10:00–19:00, Sunday Mass at 9:30, tel. 380-711-336).

• *Continuing on Horní street, you'll come to the...*

Main Square (Náměstí Svornosti): Lined by a mix of Renaissance and Baroque homes of burghers (all built upon 12th-century Gothic foundations), the main square has a grand charm. There's continuity here. Lékárna, with the fine, red, Baroque facade on the lower corner of the square, is still a pharmacy, as it has been since 1620. McDonald's tried three times to get a spot here but was turned away. The Town Hall flies the Czech flag and the town flag, which shows the rose symbol of the Rožmberk family, who ruled the town for 300 years.

Imagine the history that this square has seen: In the 1620s, the rising tide of Lutheran Protestantism threatened Catholic

Europe. Krumlov was a seat of Jesuit power and learning, and the intellectuals of the Roman church allegedly burned books on this square. Later, when there was a bad harvest, locals blamed witches—and burned them, too. Every so often, terrible plagues rolled through the countryside. In a nearby village, all but two

Edvard Beneš and the German Question

Czechoslovakia was created in 1918, when the vast, multiethnic Hapsburg Empire broke into smaller nations after losing World War I. The principle that gave countries such as Poland, Czechoslovakia, and Romania independence was called "self-determination": Each nation had the right to its own state within the area where its people were in the majority. But the peoples of Eastern Europe had mixed over the centuries, making it impossible to create functioning states based purely on ethnicity. In the case of Czechoslovakia, the borders were drawn along historical rather than ethnic boundaries. While the country was predominantly Slavic, there were also areas with overwhelmingly German and Hungarian majorities. One of these areas—a fringe around the western part of the country, mostly populated by Germans—was known as the Sudetenland.

At first, the coexistence of Slavs and Germans in the new republic worked fine. German parties were important power brokers and participated in almost every coalition government. Hitler's rise to power, however, led to the growth of German nationalism, even outside Germany. Soon 70 percent of Germans in Czechoslovakia voted for the Nazis. In September 1938, the Munich Agreement ceded the Sudetenland to Germany—and the Czech minority had to leave (for more on the Munich Agreement, see "The Never-Used Fortifications," page 218).

Edvard Beneš was the first Czechoslovak secretary of state (1918–1934) and later became the country's second president (1934–1948). Beneš led the Czechoslovak exile government in London during World War II. Like most Czechs and Slovaks, Beneš believed that after the hard feelings produced by the Munich Agreement, peaceful coexistence of Slavs and Germans in a single state was impossible. His postwar solution: move the Sudeten Germans to Germany, much as the Czechs had been forced out of the Sudetenland before. Through skillful diplomacy, Beneš got

residents were killed by a plague.

But the plague stopped before devastating the people of Český Krumlov, and in 1715—as thanks to God—they built the plague monument that stands on the square today. Much later, in 1938, Hitler stood right here before a backdrop of long Nazi banners to celebrate the annexation of the Sudetenland. And in 1968, Russian tanks spun their angry treads on these same cobblestones to intimidate locals who were demanding freedom. Today, thankfully, this square is part of an unprecedented time of peace and prosperity for the Czech people.

• *The following three museums are grouped around the main square.*

the Allies to sign on to this idea.

Shortly after the end of World War II, three million people of German ancestry were forced to leave their homes. Millions of Germanic people in Poland, Romania, Ukraine, and elsewhere met with a similar fate. Many of these families had been living in these areas for centuries. The methods employed to expel them included murder, rape, and plunder. (Today, we'd call it "ethnic cleansing.")

In 1945, Český Krumlov lost 75 percent of its population, and Czechs moved into vacated German homes. Having easily acquired the property, the new residents didn't take much care of the houses. Within a few years, the once-prosperous Sudetenland was reduced to shabby towns and uncultivated fields—a decaying, godforsaken region. After 1989, displaced Sudeten Germans—the majority of whom now live in Bavaria—demanded that the Czechoslovak government apologize for the violent way in which the expulsion was carried out. Some challenged the legality of the decrees, and for a time the issue threatened otherwise good Czech–German relations.

Although no longer such a hot-button diplomatic issue, the so-called Beneš Decrees remain divisive in Czech politics. While liberals consider the laws unjust, many others—especially the older generations—see them as fair revenge for the behavior of the Sudeten Germans prior to and during the war. In the former Sudetenland, where Czech landowners worry that the Germans will try to claim back their property, Beneš is a hugely popular figure. His bust in Český Krumlov's Hotel Růže is one of the first memorials to Beneš in the country. The bridge behind the Old Town has been named for Beneš since the 1990s. The main square—the center of a thriving German community 70 years ago—is now ironically called "Square of Concord."

Puppet Museum: You'll see fascinating displays in three small rooms of more than 300 movable creations (overwhelmingly of Czech origin, but also some from Burma and Rajasthan). At the model stage, children of any age can try their hand at pulling the strings on their favorite fairy tale (80 Kč, daily 10:00–21:00, Radniční 29, tel. 380-713-422, www.inspirace.krumlov.cz). For more on Czech puppets, see page 138.

Torture Museum: This is just a lame haunted house: dark, with sound effects, cheap modern models, and prints showing off the cruel and unusual punishments of medieval times (80 Kč, daily 9:00–20:00, English descriptions, Náměstí Svornosti 1, tel. 380-766-343).

Egon Schiele Art Center: This classy contemporary art gallery has temporary exhibits, generally featuring 20th-century Czech artists. The top-floor permanent collection celebrates the Viennese artist Egon Schiele (pronounced "Sheila"), who once spent a few weeks here during a secret love affair. A friend of Gustav Klimt and an important figure in the Secessionist movement in Vienna, Schiele lived a short life, from 1890–1918. His cutting-edge lifestyle and harsh art of graphic nudes didn't always fit the conservative, small-town style of Český Krumlov, but townsfolk are happy enough today to charge you to see this relatively paltry collection (180 Kč, daily 10:00–18:00, Široká 70, tel. 380-704-011). The Schiele collection in Vienna's Belvedere Palace is far better.

• *From the main square, walk up Radniči street and cross the...*

Barber's Bridge (Lazebnicky Most): This wooden bridge, decorated with two 19th-century statues, connects the Old Town and the Castle Town. In the center stands a statue of St. John of Nepomuk, who's also depicted by a prominent statue on Prague's Charles Bridge (see page 64). Among other responsibilities, he's the protector against floods. In the great floods of August 2002, the angry river submerged the bridge (but removable banisters minimized the damage). Stains just above the windows of the adjacent building show how high the water rose.

• *After crossing the bridge, hike on up the hill. Your next stop is Krumlov Castle.*

SIGHTS

▲▲Krumlov Castle (Krumlovský Zámek)

No Czech town is complete without a castle—and now that the nobles are gone, their mansions are open to us common folk. The Krumlov Castle complex includes bear pits, the castle itself, a rare Baroque theater, and groomed gardens (www.castle.ckrumlov.cz).

Round Tower (Zâmecká Věž)—The strikingly colorful round tower marks the location of the first castle, built here to guard the medieval river crossing. With its 16th-century Renaissance paint job colorfully restored, it looks exotic, featuring fancy astrological decor, terra-cotta symbols of the zodiac, and a fine arcade. Climb its 162 steps for a great view (30 Kč, daily 9:00–18:00, last entry 17:30).

Bear Pits—At the site of the castle drawbridge, the bear pits hold a family of European brown bears, as they have since the Rožmberks added bears to their coat of arms in the 16th century to demonstrate their (fake) blood relation to the distinguished Italian family of Orsini (the name means "bear-like"). Featured on countless coats of arms, bears have long been totemic animals for Europeans. Pronouncing the animal's real name was taboo in many cultures, and Czechs still refer to bears only indirectly. For example, in most Germanic languages the word "bear" is derived from "brown," while the Slavic *medvěd* literally means "honey-eater."

Castle—The immense castle is a series of courtyards with shops, contemporary art galleries, and tourist services. The interior is

accessible only by tour, which gives you a glimpse of the places where the Rožmberks, Eggenbergs, and Schwarzenbergs dined, studied, worked, prayed, entertained, and slept. (By European standards, the castle's not much, and the tours move slowly.) Imagine being an aristocratic guest here, riding the dukes' assembly line of fine living: You'd promenade through a long series of elegant spaces and dine in the sumptuous dining hall before enjoying a concert in the Hall of Mirrors, which leads directly to the Baroque Theater (described next). After the play, you'd go out into the château garden for a fireworks finale.

Cost, Hours, and Tours: To see the interior, you must take a 60-minute escorted tour: Tour I (Gothic and Renaissance rooms, of the most general interest) or Tour II (19th-century castle life). Tours run June–Aug Tue–Sun 9:00–12:00 & 13:00–18:00, spring and fall until 17:00, closed Mon and Nov–March. Tours in Czech cost 90 Kč, leave regularly, and include an adequate flier in English that contains about half the information imparted by the guide (generally a student who's just memorized the basic script). English tours are preferable, but cost more (160 Kč), run less frequently, and are often booked solid. Make your reservation when you arrive in town—just walk up to the castle office—or you can call 380-704-721, though the number is often busy. You'll be issued a ticket with your tour time printed on it. Be in the correct courtyard at that time, or you'll be locked out.

▲▲**Baroque Theater (Zámecké Divadlo)**—Europe once had several hundred fine Baroque theaters. Using candles for light and fireworks for special effects, most burned down. Today, only two survive in good shape and are open to tourists: one at Stockholm's Drottningholm Palace, and one here, at Krumlov Castle. During the 45-minute tour, you'll sit on benches in the theater and then go under the stage to see the wood-and-rope contraptions that enabled scenes to be scooted in and out within seconds (while fireworks

Roma in Eastern Europe

Numbering 12 million, the Roma people constitute a bigger European nation than the Czechs, Hungarians, or the Dutch. The term "Gypsies," which used to be the common name for this group, is now considered both derogatory and inaccurate. It was derived from "Egypt"—the place that medieval Roma were mistakenly thought to have come from. In the absence of written records, the solution to the puzzle of Roma ancestry had to wait for 19th-century advances in the science of linguistics.

The Roma are descended from several low north-Indian castes (one of which may have given the Roma their name). A thousand years ago the Roma began to migrate through Persia and Armenia into the Ottoman Empire, which later stretched across much of southeastern Europe. Known for their itinerant lifestyle, expertise in horse trading, skilled artisanship, and flexibility regarding private property (as in, "what's yours is mine"), the Roma were both sought out and suspected in medieval Europe. In a similar way, *gadjos* (non-Roma) and their customs came to be distrusted by the Roma.

The Industrial Revolution removed the Roma's few traditional means of earning a livelihood, making their wandering lifestyle difficult to sustain. In the 1940s Hitler sent hundreds of thousands of Roma to the gas chambers. After the war, communist governments in Eastern Europe implemented a policy of forced assimilation: Roma were required to speak the country's major language, settle in *gadjo* towns, and work in new industrial jobs. Today, few Roma can speak their own language well. Rather than producing well-adjusted citizens, the policy eroded time-honored Roma values and shattered the cohesiveness of their

and smoke blinded the audience). Due to the theater's fragility, the number of visitors is strictly regulated. There are only five English tours a day, limited to 25 people per group and generally sold out in advance. While it's a lovely little theater with an impressive 3-D effect that makes the stage look deeper than it really is, I wouldn't bother with the tour unless you can snare a spot on an English one. The theater is used only once a year for an actual performance, with attendance limited to Baroque theater enthusiasts. You can call 380-704-721 to establish English-language tour times and reserve a space; but as with the castle tour, you will likely do best by visiting the ticket office in person (180 Kč, tours daily May–Oct only; English departures at 10:00, 11:00, 13:00, 14:00, and 15:00; buy theater tour tickets at castle ticket office).

Castle Gardens—This 2,300-foot-long garden crowns the castle complex. It was laid out in the 17th century, when the noble traditional communities. It left the new Roma generation prone to sexual, alcohol, and drug abuse, and filled state-run orphanages with deprived Roma toddlers. When the obligation and right to work disappeared with the communist regimes in 1989, rampant unemployment and dependence on welfare joined the list of Roma afflictions.

As people all over Eastern Europe found it difficult to adjust to the new economic realities, they again turned on the Roma as scapegoats, fueling the latent racism that is so characteristic of European history. Many Roma now live in segregated ghettos, where even the most talented Roma children are forced to attend schools for the mentally disabled. Those who make it against the odds and succeed in mainstream society typically do so by turning their backs on their Roma heritage.

In this context, the Roma in Český Krumlov are a surprising success story. The well-integrated, proud Roma community (numbering 1,000 strong, or 5 percent of the town's population) is considered a curious anomaly even by experts. Their success could be due to a number of factors: It could be the legacy of the multicultural Rožmberks, or the fact that almost everyone in Český Krumlov is a relative newcomer. Or maybe it's that local youngsters, regardless of skin color, tend to resolve their differences over a beer in the "Gypsy Pub" (Cikánská Jizba, see page 196), with a trendy Roma band setting the tune.

While provincial politicians throughout the rest of Eastern Europe become national leaders by moving Roma into ghettos, Český Krumlov is living proof that Roma and *gadjos* can coexist happily.

family would light it with 22,000 oil lamps, torches, and candles for special occasions. The lower part is geometrical and symmetrical—French-style. The upper is rougher—English-style (free, May–Sept daily 8:00–19:00, April and Oct daily 8:00–17:00, closed Nov–March).

Near Český Krumlov

Zlatá Koruna Abbey—Directly above the river at the end of a three-hour float by raft or canoe (see "Activities," next section), this abbey was founded in the 13th century by the king to counter the growing influence of the Vítek family, the ancestors of the mighty Rožmberks. As you enter the grounds, notice the central linden tree, with its strange, cape-like leaves; it's said to have been used by the anti-Catholic Hussites when they hanged the monks. The short guided abbey tour takes you through the rare two-storied

Gothic Chapel of the Guardian Angel, the main church, and the cloister. After the order was dissolved in 1785, the abbey functioned shortly as a village school, before being turned into a factory during the Industrial Revolution. Damage from this period is visible on the cloister's crumbling arches. The abbey was restored in the 1990s and opened to the public only a few years ago (85 Kč, tours in Czech run every 45 minutes, Tue–Sun 9:00–15:15, until 16:15 June–Aug, closed Mon and Oct–March, call 380-743-126 to prearrange an English tour, access via river float).

Šumava Mountains—The Šumava Mountains (SHOO-mah-vah) are geologically one of Europe's oldest ranges. Separating Bohemia from Bavaria, this long ridge, known in German as the Böhmerwald (Czech Forest), was the physical embodiment of the Iron Curtain for 40 years: The first 10 miles or so within the Czech border were a forbidden no-man's-land, where hundreds of Czechs were shot as they tried to run across to Germany. In 1989, the barbed wire was taken down, and the entire area—more than 60 miles long—was declared the Šumava-Bayerische Wald National Park. No development is permitted within the park, and visitors can't camp outside of designated areas. Since there's little industry nearby, these mountains preserve some of the most pristine woods, creeks, and meadows in Eastern Europe.

The gateway most easily accessible from Český Krumlov is the trailhead village of **Nová Pec,** a scenic 90-minute train ride away (5 direct trains/day). Nová Pec is located just below the slopes of the tallest mountain on the Czech side of the border, Plechý, a top destination for hiking, biking, and cross-country skiing. Nová Pec's TI, which is 100 yards to the right of the train station, sells hiking and biking maps. You can rent bikes at the train station (150 Kč/day with train ticket, slightly more without one, reserve a few days ahead by calling 972-543-891 or emailing zstvlrdop @mail.cd.cz) or three miles away toward Plechý next to the Plešný parking lot (mobile 723-380-138).

Sleeping near Nová Pec: Both of these recommended B&Bs are about one mile out of Nová Pec.

Pension Hubertus sits on a sloping meadow and operates its three rooms on solar power. Owner Eva will pick you up from the train station if you ask (420–480 Kč/person, mobile 602-253-572, www.ubytovani.net—search for Hubertus).

Pension Za Pecí is brand-new, with five rooms run by two generations, the younger of whom is proficient in English—a rare treat in this German-speaking part of the country (400 Kč/person, optional dinner-100 Kč, tel. 388-336-103, mobile 775-977-469, www.zapeci.com, mifudy@seznam.cz).

ACTIVITIES

Český Krumlov lies in the middle of a valley popular for canoeing, rafting, hiking, and horseback riding. Boat-rental places are convenient to the Old Town, and several hiking paths start right in town.

▲▲▲Canoeing and Rafting the Vltava

Splash a little river fun into your visit by renting a rubber raft or hard plastic canoe for a quick 30-minute spin around Český Krumlov. Or go for a three-hour float and paddle through the Bohemian forests and villages of the nearby countryside. You'll end up at Zlatá Koruna Abbey (described above), where the rafting company will shuttle you back to town—or provide you with a bicycle to pedal back on your own along  a bike path. This is a great hot-weather activity. Though the river is far from treacherous, be prepared to get wet.

On any trip, you'll encounter plenty of inviting pubs and cafés for breaks along the way. There's a little whitewater, but the river is so shallow that if you tip, you simply stand up and climb back in. (When that happens, pull the canoe up onto the bank to empty it, since you'll never manage to pour the water out while still in the river.)

Choose from a kayak, a canoe (fastest, less work, more likely to tip), or an inflatable raft (harder rowing, slower, but very stable). Prices are per boat (2–6 people) and include a map, a waterproof container, and transportation to or from the start and end points. Here are your options:

Quickie Circle-the-Town Float: The easiest half-hour experience is to float around the city's peninsula, starting and ending at opposite sides of the tiny isthmus. Heck, you can do it twice (350 Kč for 1 or 2 people in a canoe or raft).

Three-Hour Float to Zlatá Koruna Abbey: This is your best basic trip, with pastoral scenery, a riverside pub on the left after two hours, and a beautiful abbey as your destination (about 9 miles, 700 Kč for 1 or 2 people). From there you can bike back or catch a shuttle bus home—simply arrange a return plan with the rental company.

Longer and Faster Trips: If you start upriver from Krumlov (direction: Rožmberk), you'll go faster with more whitewater, but the river parallels a road so it's a little less idyllic. Longer trips in either direction involve lots of paddling, even though you're going downstream. Rafting companies can review the many day-trip options with you.

Rental Companies: Several companies offer this lively activity. Perhaps the handiest are **Půjčovna Lodí Maleček Boat Rental** (open long hours daily April–Oct, closed Nov–March, at recommended Pension Myší Díra, Rooseveltova 28, tel. 380-712-508, www.malecek.cz, lode@malecek.cz) and **Cestovní Agentura Vltava** (April–Oct daily 9:00–18:00, closed Nov–March, in Pension Vltava at Kájovská 62, tel. 380-711-988, www.ckvltava.cz). Vltava also rents mountain bikes (320 Kč per day) and can bring a bike to the abbey for you to ride back.

Hiking

For an easy 20-minute hike to Křížový Vrch (Hill of the Cross), walk to the end of Rooseveltova street, cross at the traffic light, then head straight for the first (empty) chapel-like Station of the Cross. Turning right, it's easy to navigate along successive Stations of the Cross until you reach the white church on the hill (closed), set in the middle of wild meadows. Looking down into the valley at the medieval city nestled within the S-shaped river, framed by the rising hills, it's hard to imagine any town with a more powerful *genius loci* (spirit of the place). The view is best at sunset.

For longer hikes, start at the trailhead by the bear pits below the castle. Red-and-white trail markers will take you on an easy six-mile hike around the neighboring slopes and villages. The green and yellow stripes mark a five-mile hiking trail up the Kleť mountain—with an altitude gain of 1,800 feet. At the top, you'll find the Kleť Observatory, the oldest observatory in the country (now a leading center for discovering new planets). On clear days, you can see the Alps (observatory tours-30 Kč, hourly July–Aug Tue–Sun 10:30–15:30, closed Mon, www.hvezdarna.klet.cz).

Horseback Riding

Head about a mile and a half out of town, beyond Křížový Vrch, for horseback rides and lessons at **Slupenec Horseback Riding Club** (1 hour outdoors or in the ring-250 Kč, all-day ride-2,000 Kč, helmets provided, Tue–Sun 10:00–18:00, closed Mon, Slupenec 1, worth a taxi trip, tel. 380-711-052, www.jk-slupenec.cz, René Srncová).

SLEEPING

Krumlov is filled with small, good, family-run pensions offering doubles with baths from 1,000–1,500 Kč and hostel beds for 300 Kč. Summer weekends and festivals (see page 178) are busiest

Sleep Code

(20 Kč = about $1, country code: 420)
S=Single, **D**=Double/Twin, **T**=Triple, **Q**=Quad, **b**=bathroom, **s** = shower only. Unless otherwise noted, prices include breakfast.

To help you sort easily through these listings, I've divided the rooms into three categories based on the price for a standard double room with bath:

$$$ Higher Priced—Most rooms 1,500 Kč or more.
  $$ Moderately Priced—Most rooms between 1,000–1,500 Kč.
   $ Lower Priced—Most rooms 1,000 Kč or less.

and most expensive; reserve ahead when possible. Hotels (not a Krumlov forte) speak some English and accept credit cards; pensions rarely do either. While you can find a room upon arrival here, it's better to book at least a few days ahead if you want to stay in the heart of town. Cars are not very safe overnight—locals advise paying for a garage.

In the Old Town

$$$ Castle View Apartments, run by local guide Jiří Václavíček, rents seven apartments. These are the plushest and best-equipped rooms I found in town—the bathroom floors are heated, all come with kitchenettes, and everything's done just right. Their website describes each of the stylish apartments (1,800–4,000 Kč depending on size, view, and season; the big 4,000-Kč apartment sleeps up to six, complex pricing scheme, reserve direct with this book to claim a 10 percent discount off their online prices, fourth night free, non-smoking, voucher for breakfast at next-door Grand Hotel, Šatlavská 140, tel. 380-726-813, www.castleview.cz, info @castleview.cz).

On Parkán Street, Below the Square

Secluded Parkán street, which runs along the river below the square, has a row of pensions with three to five rooms each. These places have a family feel and views of the looming castle above.

$$$ Hotel Mlýn, at the end of Parkán, is a newly opened and tastefully furnished hotel with more than 30 rooms and all the amenities (Sb-2,200 Kč, Db-2,800 Kč, elevator, parking extra, Parkán 120, tel. 380-731-133, fax 380-747-054, www.hotelmlyn.eu, info@hotelmlyn.eu).

Český Krumlov

$$ Pension Olšakovský, which has a delightful breakfast area on a terrace next to the river, treats visitors as family guests (Db-1,050–1,250 Kč, includes parking, Parkán 114, tel. & fax 380-714-333, mobile 604-430-181, www.ckrumlov.cz/penzionekolsakovsky, J.Olsakovsky@post.cz). **Pension u Vltavy,** next door, is similar (Db-1,000–1,300 Kč, tel. & fax 380-716-396, mobile 605-175-758, www.ckrumlov.cz/uvltavy).

On Latrán Street, at the Base of the Castle

A quiet, cobbled pedestrian street (Latrán) runs below the castle just over the bridge from the Old Town. It's a 10-minute walk downhill from the train station. Lined with characteristic shops, the street has a couple of fine little family-run, eight-room pensions.

$$ Lobo Pension fills a modern, efficient, concrete building with eight fresh, spacious rooms. The pension operates a shuttle bus to Linz for 450 Kč per person (Db-1,100 Kč, Tb-1,500 Kč, includes parking, Latrán 73, tel. & fax 380-713-153, www.pensionlobo.cz, pensionlobo@cmail.cz).

$ Pension Danny is a little funkier, with homier rooms and a tangled floor plan above a restaurant (Db-990 Kč, apartment Db-1,190 Kč, breakfast in room, Latrán 72, tel. 380-712-710, www.pensiondanny.cz, pensiondanny@tiscali.cz).

On Rooseveltova Street, Between the Bus Station and the Old Town

Rooseveltova street, midway between the bus station and the Old Town (a four-minute walk from either), is lined with several fine little places, each with easy free parking. The key here is tranquility—the noisy bars of the town center are out of earshot.

$$ Little Pension Teddy has seven decent riverview rooms that share a common balcony (Db-1,200 Kč with this book in 2008, cash only, a bit smoky, Internet access in the bar—1 Kč/min, Rooseveltova 38, tel. 380-711-595, www.teddy.cz, info@teddy.cz).

$$ Pension Myší Díra (Mouse Hole) hides eight sleek, spacious, bright, and woody Bohemian contemporary rooms overlooking the Vltava River just outside the Old Town (Db-1,000–1,690 Kč, bigger deluxe riverview Db-1,200–1,990 Kč, prices depend on day and season, breakfast in your room, Rooseveltova 28, tel. 380-712-853, fax 380-711-900, www.malecek.cz). The no-nonsense reception, which closes at 20:00, runs the recommended boat rental company (Půčovna Lodí Malaček, at the same address), along with three similar pensions with comparable prices: Pension Wok down by the river, Pension Margarita farther along Rooseveltova, and Pension u Hada.

$$ Pension Anna is well-run, with two doubles, five apartments, and a restful little garden. Its apartments are spacious suites, with a living room and stairs leading to the double-bedded loft (Db-1,250 Kč, Db apartment-1,550 Kč, extra bed-350 Kč, Rooseveltova 41, tel. & fax 380-711-692, pension.anna@quick.cz). If you book a standard Db and they bump you up to an apartment, don't pay more than the Db rate.

Hostels

There are several hostels in town. Hostel 99 (closest to the train station) is clearly the high-energy, youthful party hostel. Krumlov House (closer to the bus station) is more mellow. Both are well-managed and each is a five-minute walk from the main square.

$ Hostel 99's picnic-table terrace looks out on the Old Town. While the gentle sound of the river gurgles outside your window late at night, you're more likely to hear a youthful international crowd having a great time. The hostel caters to its fun-loving young guests, offering free inner tubes for river floats, rental bikes, and a free keg of beer each Wednesday. The adjacent and recommended Hospoda 99 restaurant serves good, cheap soups, salads, and meals (65 beds in 4- to 10-bed coed rooms-300 Kč, D-700 Kč, T-990 Kč, Internet access-1 Kč/minute, laundry-200 Kč/load, use the lockers, no curfew or lockout, 10-min downhill walk from train station or two bus stops to Spicak, Vezni 99, tel. & fax 380-712-812, www.hostel99.com, hostel99@hotmail.com).

$ Krumlov House Hostel is take-your-shoes-off-at-the-door, shiny, hardwood-with-throw-rugs mellow. Efficiently run by a Canadian, it has a hip and trusting vibe and feels welcoming to travelers of any age (24 beds, 6 beds in two dorms-300 Kč per bed, Db-800 Kč, 2-person apartment-900 Kč, family room, no breakfast but there is a guests' kitchen, DVD library, laundry facilities, Rooseveltova 68, tel. 380-711-935, www.krumlovhostel.com).

EATING

Krumlov, with a huge variety of creative little restaurants, is a fun place to eat. In peak times, the good places fill fast, so make reservations or eat early.

Na Louži seems to be everyone's favorite little Czech bistro, with 40 seats in one 1930s-style room decorated with funky old advertisements. They serve inexpensive, tasty Czech cuisine and hometown Eggenberg beer on tap. If you've always wanted to play the piano for an appreciative Czech crowd in a colorful little tavern...do it here (daily 10:00–23:00, Kájovská 66, tel. 380-711-280).

Krčma u Dwau Maryí (Tavern of the Two Marys) is a characteristic old place with idyllic riverside picnic tables, serving ye olde Czech cuisine and drinks. The fascinating menu explains the history of the house and makes a good case that the food of

Český Krumlov

the poor medieval Bohemians was tasty and varied. Buck up for buckwheat, millet, greasy meat, or the poor-man's porridge (daily 11:00–23:00, Parkán 104, tel. 380-717-228).

Cikánská Jizba (Gypsy Pub) is a Roma tavern filling one den-like, barrel-vaulted room. The Roma staff serves Slovak-style food (Slovakia is where most of the Czech Republic's Roma population came from). Krumlov has a long Roma history, and even today 1,000 Roma people live in the town (see sidebar, page 188). While this rustic little restaurant—which packs its 10 tables under a mystic-feeling Gothic vault—won't win any cuisine awards, you'll never know what festive and musical activities will erupt, particularly on Friday nights when the owner's son's band Cindži Renta (Wet Rag) performs here (Mon–Sat 15:00–24:00, closed Sun, 2 blocks toward castle from main square at Dlouhá 31, tel. 380-717-585).

Restaurace u Dobráka (Good Man) is like eating in a medieval garage, with a giant poster of Karl Marx overseeing the action. Lojza, who's been tossing steaks on his open fire for years, makes sure you'll eat well. Locals know it as the best place for grilled steak and fish—expect to pay 350 Kč for a full meal. He charges too much for his beer in order to keep the noisy beer-drinkers away (open daily 17:30–24:00 from Easter until Lojza "has a shoebox full of money," Široká 74, tel. 380-717-776).

Laibon is the modern vegetarian answer to the carnivorous Middle Ages. Settle down inside or head out onto the idyllic river terrace, and lighten up your pork-loaded diet with soy goulash or Mútábúr soup (daily 11:00–23:00, Parkán 105).

Rybářská Restaurace (Fisherman's Restaurant) doesn't look particularly inviting from outside, but don't get discouraged. This is *the* place in town to taste freshwater fish you've never heard of (and never will again). Try eel, perch, shad, carp, trout, and more. Choose between indoor tables under fishnets or riverside picnic benches outside (daily 11:00–22:00, on the island by the mill-wheel).

Krčma v Šatlavské is an old prison gone cozy, with an open fire, big wooden tables under a rustic old medieval vault, and tables outdoors on the pedestrian lane. It's great for a late drink or game cooked on an open spit. *Medovina* is the hot honey wine (daily 12:00–24:00, on Šatlavská, follow lane leading to the side from TI on main square, mobile 608-973-797).

Restaurace Barbakán is built into the town fortifications, with a terrace hanging high over the river. It's a good spot for old-fashioned Czech cooking and beer, at the top of town and near the recommended Rooseveltova street accommodations (open long hours daily, reasonable prices, Horní 26, tel. 380-712-679).

Hospoda 99 Restaurace serves good and cheap soups, salads, and meals. It's the choice of hostelers and locals alike for its hamburgers, vegetarian food, Czech dishes, and cheap booze (meals served 10:00–22:00, bar open until 24:00, at Hostel 99, Vezni 99, tel. 380-712-812). This place is booming until late, when everything else is hibernating.

Dobrá Čajovna is a typical example of the quiet, exotic-feeling teahouses that flooded Czech towns in the 1990s as alternatives to smoky, raucous pubs. While directly across from the castle entrance, it's a world away from the touristic hubbub. As is so often the case, if you want to surround yourself with locals, don't go to a traditional place...go ethnic. With its meditative karma inside and a peaceful terrace facing the monastery out back, it provides a relaxing break (daily 13:00–22:00, Latrán 54, mobile 777-654-744).

TRANSPORTATION CONNECTIONS

Almost all trains to and from Český Krumlov require a transfer in the city of České Budějovice, a transit hub just to the north. České Budějovice's bus and train stations are next to each other.

From Český Krumlov by Train to: České Budějovice (6/day, 1 hr), **Prague** (8/day, change usually required, 4 hrs—bus is faster, cheaper, and easier), **Vienna** (5/day, with at least one change, 5–6 hrs, overnight possible, 10 hrs), **Budapest** (4/day with at least one change, 11–13 hrs).

From Český Krumlov by Bus to: Prague (7/day, 3.5 hrs, 180 Kč; 2 of the daily departures—12:00 and 16:45—can be reserved and paid for at TI, or simply buy tickets from driver), **České Budějovice** (transit hub for other destinations; about 2/hr, 30–50 min, 30 Kč). The Český Krumlov bus station, a five-minute walk out of town, is just a big parking lot with numbered stalls for various buses (bus info tel. 380-711-190, timetables online at http://jizdnirady.atlas.cz).

From České Budějovice to Třeboň, Telč, and Třebíč: An express bus goes from České Budějovice to the Moravian city of **Brno** (5/day Mon–Fri, 2/day Sat–Sun, 4.5 hrs). Along the way, it

Český Krumlov

stops at **Třeboň** (30 min from České Budějovice), **Telč** (2 hrs from České Budějovice), and **Třebíč** (3.25 hrs from České Budějovice).

By Shuttle Bus or Private Car to Linz and Beyond: If you get to Linz, Austria, by bus or car, you'll have your choice of fast trains that run hourly from Linz to Munich, Salzburg, and Vienna. **Pension Lobo** in Český Krumlov runs a shuttle bus service to Linz (450 Kč, 90 min, departs daily at 11:00, 2 people minimum, tel. 380-713-153). A taxi to Linz costs 2,000 Kč (sometimes less). If money is no object, hiring a private car can be efficient, especially to Budapest (the TI has referrals).

TŘEBOŇ, TELČ, AND TŘEBÍČ

Many travelers to South Bohemia visit only Český Krumlov. While it's delightful, three nearby towns are less packaged, more authentic, and—for many—equally worthwhile.

If you draw a line between České Budějovice (the capital of South Bohemia) and Brno (the capital of Moravia), you'll go right through the "Three Ts": Třeboň is an inviting medieval town famous for its peat spas, network of manmade lakes, and fish specialties. Tiny Telč has the Czech Republic's most impressive main square. And busy Třebíč is home to the country's most intact historic Jewish quarter.

Getting Around the "Three Ts"

An express bus line between the big cities of České Budějovice and Brno stops in Třeboň, Telč, and Třebíč (5/day Mon–Fri, 2/day Sat–Sun; České Budějovice to Třeboň—30 min, to Telč—2 hrs, to Třebíč—3.25 hrs, to Brno—4.5 hrs). You can reach České Budějovice easily by direct train from Prague (almost hourly, 2.5 hrs) or from Český Krumlov (6/day, 1 hr). In České Budějovice, the bus and train stations are next to each other. Direct buses also connect these towns to Prague and other destinations; see "Transportation Connections" for each destination.

Planning Your Time

With good planning—letting bus departures dictate the amount of time you spend in each town—you could reasonably leave Český Krumlov early in the morning, visit Třeboň and Telč, and arrive in Třebíč by evening. With more time, consider an evening in Telč for village relaxation and hiking, or move on to Třebíč for a bigger, more city-like feel.

Třeboň

Třeboň (TREH-bohn, pop. 18,000), a well-preserved medieval town centered around an inviting Renaissance square, is a charming place to explore a unique biosphere of artificial lakes that date back to the 14th century.

Over the centuries, people have transformed what was a flooding marshland into a clever and delightful combination of  lakes, oak-lined dikes, wild meadows, Baroque villages, peat bogs, and pine woods. Rather than unprofitable wet fields, the nobles wanted ponds that swarmed with fish—and today Třeboň remains the fish-raising capital of the Czech Republic. Landscape architects in the 16th century managed to strike an amazing balance between civilization and nature, which today is a protected ecosystem (about 15 percent covered by water) with the biggest diversity of bird species in Eastern Europe. Nature enthusiasts come here to bird-watch, bike along dikes held together by the roots of centuries-old oaks, and devour the best fish specialties in the country.

While Třeboň enjoys plenty of tourism, its fish industry makes its relative affluence feel a little less touristy than other popular towns. Its peat spas have attracted patients from all over the world for decades—but since the facilities are small, Třeboň is never as overrun as some other, more famous spa towns.

Planning Your Time

With a full day in Třeboň, spend the morning enjoying the square, climbing up the Town Hall Tower, touring the Dean Church, and visiting the "Man and the Landscape" exhibition in the castle. (The castle itself and the brewery are less interesting.) After trying fish soup and trout for lunch, rent a bike and follow the educational trail along the ancient dikes. If it's hot, bring a bathing suit.

Soaking yourself in the peat of the spas is unforgettable; unfortunately, since the spa treatments are overbooked, it's difficult to get a spot. If you get in, build your day around it (see page 204).

If you're here in October and November, lend a hand in the fascinating ritual of clearing the fish ponds, warming yourself with shots of potato rum as you wade through the mud.

ORIENTATION

The old town—separated from newer construction by city walls, Renaissance gates, a water channel, and a castle garden—encircles the main square, Masaryk Square (Masarykovo Náměstí). Sights, hotels, restaurants, and ATMs are all within a couple blocks of Masaryk Square. From the train station, enter the square through the east gate. Standing in the middle of the square and facing west (with the station and gate at your back), the street to the left leads to the brewery and to Svět lake. The castle—which houses the "Man and the Landscape" exhibit—is at the far (west) end of the square.

Tourist Information

The TI, next to the Town Hall on Masaryk Square, hands out an exhaustive, glittering brochure called *The Region of Třeboň*, which includes a town map. They can reserve an English-speaking local guide with several days' advance notice (Mon–Fri 9:00–12:00 & 13:00–18:00, Sat–Sun 9:00–12:00 & 13:00–19:00, tel. 384-721-169, www.trebon-mesto.cz).

Arrival in Třeboň

The train station and the local bus stop are within easy walking distance from Masaryk Square.

By Train: Get off at the Třeboň–Lázně station, *not* the Třeboň–Město station. From Třeboň–Lázně, walk along the road directly in front of the station and you'll reach Masaryk Square in five minutes.

By Bus: The bus from Prague leaves you at the main bus station, a 20-minute walk (or 100-Kč taxi ride, tel. 384-722-200) west of the old town. Most buses arriving from České Budějovice continue from the main station to the Sokolská stop, which is a short walk through the castle park to Masaryk Square.

Helpful Hints

Internet Access: The user-friendly **Town Library** (Mon–Fri 8:00–17:00, closed Sat–Sun) and **Café Bar–Computer Center Roháč** (daily 18:00–2:00 in the morning) are in the same building by the castle park, at Na Sadech 349. **Lázně Berta** is just outside the east gate (daily 6:00–22:00).

Bike Rental: Hotel Zlatá Hvězda (on Masaryk Square, tel. 384-757-111) and the newsstand directly across the square at #85 (tel. 384-722-867) rent decent mountain and trekking bikes (40 Kč/hr, 100 Kč/half-day, 200 Kč/day, hotel requires driver's license as a deposit).

SIGHTS

Masaryk Square (Masarykovo Náměstí)—Třeboň's fine main square is typical of squares in the region, lined with colorful facades artfully blending both Renaissance and Baroque building styles. It was built by the town's 17th-century burghers, whose wealth came from the booming fish industry. The rectangular market plaza—with a humble plague column and fountain in the middle—feels just right. Grab a seat at one of the outdoor cafés, and watch local life circulate with the serenity of ducks on a lake.

While the tranquility comes naturally today, until 1989 it was a government requirement. At the square's lower end, above the bank door, a **propaganda relief** in the Social Realist style extols the virtue of working hard and stowing your money here for the common good. Higher up, a happy fisherman cradles a big fish, the reason for his wealth—and, since the 16th century, the wealth of Třeboň.

The **Town Hall Tower,** whose moderate height of 100 feet just fits with the size of the square, is worth the climb. Surveying the view from its top, you feel as if you can reach out and touch the circular old town. Beyond that, the lakes glimmer against the green backdrop of stately oaks (15 Kč, June–Sept daily 10:00–18:00, unpredictable hours Oct–May).

Across from the Town Hall, the impossible-to-miss, rampart-like white gable marks the famous 16th-century **Inn at the White Horse** (U Bílého Koníčka—look for the small horse on the facade).

At the other end of the square, notice the only modern building here, a **Spar supermarket.** Some 30 years ago, when the square was veiled in the shabby gray of communism, the regime decided to give it a facelift with a modern building that fit the ancient space like a UFO. After 1989, locals carefully added a facade and a new roof to the concrete box, effectively blending the former eyesore into the Old World townscape.

Castle (Zámek)—The castle is covered with rectangular sgraffiti, a characteristic decoration of the late 1500s (made by etching a design in plaster, revealing a different color underneath). As with other South Bohemian towns, all this sgraffiti is a reminder that the 16th century was Třeboň's heyday. Třeboň belonged to the Český Krumlov–based Rožmberk family. In 1600, Petr Vok—the last of the Rožmberks—moved here permanently after selling Český Krumlov to the emperor. He brought along his archive, still considered the most valuable collection of medieval documents in this part of Europe. The castle can only be visited with an escorted tour. Your best basic castle visit is Route A, which includes Petr Vok's Renaissance rooms. Route B covers the 19th-century apartments, kitchens, and stables of the later, equally distinguished Schwarzenbergs (60 Kč, buy at "cash box" ticket desk, tours go hourly or more, in Czech with English flier, April–Oct Tue–Sun 9:00–11:45 & 12:45–17:00, closed Mon and Nov–March, tel. 384-721-193).

▲"Man and the Landscape" Exhibit—Located inside the castle, this is the best sight in town. Surprisingly modern, thoughtfully described in English, and further illuminated by excellent little video-on-command terminals, the exhibit covers the things that make this town distinct: lake-making, the fish industry, the peat spa treatment, and the natural environment. A highlight is the theater (just after the stuffed animals) where you can watch a 13-minute video that takes you fishing early in the morning, and a 20-minute video racing you through a year with nature in Třeboň. An hour here is time well-invested (50 Kč, Tue–Sun 9:00–17:00, closed Mon, enter from garden just outside castle and city wall, tel. 384-724-912).

City Wall and Park—The greenbelt that circles the town just outside its 16th-century wall makes for a delightful 15-minute walk. Along the way, you'll pass the town's famous but underwhelming spas.

Dean Church and Augustine Monastery (Děkanský Kostel a Augustiánský Klášter)—This Gothic church, with its unusual double nave (and obtrusive columns down the middle) is worth a look if open during your visit. A highlight is its delicately curved statue of the Madonna and Child (c. 1390, painted limestone). Its Ivory Soap sweetness and a slinky S-shaped body are typical of late "beautiful style" Gothic. The artist, while anonymous, is known as the "Master of the Třeboň Madonna." The church once showcased more marvelous Gothic sculptures and altars, but these were deemed too valu-

able, so they were zipped off to the Museum of Medieval Art in Prague's St. Agnes Convent (see page 57). Frescoes in the adjoining cloister, badly neglected until after 1989, show scenes from the life of St. Augustine. While the monastery library is long gone, Augustinians were some of the most ardent medieval copyists in the time before Gutenberg's moveable type revolutionized printing. Through the efforts of monks in this monastery, Třeboň became a center of medieval learning for Czechs and Austrians alike (30 Kč, July–Aug daily 9:00–11:30 & 13:30–17:00, or pop in just before the nearly nightly 18:30 Mass, if closed ring the parish home next door, Husova 142, rectory tel. 384-722-390).

ACTIVITIES

Boating and Swimming—A motorboat sets out from the small wharf behind the brewery once an hour for a 30-minute (60 Kč) or 45-minute (90 Kč) cruise over the second-largest of Třeboň's lakes, Svět (daily 10:00–19:00). The nearest sandy beach is a 10-minute walk, to the right from the wharf along the dike.

Biking—The area is flat, so biking is a fun and convenient way to get around. A bike trip along the dirt trails on the ancient dikes is a fine way to experience the land and water. Either buy a cycling map from the TI, or follow the clearly marked 24-mile educational trail that snakes along channels and through traditional villages.

Hiking—The best hiking is in the area of Nová Řeka (New River), directly east of town. Or catch a bus (or drive) to Chlum u Třeboně, and hike in the blueberry-filled pine woods along the Austrian border.

Peat Spa (Bertiny Lázně)—Třeboň is an important peat spa. Patients from all over the world come here for weeklong stays to get buried in the black, smelly sludge that's thought to cure aching joints and spines. Well...I guess it doesn't hurt to try. The complete peat bath *(slatinná koupel celková)* is combined with a full-body massage (don't try to sneak away before the nurse is finished with

The Lakes

The medieval lake-builders of Třeboň created an ingenious landscape of regulated channels, marshes turned into lakes, and fields changed into marshes. Birds and animals new to the region began to dwell here. Peat provided a rich soil for pines and blueberry bushes.

The good lake-builders knew that small is beautiful… but, of course, not all of them were good. The most famous of Třeboň lake-builders was Jakub Krčín, the architect of the largest lakes, Svět and Rožmberk. Krčín was a man driven more by his ego than by practical considerations. Much of the water in his huge, deep lakes is dead, lacking enough oxygen to support large fish colonies. His predecessor, Štěpánek Netolický—while less celebrated—was more of a fishing expert. He built small, and his lakes were successful. His Golden Channel, which connects dozens of lakes, is the region's biggest marvel.

The Třeboň lakes were built for flood control as well as fishing. The marshy area around the town used to be regularly flooded by the Lužnice River. The artificial lakes were designed to absorb the floods. In 2002, the largest floods in Czech history tested the work of those medieval lake-builders. While the 20th-century dams built on the Vltava River to protect Prague failed, Třeboň's 16th-century dams held, vindicating Krčín and keeping Třeboň's feet dry.

you). It's worth it to have the opportunity to fully judge the power of peat and experience the surreal *One Flew Over the Cuckoo's Nest* atmosphere of Czech medical institutions.

While spa treatments can be booked months ahead, you can often snare a spot if there's a cancellation; if you ask your hotelier to make a reservation for you when you book your room; or if you contact the spa at least two weeks in advance (email sestra@berta .cz or call 384-754-413). To get to the spa, go through the east gate; the spa is just off to your left.

SLEEPING

Although there are many pensions in Třeboň, most only take spa guests who stay for a couple of weeks. These two hotels welcome guests even for one- or two-night stays on short notice.

$$$ Hotel Galerie has 12 renovated rooms and an artistically decorated breakfast room. Notice the slightly buried storage room by the reception hall that now serves as a semi-open wine cellar—since Třeboň stands on floating sands, no house in

Sleep Code

(20 Kč = about $1, country code: 420)
S = Single, **D** = Double/Twin, **T** = Triple, **Q** = Quad, **b** = bathroom,
s = shower only. Unless otherwise noted, credit cards are
accepted and prices include breakfast.

To help you sort easily through these listings, I've divided
the rooms into three categories based on the price for a standard double room with bath:

$$$ **Higher Priced**—Most rooms 1,500 Kč or more.
$$ **Moderately Priced**—Most rooms between 1,000–
1,500 Kč.
$ **Lower Priced**—Most rooms 1,000 Kč or less.

town has a basement. The Galerie manager can usually set up a
spa appointment even at the last minute—ask when you reserve
(Sb-1,000 Kč, Db-1,500 Kč, Tb-1,800 Kč, these prices valid with
cash and this book in 2008, request this price when you reserve,
Rožmberská 35, tel. 384-385-293, fax 384-385-294, mobile 724-
093-876, www.hotel-trebon.cz, galerie@hoteltrebon.cz). The hotel
also runs a decent restaurant on the ground floor with tasty, cheap
lunch specials.

$ **Hotel Bílý Koníček,** on Masaryk Square, has managed to
revamp all 23 of its rooms. Although still only a pale shadow of
what was once a Renaissance inn—founded in 1544 and famous
throughout the country—its rooms are a good value (standard
Db-1,000 Kč, tel. 384-721-213, Masarykovo Náměstí 27, www
.hotelbilykonicek.cz, hotel@hotelbilykonicek.cz). Breakfast is not
included—that's probably a good thing, since the sausage-oriented
ground-floor restaurant is best avoided. Instead, walk around the
corner by the Town Hall to a little Happy Café bakery that serves
a large selection of fine pastries and good coffee from 7:00.

EATING

Since the 1200s, Třeboň has lived on a steady diet of fish. The variety of fish raised here is amazing...as are the chefs. Austrians and
Czechs alike drive for hours just to dine here. While you can find
trout and carp throughout the country, the perch and pike from
the lakes are unique. The pine woods south of the lakes are filled
with blueberries—when it's the season, the blueberry dumplings
are another must.

Šupina and Šupinka Restaurant (Scale and Little Scale) is
run by the local fishers' union, which makes sure the meals are top-

notch. While the modern interior may not seem very atmospheric to visitors, it doesn't bother locals, who have good reason to consider this one of the best fish restaurants in the country. Dig into the rare and refined appetizers, which include fried carp sperm, cod liver, pickled herring, and local crab. If you have only one fish dinner in the Czech Republic, the native pike perch here would be your best choice (daily 10:30–24:00; from Masaryk Square, walk past the Spar supermarket, then turn right into Novohradská Brána; tel. 384-721-149).

Na Rožmberské Baště is a little eatery with warm wooden walls and nets and fishing rods hanging from the ceiling (you can borrow one and bring in your own catch to be cooked). They serve tasty and cheap meals made from everything that swims in the surrounding lakes (Mon–Sat 10:30–23:30, Sun 10:30–22:30, on Rožmberská, tel. 384-721-893).

Schwarzenberská Pivnice is a large and colorful brewery/pub serving every variety of local Regent beer, including the fresh yeast kind you won't find in regular pubs. This is a drinking place—the only snacks available are Czech munchies, such as pickled sausage *(utopenec)* and pickled brie *(nakládaný hermelín;* Mon–Fri 11:00–22:00, Sat–Sun 12:00–23:00, in Regent Brewery).

TRANSPORTATION CONNECTIONS

While buses between Třeboň and Prague are about as fast as the train (2.5 hrs), bus departures are less frequent, and the bus station is far from the center of Třeboň.

From Třeboň by Train to: Prague (7/day, 2.5 hrs, transfer at Veselí nad Lužnicí). If going from Prague to Třeboň, get off at Třeboň–Lázně, not Třeboň–Město.

By Bus to: Prague (2/day, 2.5 hrs), **Český Krumlov** (10/day to České Budějovice, 30 min, then transfer to Český Krumlov—see page 176), **Telč** (5/day Mon–Fri, 2/day Sat–Sun, 90 min), **Třebíč** (5/day Mon–Fri, 2/day Sat–Sun, 2.75 hrs), **Brno** (5/day Mon–Fri, 2/day Sat–Sun, 4 hrs).

Telč

Telč (pronounced "telch," pop. 6,000) is famous for its castle and its glorious square, considered by many to be the country's best. The old town—just a fat square with a thin layer of buildings—is surrounded by a sophisticated system of protective ponds and defense walls. The general lay of the land has changed little since the 1300s. After 1800, all new construction took place outside the core. Today, Telč remains an unspoiled, sleepy Czech town where neighbors chat in pastry shops, Vietnamese traders in medieval arcade stalls sell dirt-cheap textiles to country folks, and the smell of goat dung from a pasture across the lake permeates the town after nightfall.

There are basically no attractions aside from the square and the castle. Telč is made to order as a lunch stop on the way to or from Slavonice, Třeboň, and Třebíč, or on the longer haul between Prague, Brno, and Vienna. An overnight stay here can be a relaxing village experience.

ORIENTATION

Everything you'll need—including ATMs, exchange offices, shops, hotels, and restaurants—is on the main square (Náměstí Zachariáše z Hradce), easily reachable on foot from the bus station. For a taxi, call 603-255-048 and expect basic English.

Tourist Information

The TI has information on activities in the area, train and bus schedules, and Internet access (Mon–Fri 8:00–18:00, Sat–Sun 10:00–18:00, shorter hours off-season, tel. 567-112-407, www .telc-etc.cz). They can also help you find a room in one of the pensions on the square (see "Sleeping," below).

Helpful Hints

Festivals: Every year during the first two weeks of July, young musicians pour into Telč from all over Europe for the French–Czech Music Academy, which hosts workshops on classical music interpretation. The young virtuosos show off their skills in a number of concerts and recitals.

The Telč Vacations (Prázdniny v Telči) festival, held during the first two weeks of August, makes the squares, gardens, and castle chambers come alive with folk music, open-air theater, and exhibitions.

Internet Access: The TI has one computer available to the public. The shop next to the TI also offers Internet access.

Bike Rental: You can rent bikes at the shop next to the TI (40 Kč/ hour, 250 Kč/day, daily 9:00–18:00, tel. 567-243-562). Locals enjoy the half-day bike trip to the castle ruin of Roštejn and back (10 miles round-trip).

Boat Rental: During the summer, you can rent a boat for a lazy lake cruise. To get to the rental boats, walk through the gate between the castle and the square, then turn right on the path along the lake (40 Kč/hr; July–Aug daily 10:00–18:00; June Fri 13:00–18:00, Sat–Sun 10:00–18:00, closed Mon–Thu; no rentals Sept–May).

SIGHTS

▲**Main Square (Náměstí Zachariáše z Hradce)**—Telč's spacious square, lined by fairy-talė gables resting on the charac-

teristic vaulted arcades that still cover local shops and bakeries, is the most impressive in the Czech Republic. The uniqueness of the square lies in its enormous size, unexpected proportions in such a small town, and the purity of its style—of the 40 houses lining the square, there isn't a single one younger than 300 years. A fire devastated the town in 1553, and it was rebuilt of stone. A plague that ravaged the region in 1780 skipped Telč, so the plague column was built on the square to thank God.

Telč Castle—In its early years, this castle belonged to the clan of the Five Roses (symbolized by a golden rose on a blue field; see the "Parting of the Roses" sidebar on page 182). In the 1500s, the nobleman Zachariáš z Hradce (for whom the grand main square is named) imported a team of Italian artists, who turned the earlier Gothic palace into a lavish Renaissance residence. (Their work also influenced most of the burgher houses in the square.) The castle can be toured only with an escort. You have two options: Tour A, the best basic castle tour, takes you through some stately Renaissance chambers. Tour B goes through the 19th-century apartments of the Lichtenstein family, who lived here until 1945. You'll most likely have a Czech-speaking guide and be given an English description to read as you go (160 Kč per tour; May–Aug Tue–Sun 9:00–12:00 & 13:00–17:00, closed Mon; April and Sept–Oct Tue–Sun 9:00–12:00 & 13:00–16:00, closed Mon; closed Nov–March; last tour 1 hour before closing). The castle is located at the end of the main square—you can't miss it.

Regional Museum of Telč—While humble, this little five-room exhibit gives an interesting insight into the town (check out the 1895 town model and the WWI and WWII photos). Everything is well-explained in the English pamphlet that you'll be loaned as you enter (30 Kč, daily 9:00–16:30, in the castle complex).

Telč

Gustav Mahler and Jihlava

Gustav Mahler (1860–1911) was the most important composer in Vienna at the turn of the 20th century. Mahler composed some of the last of the classical symphonies and was the first to venture into the musical never-never-land of atonality (while his contemporary Arnold Schönberg, also Jewish, took up residence there). The age of harmony ended—by 1910 there was nothing to hold the world together, and art preceded the shots of World War I.

Mahler, born in the nearby village of Kaliště, spent the first 15 years of his life in Jihlava, at a house at Znojemská 4 that now functions as a vibrant cultural center and the composer's museum (tel. 567-306-239, www.dum-gustava-mahlera.cz). This is a worthwhile stop for music buffs en route from Prague to Telč.

Gallery of Jan Zrzavý—Tucked away in the garden to the right of the castle entrance, this small gallery is worth a peek to learn about pointillism. Zrzavý, one of the most prolific Czech painters, had a style similar to earlier Impressionists, but used dots (or points) instead of lines to construct images. Paintings in the five-room gallery evolve from his teen years on through the troubled first half of the 20th century, but without the angst you might expect. Don't try to make much sense of it. Just enjoy looking at the artist's slices of local life, from steelworks to villages, represented in his unusual style (30 Kč; April–Oct Tue–Sun 9:00–12:00 & 13:00–17:00, closed Mon; Nov–March Tue–Sun 9:00–12:00 & 13:00–16:00, closed Mon).

SLEEPING

Many families living on or near the main square have turned parts of their homes into pleasant pensions that meld perfectly with the mellow feel of this town. At a pension, you get nicer rooms and more personal service for about half the price of the hotels, which bank on being the only places in town able to accommodate big groups.

$$$ Hotel Telč, under the church tower across the square from the castle, has 10 simply furnished rooms (Sb-1,265 Kč, Db-1,580–1,870 Kč, extra bed-200 Kč, tel. 567-243-109, www.hoteltelc .cz, hotel.telc@tiscali.cz).

$$$ Hotel Celerin, also on the main square, is slightly bigger than Hotel Telč. Some of its comfy rooms have traditional burgher furniture (Sb-900–1,100 Kč, Db-1,400–1,600 Kč; rooms #4, #5, #9, and #10 face the square and are more expensive; tel. 567-243-477, fax 567-213-581, www.hotelcelerin.cz).

$ Penzion Patricia is run by a former high-school teacher (and her four-legged friends Bibi and Borka) who, after 14 years in the US, returned to Telč with a mission: to turn her family's house into a showcase of Telč's hospitality. The eight rooms vary in size and style, but all come with queen-size beds imported from California. Breakfast is served on a terrace under the Romanesque church tower, and bonfires are lit in the garden on the former town walls where you can munch seasonal fruits (Sb-500 Kč, Db-800 Kč, Internet access, next to Hotel Telč on the main square at #38, tel. 567-213-342, www.penzionpatricia-telc.wz.cz, patricia_telc @volny.cz).

$ Penzion Steidler has the most tastefully furnished rooms in town and a blooming narrow garden that stretches all the way to the lake (Sb-500 Kč, Db-800 Kč, look for house #52 on the main square, tel. 567-243-424, mobile 602-790-975 or 721-316-390, www.telc-accommodation.eu, steidler@volny.cz).

$ Penzion Danuše is a well-managed, quiet place with four solid rooms (Db-1,000 Kč, 30 yards off the main square at the corner of Palackého and Hradební 25, tel. 567-213-945, mobile 603-449-188, danuse.telc@quick.cz).

EATING

All of these eateries are on the main square.

Šenk pod Věží (Under the Tower) is ideal for a fancy meal of Czech cuisine with extra touches. It has two small, atmospheric rooms with 100-year-old photographs and tranquil outside seating in the back on the former town wall (daily 11:00–22:00, tel. 567-243-889).

Osvěžovna u Marušky, also directly beneath the tower, is popular with young locals who congregate here for coffee and cigarettes as much as for the food and beer. The walls are decorated by local artists and vacationing out-of-towners, and jazz and classical concerts take place here twice a month (daily 11:00–24:00, mobile 603-398-128).

Pizzerie, on the corner by the plague column, has the best outside seating on the square and two modern, high-ceilinged rooms in the basement. Locals of all generations converge here for a surprisingly good and cheap Czech interpretation of the Italian theme. Sweet Czech ketchup rules the day, drowning every item on the long menu—be it pizza or pasta—in the same distinct flavor. Sicilian purists would not be amused (daily 11:00–22:00).

TRANSPORTATION CONNECTIONS

From Telč to: Třeboň (5 buses/day Mon–Fri, 2/day Sat–Sun, 90 min), **Třebíč** (5 buses/day Mon–Fri, 2/day Sat–Sun, 45 min), **Brno** (5 buses/day Mon–Fri, 2/day Sat–Sun, 2.5 hrs), **Slavonice** (2 trains in morning, 3 in afternoon, 1 hr), **Prague** (3/day, 4–5 hrs, requires 2 changes—bus is better; 5 buses/day Mon–Fri, 3/day Sat–Sun, 2–3 hrs, more with a transfer in Jihlava—3 hrs total). Note that some buses to Prague may arrive at the Roztyly station (on the red Metro line), not the main bus station, Florenc.

Třebíč

A few miles east of Telč is the big, busy town of Třebíč (TREH-beech, pop. 40,000), with another wonderful main square and, just over its river, the largest intact Jewish ghetto in the country. While Prague's Jewish Quarter is packed with tourists, in Třebíč you'll have an entire Jewish town to yourself. Třebíč's Jewish settlement was relatively small. Its remains, while lonely and neglected, are amazingly authentic.

ORIENTATION

Three hours in Třebíč is sufficient—everything's close by. The main square affords a fun slice-of-local-life look at a humble yet vibrant community, while the near-ghost town across the river was once the Jewish ghetto. The two main streets that run parallel to the river (which separates the ghetto from the Christian town) are connected by a maze of narrow passages, courtyards, and tunnels.

Tourist Information

The TI has two helpful branches: one on the main square and one in the ghetto's Rear Synagogue (both open daily 10:00–12:00 & 13:00–17:00, rental bikes at main square location, tel. 568-823-005, www.kviztrebic.cz).

Arrival in Třebíč

From the train station (with safe 24-hour luggage storage), cross the street behind the large waiting hall, and walk to the main square. To continue on to the ghetto, cross the river, following *Židovské Město* signs, marked with Stars of David. The cemetery is uphill.

Helpful Hints

Festival: Třebíč's annual Šamajim festival of Jewish music and film brings Jews and their culture back into the old ghetto for one week a year in early August (details at TI).

Local Guide: If you want a deeper look into the life of Moravian Jews, as well as today's Třebíč, call the knowledgeable young guide **Alena Gottliebová** (450 Kč/hr, tel. 568-850-249, mobile 777-197-835, info@amigoski.cz).

SIGHTS

▲**Charles Square (Karlovo Náměstí)**—Třebíč's main square is the third-biggest in the Czech Republic. A market square since the 13th century, it's still busy with a farmers' market every morning. Třebíč was historically a mix of Christians and Jews, all living on the easy-to-defend bit of land between the river and the hill. As you'll see, that area is pretty tiny—and eventually the Christian community packed up and moved across the river for more space, establishing this square as the town's nucleus.

The statue of two Macedonian brothers—the saints Cyril and Methodius, who brought Christianity to Moravia and the Slavs in their own language, rather than Greek or Latin—was erected a thousand years after Methodius' death in 885. But forget all that history. Just circle the square surveying today's Moravian scene. There are several fine pubs and cafes from which to people-watch. The small gallery in the four delightful vaulted rooms of the Painted House on the upper corner of the square is worth checking out to feel the artistic pulse of Moravia (next to the TI, displays temporary exhibits).

Opposite the bell tower, at #11, a lane leads across the river into the Jewish quarter, taking you directly to the Rear Synagogue (with a TI and small museum). Notice the fine views of the ghetto from the bridge.

▲**Jewish Ghetto (Židovské Město)**—The population of Třebíč's ghetto peaked in the 19th century at about 1,500. Only 10 Třebíč

Jews survived the Holocaust. In the 1970s, the ghetto was slated for destruction, to be replaced by another ugly communist high-rise housing complex. But because the land proved unable to support a huge building project, the neighborhood survived. Today, it's protected by the government as the largest preserved Jewish quarter in Europe.

Třebíč

Coming here, you enter a place where time has stopped: The houses are essentially as the Jews left them more than 60 years ago. Many of the houses were resettled by Roma (see sidebar, page 188), who have done little to change the look and feel of the place. In Třebíč today, only one woman has a Jewish father. (Because you must have a Jewish mother to be legally Jewish, the Jewish population is officially zero.) The government wants the ghetto to be a living neighborhood, not a museum. Lines of drying clothes and kids kicking around a soccer ball on the cobblestones make today's ghetto come alive. After dark, it's *the* place for edgy nightlife.

The **Rear Synagogue** (Zadní Synagoga) is the visitor center, with a branch of the TI, plus displays of artifacts and a model of the once-thriving local Jewish community (40 Kč, daily 10:00–12:00 & 13:00–17:00). At the TI, confirm the hours of the nearby cemetery (listed below).

The **Front Synagogue** (Přední Synagoga) has functioned since 1954 as a Hussite Christian church. While generally locked, you can peek through its gate to see how the synagogue was retooled for the plain Hus-style worship.

Jewish Cemetery—A 20-minute walk above the ghetto, this evocative memorial park is covered with spreading ivy, bushes of wild strawberries, and a commotion of 9,000 gravestones (the oldest dating to 1631). Notice how the tombstones follow the assimilation of the Jews, from simple markers to fancy 19th-century headstones that look exactly like those of the rich burghers in Christian cemeteries (daily May–Sept 8:00–20:00, March–April and Oct 8:00–18:00, Nov–Feb 9:00–16:00, confirm hours at the Rear Synagogue TI before ascending the hill).

St. Procopius Basilica—This enormous church looms over the town on a hill a five-minute walk above the main square and the ghetto. In a region of Baroque churches, this rich fusion of late Romanesque and early Gothic styles is a striking contrast. Unfortunately, it's viewable only with a tour (40 Kč, 45-min tours start every 30 min, May–Sept Tue–Fri 9:00–12:00 & 13:00–17:00, Sat–Mon 13:00–17:00, shorter hours and less-frequent tours Oct–April, tel. 568-610-022).

SLEEPING

$$ Hotel Winkler, near the bus station, is an attractive little place with 15 comfortable rooms and flowers in the windows (Sb-1,155 Kč, Db-1,375 Kč, V. Nezvala 8, tel. 568-841-506, www.hotel-winkler.cz, recepce@hotel-winkler.cz).

$ Penzion u Synagogy, next to the Rear Synagogue, is as close as you can get to living in a Jewish ghetto, and includes free entry into the visitor center at the synagogue (Sb-300 Kč, Db-500

Třebíč

Kč, extra bed-120 Kč, Subakova 43, check in at Rear Synagogue TI, tel. 568-823-005, www.kviztrebic.cz).

$ Travellers' Hostel, near the Front Synagogue, has 55 dorm beds fitted into the meticulously restored home of a 16th-century baker. The oven still turns out warm bread, and a beer tap was installed even before the new roof, ensuring no guest leaves this party place without the two key elements of life (250 Kč per bunk in 8- to 10-bed dorm, 330 Kč in 4-bed dorm, Sb-600 Kč, Db-800 Kč, includes sheets and breakfast, Žerotínovo 19, tel. & fax 568-422-594, mobile 777-637-417, trebic@travellers.cz).

EATING AND DRINKING

Neptune Restaurant, facing the Front Synagogue, serves good soup, fish dishes, and cheap daily lunch specials. This is the best place in the Jewish quarter, with fine indoor or outdoor seating (daily 11:00–22:00, mobile 776-350-850).

Měsíční Čajovna (Moon Teahouse), on the upper street in the middle of the ghetto, is made for contemplating times-gone-by in the company of young English-speaking locals (Sun and Tue–Fri 15:00–21:00, Sat 16:00–23:00, closed Mon, Skalní 2).

Občerstvení Jordan, in the midst of the action at #23 on the main square, has outside seating perfect for a fast salad, sandwich, or ready-made daily special. Go inside and order by pointing at what you want (Mon–Fri 6:30–18:00, Sat 8:00–12:00, Sun 14:00–18:00).

TRANSPORTATION CONNECTIONS

From Třebíč to: Telč (5 buses/day Mon–Fri, 2/day Sat–Sun, 45 min), **Třeboň** (5 buses/day Mon–Fri, 2/day Sat–Sun, 2.75 hrs), **Brno** (5 buses/day Mon–Fri, 2/day Sat–Sun, 75 min; also 10 trains/day, 75 min), **Prague** (nearly hourly trains, 4–5 hrs, transfer in Brno—bus is better; 7 buses/day, 2.5 hrs). Note that some buses to Prague may arrive at the Roztyly station (on the red Metro line), not the main bus station, Florenc.

Třebíč

SLAVONICE

Slavonice (SLAH-voh-neet-seh)—a charming little town of 2,700 people less than three miles from the Austrian border—is a perfect base for venturing into the most romantic of Czech landscapes. The town features two once-elegant Renaissance squares separated by a Gothic church and Town Hall. In the surrounding countryside, hulking castle ruins top forested hills, deep woods surround lonely meadows, and WWII bunkers covered with sprawling blueberry bushes evoke the harsh realities of being a border town.

Centuries ago, this thinly populated borderland between Bohemia, Moravia, and Austria was filled with thieves and thugs—and was, therefore, nearly impossible to tax. Founded in the 1200s, the town was originally named Zlabings by the German settlers invited to colonize and civilize the region.

During the 14th century, when the main trading route between Prague and Vienna passed through here, Zlabings boomed. Most of the town's finest buildings date from this period. After the Thirty Years' War (1618–1648), the town declined, and thanks to its ill fate, few new buildings broke the medieval harmony.

Following World War II, Zlabings' German residents—90 percent of the population—were forced out by vengeful Czechs (see "Edvard Beneš and the German Question" sidebar on page 184). Czech people moved in and simply occupied the homes of the former residents—sitting on their sofas and even wearing their clothes.

The town became fully Czech (and was officially renamed Slavonice), and a curtain of barbed wire sealed it from the West on three sides. This region—always sparsely populated, and even more so after its predominantly German population was removed—grew wilder and full of forests throughout the Cold War, when it earned the nickname "Czech Canada" (Česká Kanada).

After 1989, the deep woods of the military zone were opened up to hikers and cyclists, the border a mile south of Slavonice was reopened, and Austrians began flocking here for a cheap lunch and shopping sprees—stoking business and bringing a new period of relative prosperity to Slavonice. The children you see playing in the streets today—the grandkids of those Czech settlers from 1945—are enjoying good times once again. But something about this town, at the end of the Czech world just 20 years ago, still feels like Česká Kanada.

ORIENTATION

Everything of interest is on Slavonice's main square, Náměstí Míru. The train and bus stations are each within a few minutes' walking distance of the center (head for the church tower, which overlooks the square).

Tourist Information

The TI, on the main square, hands out useful tourist maps of the Slavonicko region and sells the detailed *Česká Kanada* hiking map. They also have good Internet access (daily 9:00–12:00 & 13:00–18:00, shorter hours off-season, Náměstí Míru, tel. 384-493-320, www.slavonice-mesto.cz).

The little-frequented roads in the area are ideal for **biking**; you can borrow bikes from each of the listed hotels (see "Sleeping," below).

SIGHTS

The city tower and the simple town museum are nothing special and probably not worth your time (both open daily June–Aug, weekends only May and Sept, closed Oct–April). Instead, consider the following attractions.

Underground Passages—The medieval cellars under the town, connected by an intricate network of underground passages, are a hit with children and thin, short people. Starting from the entrance (on the main square, next to the TI), you can slip on boots and an overcoat and follow the flashlight of your guide, squeezing through a 30-minute subterranean tour of the town. While you'll see little more than dirty bricks, it's certainly a unique experience. It costs 40 Kč to join an existing tour. If you're visiting at a time when a tour isn't already scheduled, you'll pay 240 Kč, the total cost of a tour for six people (July–Aug daily 9:00–18:00, call mobile 775-906-330 to arrange a visit).

Sudetenland Defenses—Just outside Slavonice, hidden in a thick forest, is a network of armadillo-like concrete pillboxes and gun

The Never-Used Fortifications

As soon as Adolf Hitler came to power in Germany in 1933, Czechoslovakia grew nervous about invasion. The area around Slavonice was part of the so-called Sudetenland: It belonged to Czechoslovakia, but was predominantly inhabited by ethnic Germans (see sidebar on page 184). Czechoslovakia began constructing a ring of fortifications along its borders. Iron-enforced concrete bunkers were connected by underground tunnels.

By September 1938, when Hitler met with the French and the British in Munich to claim the Sudetenland, these fortifications were filled with 1.5 million mobilized Czechs and Slovaks. Morale was high, and nobody doubted that the French and British would honor treaties with Czechoslovakia and help the young democracy. But instead, British Prime Minister Neville Chamberlain proclaimed to the British public, "Why should we care about the fate of a quarreling people about whom we know nothing?"—and signed off on the Munich Agreement, ceding the German areas of Czechoslovakia to Hitler without even inviting Czech representatives to the negotiations. (Chamberlain won a Nobel Prize for this appeasement policy.) Alone, the Czechoslovak army—outnumbered by the Germans three to one—stood no chance. The frustrated soldiers were ordered home, and Czechs were forced out of the Sudetenland. Half a year later, Hitler occupied the rest of the territory.

Today, the never-used bunkers along the hiking trails around Landštejn stand witness to the futility of appeasement policies and to the Czechs' bitter sense of betrayal. At the close of the war, this feeling led to the Czechs' siding with the Soviet Union, rather than with the unreliable French and British Allies. Ironically, the Munich Agreement probably saved Czechoslovakia from the fate of Poland, which was reduced to rubble during the war. Nevertheless, it took until 1989 for the Czechs to get over the frustration of the Munich Agreement in 1938, the communist take-over in 1948, and the failed "Prague Spring" uprising in 1968—moments when instead of being able to win their freedom, the Czechs had to give up without firing a single shot.

emplacements built by the Czechs in the 1930s, in anticipation of the Nazi takeover (see "The Never-Used Fortifications," above). The camouflaged mini-forts, barbed wire, and toy-like tank barriers evoke the futility of standing up to the Nazi war machine and cause you to ponder the fine line between heroism and folly. A local duo is working to turn this area into the Museum of Fortifications. To get there, hike from Slavonice (1.25 miles) along the red-marked trail in the direction of Landštejn (see "Suggested Day Hike," below); or drive on the Slavonice–Stálkov road out of town and look for the *Muzeum Opevnění* sign on the left (park where you can and walk along the tiny road, then go through the lonely woods as if you were a 20th-century invader). You'll reach two bunkers fully equipped with 1930s periscopes and machine guns (daily July–Aug and on weekends May–June and Sept).

Landštejn Castle (Hrad Landštejn)—This region of thick forests and softly rolling hills is overseen by the stark ruins of the Gothic castle that once guarded the border. While the castle itself is barren and looks like it was made of recently poured concrete, the commanding view from the top is worth the climb (40 Kč; June–Aug Tue–Sun 9:00–16:30, closed Mon; May and Sept Tue–Sun 9:00–15:30, closed Mon; April and Oct Sat–Sun 9:00–15:30, closed Mon–Fri; closed Nov–March; simple café inside castle gate, fancy Landštejnský Dvůr restaurant, two pubs by parking lot under castle; tel. 384-498-580, www.hradlandstejn.cz). On summer weekends, the castle serves as a venue for open-air folk and rock concerts.

Landštejn Castle is seven miles west of Slavonice, on the road to Nová Bystřice. Hardy travelers can reach the castle on foot (follow red-marked trail, see "Suggested Day Hike," below) or by bike (follow the road or get map at TI to go through the countryside). You can also reach it by bus (Slavonice–Nová Bystřice line, 3/day, weekdays only, 15 min, ask to be let off at Landštejn) or car (drive towards Nová Bystřice).

Suggested Day Hike: For a 14-mile hike, follow the red-marked trail from Slavonice to Landštejn via the work-in-progress Museum of Fortifications (see "Sudetenland Defenses," earlier in this section), visit the castle (have lunch here), then descend along the yellow-marked trail in the direction of Dačice to Velký Troubný lake, a perfect swimming spot. From there, return to Slavonice along the red-and-white-marked nature trail.

SLEEPING

All three recommended hotels are on the main square.

$$ Dům u Růže has 12 rooms in a restored late-19th-century house. Each room has its own bath and kitchen; the sauna and pool are free for hotel guests (Sb-1,290 Kč, Db-1,590 Kč, Tb-1,890 Kč, free parking, Náměstí Míru 452, tel. 384-493-004, mobile 603-493-879, www.dumuruze.cz, hotel@dumuruze.cz). They also rent bikes (30 Kč/hr, 200 Kč/day).

$$ Hotel Besídka, between the two parts of the square separated by the church, hides eight ultra-modern, bright rooms behind a magnificent Renaissance facade. The striking combination of

Sleep Code

(20 Kč = about $1, country code: 420)
S = Single, **D** = Double/Twin, **T** = Triple, **Q** = Quad, **b** = bathroom, **s** = shower only. Unless otherwise noted, credit cards are accepted and prices include breakfast.

To help you sort easily through these listings, I've divided the rooms into two categories based on the price for a standard double room with bath:

$$ Higher Priced—Most rooms 1,000 Kč or more.
$ Lower Priced—Most rooms less than 1,000 Kč.

ancient and postmodern styles makes it perhaps the coolest hotel in the country. Maybe that's because the rooms were designed by (and are named after) the architects-cum-actors of Prague's popular avant-garde theatre, Sklep, who still converge here every New Year (Db-1,490 Kč, extra bed-490 Kč, free Wi-Fi, Horní Náměstí 522, tel. & fax 384-493-293, www.besidka.cz). The hotel also runs a restaurant (see below).

$ Hotel Arkáda is more spartan (although all of the rooms have been recently renovated) and seems designed for hikers (Sb-620 Kč, Db-980 Kč, Náměstí Míru 466, tel. 384-408-408, fax 384-408-401, www.hotelarkada.cz, info@hotelarkada.cz).

EATING

Restaurant Besídka is a welcoming place, with modern, artsy decor, a solid Czech menu, excellent pizzas, and divine blueberry dumplings. Their entertaining menu has choices ranging from "Castro Breakfast" to "Cold and Chilly Tidbits" (daily 11:00–22:00, tel. 384-493-293, see Hotel Besídka listing, page 219).

TRANSPORTATION CONNECTIONS

The only way in and out of Slavonice is by train from Telč (2 trains in morning, 3 in afternoon, 1 hr; see Telč's "Transportation Connections," page 212).

Slavonice

MORAVSKÝ KRUMLOV

Don't mistake the shabby industrial town of Moravský Krumlov (MOH-rahv-skee KROOM-loff) for its enchanting Bohemian counterpart, Český Krumlov. A "bend in the river" (the literal meaning of "Krumlov") is the only thing these two towns have in common.

Moravský Krumlov has two restaurants, and every store is closed by 17:00. In the evening, steam from the nearby nuclear power plant envelops the setting sun. The clumsy ugliness of the circa-1950s main square (rebuilt after the town was bombed by Russians in 1945) can feel strangely exotic after you've visited picture-perfect villages elsewhere in the country.

But despite its flaws, there's one big reason to visit Moravský Krumlov: discovering the masterpiece of the Czech Republic's greatest painter, Alfons Mucha, tucked away in the town's decaying castle. Laying eyes on Mucha's grand work in this improbable setting gives you the feeling of having discovered a true "back door."

While Mucha's masterpiece, *Slav Epic,* will be in Moravský Krumlov in 2008, its location for 2009 is unclear. If you'll be visiting then, call 515-322-225 or 515-322-789 to see if it's still displayed here.

SIGHTS

▲▲▲Mucha's *Slav Epic*

Every year, 20,000 people come to Moravský Krumlov solely to see Alfons Mucha's epic 20-canvas masterpiece. Mucha's huge paintings depict momentous events in Slav history.

His work is more than a timeline chronicle. *Slav Epic* rises above the typical shallow, overly nationalistic products of the politicized 19th century. A brilliant craftsman and designer, Mucha

History of Mucha's *Slav Epic*

Alfons Mucha (1860–1939), born in the nearby town of Ivančice, made a hugely successful commercial career for himself in Paris and in the US as *the* Art Nouveau poster artist and illustrator. In

Paris, Mucha conceived the idea of dedicating the second half of his life to a work that would edify his nation. Throughout history, bards in every culture have composed poems eulogizing the best moments of their tradition. Mucha would do the same for the Czechs and the Slavs, on a grand, epic scale... and on canvas.

Mucha convinced the Chicago industrialist Charles Crane to sponsor his project. Both men believed that the purpose of a truly patriotic work was to inspire human beings to understand one another better, and thereby bring humanity closer together. Mucha returned home, and by 1912, finished the first three paintings (each 25 by 20 feet). It took another 16 years before Mucha could dedicate the cycle of 20 enormous canvases to the Czech nation and the city of Prague. The response of his fellow artists was lukewarm—in the experimental age of Picasso, Mucha's slinky style and overt nationalism were out of fashion.

During the war, the patriotic work was hidden from the Nazis and became damaged in the process. After years of restoration, the paintings were unveiled in 1963 in Moravský Krumlov's castle, near Mucha's birthplace.

captures the viewer's attention with his strong composition and sense of color. Like any true artistic masterpiece, Mucha's work goes beyond the style of the time, beyond Art Nouveau, beyond Slavic.

Consider contemplating Mucha's canvases on three levels. First, with the help of the handout that you'll get at the ticket office, decipher the history. The great feast is the celebration of the Slavic pagan god, the zealous preacher is Jan Hus (the revolutionary Czech priest), and the subdued old man contemplating the dark horizon is the first Czech exile and great educator, John Amos Comenius (for more about Comenius, see sidebar on page 236). Red is the color of war; white is the color of peace; blue is the past; and orange is the future.

When you get tired of being told what's what, step back

and figure out Mucha's intention. His technique will help you. The grand-scale background—which shows the historic events—is executed in egg-based tempera. Against that low-resolution, foggy base, clear details come into focus: the terrified couple, the mother with the child, the bearded sage with the young man, the face of the lady-in-waiting. These figures are painted in oil, and the lucid detail tells the experience of a single, often-anonymous individual. The people within *Slav Epic* suggest that Mucha's artwork is not about monumental depiction of a particular event, but about the fate of the individual against the backdrop of history. The entire weight of events is condensed into the expressions shown on their faces. In the scene showing a print shop, the young man in the foreground is Mucha's own self-portrait.

Finally, step even farther back and contemplate the painting as a work of an Impressionist or an abstract artist. The fusion of colors stands far beyond any particular meaning. Like the tones of a 19th-century symphony, Mucha's visual concert has the power to stir the deepest emotions.

Cost, Hours, Location: 80 Kč, April–Oct Tue–Sun 9:00–12:00 & 13:00–16:00, July–Aug until 17:00, closed Mon, closed Nov–March. The ticket office sells a few brochures and pictures. Notice how out-of-place Mucha's characteristic posters feel here. Allow two hours to see *Slav Epic*—it's hard to appreciate the work in less time.

SLEEPING

(20 Kč = about $1, country code: 420)
$ Hotel Epopej (Epic) was built in the early 1960s on the town's main square (Náměstí T.G. Masaryka) to accommodate far more visitors than actually ended up coming. The hotel and the restaurant deteriorated until both were closed down. Fortunately, the economic boom of recent years brought the need for a new, modern, business-class facility. The hotel's 20 rooms were renovated and equipped with modern amenities. Whether you're traveling to Moravský Krumlov to spend more time in the company of lanky Slavic heroes—or if you're simply stranded in Moravský Krumlov overnight—you won't regret your stay here (Sb-550 Kč, Db-900 Kč, Tb-1,350 Kč, tel. 515-321-317, fax 515-322-373, www.hotel-epopej.cz, hotelepopej@seznam.cz).

EATING

Restaurant Epopej, on the ground floor of the hotel listed above, is popular with locals attracted by both the varied menu (available in English) and cheap lunch specials (advertised only in Czech). Ask the waiter for today's special, and avoid the greasy Chinese dishes made by the restaurant's Vietnamese chef (daily 10:00–22:00). If you have time and money to waste, a slot-machine room *(Herna)*, located behind the restaurant bar, will be more than willing to oblige (daily until 2:00 in the morning).

TRANSPORTATION CONNECTIONS

With easy connections in and out, only one hotel worth recommending, and no excuse to spend more time in Moravský Krumlov than it takes to see Mucha's masterpiece, I'd sleep elsewhere.

From Moravský Krumlov to: Mikulov (2 trains per afternoon, 1.5 hrs, transfer in Hrušovany), **Brno** (10 trains/day, 45 min; bus connections mainly on weekdays). Since Brno is right on the Prague–Vienna and Prague–Bratislava–Budapest train lines, Moravský Krumlov is a handy stop in the middle of a long travel day. (Consider taking the SC Pendolino train from **Prague's Holešovice Station** to **Brno,** which is a bit faster than other trains; 2.5-hr trip.)

By Car: If you're driving to Moravský Krumlov, figure about 30 minutes from Třebíč or Mikulov, and one hour from Telč or Slavonice.

OLOMOUC

Olomouc (OH-loh-moats), the historical capital of Moravia, is a showcase of Baroque city planning. Today, it's the Czech Republic's fifth-largest city (pop. 100,700) and harbors Moravia's most prestigious university. Students rule the town. With its wealth of cafés, clubs, and restaurants, Olomouc is the place to taste vibrant local culture—without the hassles and scams of Prague.

Olomouc has pride. It's at a crossroads about 150 miles from each of the other great cities of the region (Prague, Wrocław, Kraków, Bratislava, and Vienna) and wants to play with the big boys. While it ruled Moravia from the 11th century until 1642, today it's clearly playing second fiddle to Prague in the modern Czech Republic. Locals brag that Olomouc has the country's second-most-important bishopric and its second university. Like Prague, it has its own fancy astronomical clock. Olomouc actually built its bell tower in the 19th century to be six feet taller than Prague's. Olomouc is unrivaled in one category: Its plague monument is the tallest and most grandiose anywhere.

Although Olomouc's suburbs sprawl with 1960s apartment complexes and factories, its historic core was spared Stalin's experiments in urban design. It's not lost in a time warp like the old-town areas of Český Krumlov, Telč, and Slavonice. It's simply workaday Moravia. Trams clatter through the streets, fancy boutiques sell stylish Versace fashions, and locals pack the busy pubs. Few tourists come here, so the town lives on its own booming economy.

In the mornings, proud farmers dig out their leeks and carrots and descend upon the colorful open-air market. Haná, the region that immediately surrounds Olomouc, is the most fertile in the Czech Republic. The big landowners here have never had trouble converting their meat, milk, and bread into gold and power. The most distinguished landowner of all has always been the Church.

Olomouc's History

The fortune and misfortune of Olomouc has always come from its strategic location at the intersection of Eastern Europe's main east–west and south–north routes: Merchants, pilgrims, kings, and armies had to pass through the city.

Until the 1640s, Olomouc was the second-largest city in the Czech lands. The king's younger brother governed Moravian politics from here, while the archbishop kept the spirits (and the lands) of Moravians in God's hands—that is, his own.

Olomouc was trashed by passing armies during the Thirty Years' War (1618–1648) and occupied by Sweden for the last eight of those years. More than 70 percent of the town's population died in battles or from plagues, and the Moravian capital was moved to Brno. In 1709, Olomouc burned to the ground...only to emerge from the ashes with a Baroque flair during the Hapsburg years. The new Olomouc—filled with churches, colleges, statues, and fountains—became the largest Baroque town in the country. But its prosperity again ended abruptly, as Prussia (occupying what is now western Poland and eastern Germany) threatened to invade Vienna—and Olomouc was right in the way. The Hapsburgs had Olomouc's students and monks leave, and replaced them with soldiers who would defend the city. They surrounded Olomouc with tall, thick walls, and what once was a cultural center became an immense fortress. The Prussians laid siege to the city, but never managed to take it. The ring of walls and moats that protected the town also ended up preventing the encroachment of modern-day architecture into the historic center.

Olomouc eventually began to thrive again, but it remains overshadowed by Brno. Today, it still comes in second as the economic powerhouse of Moravia. But ever since Palacký University was founded here in 1946—on the grounds of the centuries-old theological university—Olomouc has become Moravia's intellectual center.

Archbishops have ruled from here for a thousand years, filling the town with churches and monasteries. In 1946, these buildings were turned into faculties of Palacký University.

Being a student town, Olomouc feels young and alive (though quiet during summer weekends and school vacations, when the students clear out). Olomouc has managed to blend the old and the new better than any other town in the country. The McDonald's on the Baroque main square is not an intruder, but simply a contented acknowledgment of modern times.

To generalize, the Moravians are seen as friendlier and more community-oriented than the more individualistic Bohemians. This shows in voting patterns. In Moravia, left-leaning parties tend to do better than the pro-business candidates who dominate the electorates in Prague and Pilsen (a city in western Bohemia). Traditions are also more prized in Moravia: Diverse regional dialects and folk customs have flourished here but have long since disappeared in Bohemia.

Anything labeled "Haná" is from this particular part of Moravia—you'll notice plenty of Haná pride among locals. Olomouc is a fine place to just kick back for a day or two in a beautiful Baroque town with its Haná-centric gaze fixed on the future.

Planning Your Time

Olomouc is a delightful mix of Baroque space and 21st-century life. Don't approach the city as a sightseer; Olomouc is to be experienced and enjoyed. The only must-see "sights"—the two squares and the plague column—can be covered in an hour. But you can happily spend additional time in the city's restaurants, bars, and clubs.

If you're passing through, hop off the train for a three-hour lunch stop on the main square. Better yet, stay the night to relax and sample the rich nightlife. I enjoy the city enough to visit it as a long day trip from Prague. On a more leisurely visit, consider the worthwhile day trips to Kroměříž (with a sumptuous château—see page 244) and the Wallachia region (see next chapter).

ORIENTATION

Olomouc's historic core is small, compact, and just five tram stops from the train station (see "Arrival in Olomouc," below). The core has two parts: the original settlement around the former royal palace and cathedral, and the royal town (west of the cathedral). The royal town is concentrated around two connected squares: Upper Square (Horní Náměstí), with the Town Hall and plague column; and Lower Square (Dolní Náměstí), with many restaurants.

Part of Olomouc's charm is that it's a Baroque town on a medieval street plan. Everything of sightseeing interest is contained within its historic core, defined by the circular greenbelt that follows the town's old wall (much like the famous Planty in Kraków).

Tourist Information

Olomouc's main TI, in the Town Hall on the Upper Square, has plenty of well-written fliers describing the town's main sights (daily 9:00–19:00, tel. 585-513-385, www.olomouc-tourism.cz; there's also

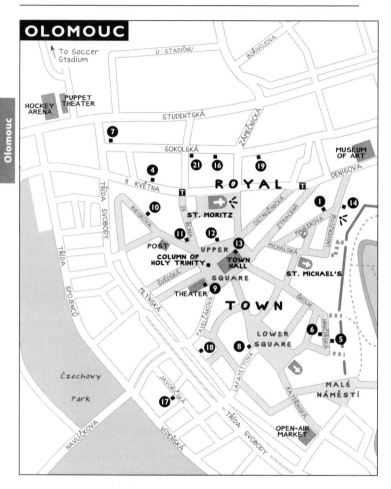

a TI at the train station—see below). They sell tickets to concerts and can set you up with a local guide (500 Kč/hr, reserve ahead).

Arrival in Olomouc

Olomouc's circa-1950s **train station** (Hlavní Nádraží) is down-right cute: Bright and happy workers and peasants still greet you with their banners and sickles.

As you exit through the main station hall, you'll see three information offices on the left. First is the railway center, with 24-hour help on train connections (tel. 585-785-620). Next is a simple TI that offers basic help—such as directions to hotels—and can sell you a good town map (Mon–Fri 5:00–19:00, Sat 7:00–13:00, closed Sun). And third is a city transit office, with information about trams and tickets.

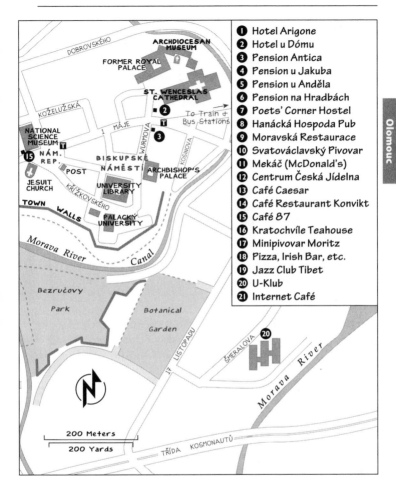

1. Hotel Arigone
2. Hotel u Dómu
3. Pension Antica
4. Pension u Jakuba
5. Pension u Anděla
6. Pension na Hradbách
7. Poets' Corner Hostel
8. Hanácká Hospoda Pub
9. Moravská Restaurace
10. Svatováclavský Pivovar
11. Mekáč (McDonald's)
12. Centrum Česká Jídelna
13. Café Caesar
14. Café Restaurant Konvikt
15. Café 87
16. Kratochvíle Teahouse
17. Minipivovar Moritz
18. Pizza, Irish Bar, etc.
19. Jazz Club Tibet
20. U-Klub
21. Internet Café

Take the **tram** into the center. Trams #2, #4, and #6 stop in front of the train station and go past the cathedral (U Dómu, third stop), then continue to Koruna (fifth stop), right by the main square. Even if you're not arriving by train, consider riding this tram for an easy orientation to the city (see "Getting Around Olomouc," next page).

Taxis are inexpensive (figure on 100 Kč to the center). Call Atlant-taxi (toll-free tel. 800-113-030) or Citytaxi (toll-free tel. 800-223-030).

Helpful Hints

Festivals: During the summer (July–Sept), the town organizes a cultural festival. Top Czech artists perform weekly under the open sky in the Town Hall courtyard or in one of the numerous churches and student clubs around town (www .okl.info). The Jesuit Konvikt (former monastery) simultane-ously hosts a Baroque music festival. Outside of festival time, when school is in session (Sept–June), Olomouc is hopping, with good independent movie theaters (www.olomouckakina .cz) and live music in bars (see "Cafés, Teahouses, Pubs, and Clubs," page 241). The town's main theater, Moravské Divadlo, puts on opera performances regularly (ticket office open Mon–Fri 9:00–18:00, closed Sat–Sun, located on the Upper Square next to Moravská Restaurace, tel. 585-223-533, pokladna @moravskedivadlo.cz).

Pharmacy: A 24-hour pharmacy is on Aksamitova street.

Internet Access: U Dominika has mellow decor and comfy chairs (Mon–Fri 9:00–21:00, Sat–Sun 10:00–21:00, across the street from Dominican monastery on the corner of Sokolská and Slovenská).

Walking Tours and Bike Rentals: Poets' Corner Hostel organizes a daily walking tour and rents wheels by the day (for details, see page 239).

Rickshaws: To cycle around on a rickshaw, look for the main stand in front of the TI on the square (50 Kč per ride, 100-Kč circuit goes around all fountains, 200 Kč also includes parks).

Local Guide: Štefan Blaho, who speaks English well, is a rare Olomouc guide, ready to connect with curious visitors who figure out how much fun Olomouc is to visit—especially with a local (500 Kč/hr, tel. 581-208-242, mobile 602-729-613, www.olomouc-guide.cz, stefan@olomouc-guide.cz).

Getting Around Olomouc

While Olomouc is walkable, I recommend taking the following tram ride for a good orientation.

Overview Tram Ride: The 10-minute tram ride from the train station (Hlavní Nádraží) to the Upper Square (stop: Koruna) is a handy way to get an overview of the city. It's easy. Trams #2, #4, and #6 make the route, going every few minutes. Tickets are good for 40 minutes, so you can hop on and off (8 Kč, buy at *tabák* shops or yellow machines, or pay a little extra to buy on board from the driver).

In front of the train station stretches a modern town center with planned communist-era apartment blocks. While there are plenty of drawbacks to the city's communist heritage, one good leftover from that era is Olomouc's fine, still-subsidized public transit. As you ride, notice that people have a choice to forgo own-ing a car because of dirt-cheap monthly passes. It's second nature here.

Going downtown from the station, you peel through the city's architectural layers of history. Crossing the three branches of the river, you pass through the university district before reaching the center. A red light at the front of the car indicates your next stop. Hop out at "Koruna," and head toward the big square (Upper Square) a block to your left.

SIGHTS

Olomouc is divided between its royal town (surrounding the magnificent Upper Square, with its famous plague column) and its bishop's town, or cathedral district (the other end of town, with the bishop's palace and the new Archdiocesan Museum). The huge university sprawls between these two former centers of power. Visitors connect the two zones with an easy 10-minute walk (described below). The sights here are listed in that order: Upper Square and its surroundings (market and churches), cross-town walk, and cathedral.

The Royal Town

Upper Square (Horní Náměstí)—Standing in front of the Town Hall, surrounded by the vast square and the town's fine noble and bourgeois residences, you can imagine the importance of Olomouc over the centuries. The fountain with an equestrian statue of Julius Caesar is dedicated to the legendary founder of the town (excavations reveal that it actually originated as a third-century Roman military camp—centuries after Caesar).

The Mahler Café is a reminder of the great composer Gustav Mahler (1860–1911). He lived and worked here until he moved to Vienna, claiming he needed better food.

Examine the town model. While designed for blind people, it gives anyone interested a feel—literally—for the medieval street plan, otherwise easily overlooked among all the Baroque grandeur.

On the square, take a look at the Town Hall, the fancy clock, the towering plague monument, and the seven mostly venerable fountains (all described below).

▲Town Hall—Olomouc's grand Town Hall is a testimonial to the city's 600 years of prominence in Moravia. The three wings around a rectangular courtyard once served as both council chambers and market halls. In the late 1400s, part of the building was converted into an armory, guards' house, and jail. On the outside, notice the beautiful Mannerist loggia, used for the entry into the council chambers and for ceremonial purposes (such as the mayor's declarations to the public). The coats of arms of many nations show that Moravia was part of the vast and multiethnic Hapsburg Empire.

The Baroque Fountains of Olomouc

Sprinkled around Olomouc's old town is a series of seven allegorical fountains with statues. Since pagan times, Olomouc—whose wealth has always been based on agriculture—has had a close relationship to water. Most of the fountains were inspired by classical mythology.

One features a statue of **Neptune,** the god of water. Another shows **Hercules** depicted as the guardian of Olomouc, holding the Moravian checkered eagle in his left hand and a mace in his right. **Jupiter,** the overlord of the gods, replaced an earlier sculpture of the only Christian saint who appeared on the fountains: St. Florian, protector from fires and floods.

The **Tritons** fountain—closely based on the one at Rome's Piazza Barberini—has the most developed composition: a pair of water spirits and a dolphin carrying a conch, with a fragile boy leading two dogs.

The culmination of the cycle is the equestrian statue of **Caesar,** who looks proudly towards Michael Hill (where legend says he founded Olomouc). The water gods Morava and Danubius carry the coats of arms of Moravia and Lower Austria, and the dog represents Olomouc's fidelity to the Austrian emperor.

The **Mercury** statue is artistically the most successful. Mercury fulfilled the same role in classical mythology as the archangel Michael in the Old Testament: He was the guide through the land of the dead and the messenger of gods.

The modern **turtle fountain,** at the end of the Town Hall, is the most entertaining. The turtle, who lives a long life, symbolizes ancient Olomouc's ability to hang in there. The city's history in maps and documents is inscribed on the turtle's pillar. Contribute to a new tradition—though the statue is only a few years old, the tail (on the dolphin statue) already shows signs of being rubbed by visitors to assure their return to Olomouc. This fountain is a meeting place for young mothers, and a fun place to watch toddlers enjoy the art.

The placement of the fountains and statues at the intersections of roads and squares—reminiscent of stage props in Baroque theater—imitates the spectacular cycle of Bernini's fountains in Rome. Since the second half of the 18th century, every view down any main street in Olomouc has ended with a sculpture. Look for these as you sightsee, and you'll better appreciate the town as theater.

The Town Hall is busy with local weddings—if you see a festively decorated car parked on the square, it's probably waiting to zip a bride and groom away. You can visit the Town Hall's interior and climb the tower only with an escort (15 Kč, 30 min, daily at 11:00 and 15:00, book tickets and depart from the TI located within the Town Hall).

▲Astronomical Clock—The huge clock on the Town Hall was once far more complex than even the one in Prague. Originally,

it depicted the medieval universe divided into three spheres, but it was periodically rebuilt to correspond with new advances in knowledge. In 1898, purists worked to restore it to its original state. (A picture of this older version is in the window located a few steps to the left of the actual clock.)

Like Prague's clock, Olomouc's astronomical clock was intentionally destroyed by the Nazis in World War II. Today's version was rebuilt in 1953 by the communists—with their kitschy flair for propaganda. In this one-of-a-kind clock made in the Social Realist style, you have earnest chemists and heroic mothers rather than saints and Virgin Marys. High noon is marked by a proletarian parade, when, for six minutes, a mechanical conga line of milkmaids, clerks, blacksmiths, medics, and teachers are celebrated as the champions of everyday society. Study the mosaic symbols of the 12 months (*leden* is January; circle down on the left—*červen* is June). The Haná region is agriculturally rich, so each month features a farm activity. As with any proper astronomical clock, there's a wheel with 365 saints, so you'll always know whose special day it is. But this clock comes with a Moscow-inspired bonus—red bands on the wheel splice in the birthdays of communist leaders (Lenin was born on the 112th day of year in 1870. Stalin's saint was Toman—day 355). Note that the clock's designers were optimists—the year mechanism (on the bottom) is capable of spinning until 9999 A.D.

▲▲▲Column of the Holy Trinity (Sousoší Nejsvětější Trojice)—The artistic pride of Olomouc is the tallest plague column in Europe. Squares throughout Eastern Europe are dotted with similar structures, erected by locals to give thanks for surviving the plague. This one was started in 1716 by a local man named Render, who announced—with a confidence characteristic of the Haná region—that he would create a work that in "its height and ornamentation would not have a peer in terms of excellence." He donated his entire fortune, employing many great artists for decades to build the monument. Sadly, he died before its

Olomouc

consecration, which occurred in the presence of the Hapsburg ruler, Maria Theresa, the Holy Roman Empress.

The Holy Trinity group on the highest point of the column features God the Father making a blessing, Christ with a cross sitting on a globe, and the dove in gold (representing the Holy Spirit) crowning everything. Tumbling with the Trinity, the archangel Michael—holding his fiery sword and shield—reminds us that the Church is in a constant struggle with evil. A third of the way down from the top of the column (past the golden cannonball—embedded there as a reminder of the 1758 Prussian siege), we see Mary—the mediator between heavenly and earthly spheres—carried off by angels during the Assumption.

The bottom third features three reliefs with allegories of the Christian virtues (Faith, Hope, and Charity), surrounded by six saints. Four of the saints are closely connected with the life of Jesus (saints Joachim and Anne—the parents of St. Mary—as well as St. Joseph and St. John the Baptist) and the other two are the patron saints of Olomouc (saints Jerome and Lawrence). This particular arrangement of saints shows that universal faith is often combined with a distinctly local myth and belief.

It all sits atop a tiny (and rarely open) chapel where Maria Theresa knelt to pray—devout, yet green with envy. Olomouc had a plague column grander than Vienna's.

Lower Square (Dolní Náměstí)—Below the Upper Square stretches the more workaday Lower Square. Enjoy live music at the beer terrace or a bite at the fine Hanácká Hospoda pub (described in "Eating," below). Find the communist-era lamppost with its twin 1970s speakers. Locals remember growing up with these mouthpieces of government boasting of successes ("This year, despite many efforts of sabotage on the part of certain individuals in service of imperialist goals, we have surpassed the planned output of steel by 195 percent"); calling people to action ("There will be no school tomorrow as all will join the farmers in the fields for an

abundant harvest"); or quelling disturbances ("Some citizens may have heard about alien forces in our society taking advantage of this week's anniversary to spread unrest. This is to reassure you that the situation is firmly under control and nothing is happening in Olomouc or in Prague. Nevertheless, for their own safety, we suggest all citizens stay home").

Open-Air Market—As was the norm in medieval times, poor people traded tax- and duty-free items just outside the town walls. The city's market remains in the same spot, just outside the town wall a long block below the Lower Square. The town's circa-1900 brick market hall is of no interest today, but around it sprawls a colorful open-air market. While Moravian farmers sell their vegetables and herbs, Vietnamese traders hawk knock-off jeans and cheap sunglasses (closed Sun, busiest on Wed and Sat, but fun any morning). The rough little snack bar sells *langoš* (a Hungarian cheese-and-grease doughnut, 13 Kč), cheap coffee, and good beer.

Churches—Olomouc has been the seat of bishops from its origin. The great number of churches—concentrated in such a small area—shows the strong presence of the Church here. Of the many churches in town, two are worth a peek (each one is a block off the Upper Square).

St. Michael's Church (Sv. Michal), located at the highest point in town, dominates Olomouc's skyline (free, open long hours daily). It's a fine, single-nave Baroque church full of illusory paintings, fake armor, and fine Gothic frescoes hidden under Baroque whitewash. As it was rebuilt after looting by the Protestant Swedes during the Counter-Reformation, the Catholic propaganda is really cranked up. The three-domed ceiling—a reminder of the Trinity—is an unusual feature. From the cloister, stairs lead down to the 11th-century "rock chapel" and its tiny lake. The chair in the dark hole on the left is an invitation to pray or meditate. This humble grotto was the site of the first hermitage here on Olomouc's high rock. As Michael is the Christian antidote to paganism, archaeologists assume that this church sits upon a pagan holy spot.

St. Moritz Church (Sv. Mořic) is a must-see for its pair of asymmetrical towers, which look more like fortresses. The church has an original Gothic vault, but its Gothic treasures are in a Prague museum. The altar and windows, while lovely, are Neo-Gothic, dating only from the 19th century. Climb the 200 steps to the tower to enjoy a commanding city view (15 Kč).

Strolling Between the Royal Town and the Cathedral

Connect the two sightseeing zones with a short walk along the city's main drag. Leaving the Upper Square on Ostružnická street, you'll pass real-estate offices (a home in a village or apartment here goes for about 1.5 million Kč, or about $75,000), and lots of bookstores (supplying 17,000 local university students).

When you hit the main road, Denisova, notice the fine gas

"From Armories Make Libraries": John Amos Comenius
(1592–1670)

This motto, which inspired the transformation of Olomouc's military fortress into a lively university campus, came from Comenius, a.k.a. Jan Amos Komenský, one of the Czech Republic's most influential teachers and writers (pull out a 200-Kč banknote to have a look at him). You'll find his dictum embedded in the pavement at the entrance to Olomouc's former central armory, which is the main university library today.

Comenius was born into the Moravian Brethren faith, which was founded on the pacifist ideals of the Czech religious reformer Petr Chelčický (c. 1390–c. 1460). Having studied at universities in Germany, Comenius returned to Moravia as a young pastor to run the Protestant schools in Fulnek and Přerov. The beginning of the Thirty Years' War had a direct impact on him: His wife and two children died in a plague epidemic, and following the defeat of the Czech Protestants by the Catholic Hapsburgs, Comenius had to choose exile over abandoning his faith. Personal misfortune went hand-in-hand with a professional one: During his escape through Poland, his entire library went up in flames, a fate that later befell many of his personal writings.

Surrounded by the chaos and destruction of war, Comenius believed that guns were no way to restore order—what the world really needed was a revolution in learning. He envisioned a liberal-arts education that would create citizens, rather than specialists, and proposed a new teaching system based on the novel principle of "school through play." To promote this idea, he wrote extensively. His works included a textbook aimed at making learning Latin fun for children, one of the first scholarly

streetlamp that lit the street in 1899, when the tram first ran. Follow the tram line toward the lacy spire of the cathedral in the distance.

The mix of facades, from Gothic to Art Nouveau, masks narrow medieval buildings. At Univerzitní street, a quick detour to the right leads past the Vertigo Bar (where students believe a mind is a wonderful thing to waste) to the grand and renovated University building on the left (with its handy Café Restaurant Konvikt and a courtyard with a nice view over the town wall).

Continuing up the main drag, you pass the Museum of Art (interesting) and the Natural History Museum (boring). If you visit the art museum (50 Kč, Tue–Sun 10:00–18:00, closed Mon, Denisova 47), save your ticket—it'll also get you into the Archdiocesan Museum (described below).

treatments of preschool education, and *Orbis Pictus* ("World in Pictures")—the first children's encyclopedia. His most famous and acclaimed work, *The Labyrinth of the World and the Paradise of the Heart* (written in Czech, not Latin), argued that all human knowledge and ambition is futile if unaccompanied by faith and charity. His fame spread across the Atlantic: In 1636, Comenius was asked to become the first president of Harvard University. Still hoping to return home (and afraid of sea journeys after he almost lost his life in a storm in the North Sea), Comenius declined the offer.

For the remainder of his wandering life, Comenius taught and wrote in Poland, Hungary, the Netherlands, England, and Sweden, never able to return home. Alfons Mucha powerfully

captured Comenius' tragic fate as a homeless exile—a fate to be shared by thousands of free-spirited Czechs—in one of the canvases of his *Slav Epic* (see page 222).

During the communist era, Comenius' grave (in Naarden, near Amsterdam) became a shrine for Czech exiles; immediately after the fall of the Iron Curtain, the site was swamped with Czechs who came to pay their respects. Today, Comenius is considered one of the founders of modern education, and his legacy is alive far beyond Olomouc. In the Czech Republic and Slovakia, Comenius' birthday is celebrated as Teachers' Day, while the Comenius' Medal is the highest UNESCO award for achievement in education.

The big square called Náměstí Republiky is marked by a fountain inspired by Bernini's Triton Fountain in Rome (see "The Baroque Fountains of Olomouc," page 232). The Jesuits—whose gorgeous church faces the square—founded the original university in the 16th century. This square marks the division between the royal town and the bishop's town. Ahead (past the square, veering a bit to the right), Mariánská street leads to the archbishop's stately 17th-century palace (closed to the public). On the slopes below the palace are Jesuit colleges (now university classrooms) and a Clarist convent, now a museum.

In the Bishop's Town, near the Cathedral

St. Wenceslas Cathedral (Dóm Sv. Václava)—This has supposedly been the resident church of Olomouc's bishops ever since the

Christian missionaries Cyril and Methodius visited in the ninth century. The present church has been rebuilt many times. While it maintains its Gothic lines, what you see is 19th-century pseudo-Gothic, with Neo-Renaissance paintings. The crypt houses a collection of liturgical ornaments—the second-largest in the country, after Loreta Church in Prague (see page 99). Just inside the door, you can trace the lineage of local archbishops back 68 men, from today's archbishop to St. Methodius in 869.

▲**Archdiocesan Museum**—Opened in 2006, this is the pride and joy of Olomouc. After his 1995 visit, Pope John Paul II asked the city to build this museum. The mission of this state-of-the-art museum is "In Glory and Praise—To Share a Thousand Years of Spiritual Culture in Moravia"...and it does just that.

This former royal castle, once the king's principal Moravian residence, later became home to Olomouc's archbishop. The exterior is a mix of Romanesque and Gothic elements. Inside, you'll wander among some of the finest medieval art in Eastern Europe (all well-described in English). The centerpiece of the treasury is a monstrance with 1,800 diamonds and seven pounds of pure gold (from 1750). The bishop's gilded coach understandably gave the Holy Roman Empress Maria Theresa more reason for envy.

Then, with slippers to protect the not-so-hardwood floor, you shuffle through the staterooms lined with well-lit paintings. Don't miss the painting depicting the ceremonial arrival of the new archbishop in Olomouc in the mid-1700s. Survey the town: Except for the McDonald's, it's all there. See how the artist, playing with perspective a bit, shows the gate on the left dividing the royal town from the bishop's town. This day was a good one for the bishop, as the secular royal town is filled with Christian pageantry (50 Kč, free on Wed and Sun, open Tue–Sun 10:00–18:00, closed Mon, Václavské Náměstí 3, same ticket also gets you into the Museum of Art at Denisova 47).

SLEEPING

$$$ **Hotel Arigone,** filling three tastefully renovated townhouses, is on the hill by St. Michael's Church. While some of the 40 rooms have 17th-century wooden ceilings and 19th-century-style furniture, most are furnished in a modern style and are accessible by elevator (Sb-1,700 Kč, Db-2,000 Kč, Univerzitní 20, tel. 585-232-350 or 585-232-351, fax 585-232-350, www.arigone.cz, hotel@arigone.cz).

$$$ **Hotel u Dómu,** a six-room place on a quiet street next to the cathedral, is run with a personal touch that makes it popular with quirky visiting professors (Sb-1,300 Kč, Db-1,800 Kč, Tb-2,000 Kč, free parking, Dómská 4, tel. 585-220-502, fax 585-220-501,

Sleep Code

(20 Kč = about $1, country code: 420)
S = Single, **D** = Double/Twin, **T** = Triple, **Q** = Quad, **b** = bathroom, **s** = shower only. Unless otherwise noted, credit cards are accepted and prices include breakfast.

To help you sort easily through these listings, I've divided the rooms into three categories based on the price for a standard double room with bath:

$$$ **Higher Priced**—Most rooms 1,500 Kč or more.
  $$ **Moderately Priced**—Most rooms between 1,000–
                 1,500 Kč.
    $ **Lower Priced**—Most rooms 1,000 Kč or less.

www.udomu.3dpano.eu, hoteludomu@email.cz).

$$$ Pension Antica, in a Baroque house filled with antique furniture and Oriental rugs, is a mixture of friendliness and tasteful opulence, courtesy of the caring owner Miroslava (apartments 1,800–2,500 Kč, Wurmova 1, tel. 585-242-368, mobile 731-560-264, www.pension.antica.cz, pension@antica.cz).

$$ Pension u Jakuba rents six self-contained, Ikea-furnished apartments in a renovated 400-year-old house on a busy street. The pension also has seven quiet, modern rooms in a newly built annex in the courtyard (Sb-790 Kč, Db-1,200 Kč, Tb-1,500 Kč, Qb-1,900 Kč, 8 Května #9, to reach the reception walk through the passage and into the courtyard, parking available, tel. 585-209-995, mobile 777-747-688, www.pensionujakuba.com, ujakuba@iol.cz).

$ Pension na Hradbách rents four modern rooms with a personal touch (Sb-700 Kč, Db-1,000 Kč, Tb-1,500 Kč, no breakfast, Hrnčířská 3, tel. 585-233-243, mobile 602-755-848, nahradbach @quick.cz).

$ Pension u Anděla, across the street, is well-suited to be on Hrnčířská (Potter's street), a quiet row of two-story village houses with brightly painted facades and window-boxes full of geraniums. Two of the four simply furnished rooms overlook the bastion and park (Db-700 Kč, no breakfast, Hrnčířská 10, tel. 585-228-755, mobile 602-512-763, www.uandela.cz).

$*Hostel:* **Poets' Corner Hostel** fills two 1930s apartments near the town center. Tastefully furnished, immaculately clean, and run by a friendly Australian couple, Greg and Francie, the hostel fits in perfectly with Olomouc's character as a student town and ultimate back-door destination for the Czech Republic. The common room has sofas, armchairs, a decent library, Czech CDs—and no TV—and holds a wealth of information on Olomouc and the surrounding area (dorm beds-300–350 Kč, Db-800 Kč, Tb-1,100 Kč, laundry service-100 Kč/load; ring the doorbell at the entryway to the right of the Umbro shop to get into Sokolská 1; mobile 777-570-730, www.hostelolomouc.com). The hostel also rents bicycles (100 Kč/day) and organizes walking tours of Olomouc that depart every morning at 10:00 from the Astronomical Clock (voluntary contribution, 200 Kč/person is fine).

EATING

Try the sour, foul-smelling, yet beloved specialty of the Haná region, Olomouc cheese sticks *(olomoucké tvarůžky)*. The milk goes through a process of natural maturation under chunks of meat. Czechs figure there are two types of people in the world: *tvarůžky*-lovers and sane people. The *tvarůžky* are so much a part of the Haná and Czech identity that when the European Union tried to forbid the product, the Czech government negotiated for special permission to continue to rot their milk. Zip a few of these stinkers in a baggie, and you can count on getting a train compartment to yourself.

Restaurants

Hanácká Hospoda, on the Lower Square, is a simple, hearty village pub that serves regional specialties to visitors and locals alike. Choose between the woody Moravian beer-hall interior or the best square seating outside. Mozart came here to escape a smallpox epidemic in Vienna, and he lived above this restaurant. Enjoy the funky menu. Dish #007, Guttery Breath of the Knight of Loštice (a.k.a. *tvarůžky*—see above), comes with a lid, mints, and the offer of a toothbrush—they only have one, so please return it. Dishes #40 to #81 are good local favorites (Mon–Sat 10:00–24:00, Sun 10:00–20:00, kitchen closes two hours earlier, Dolní Náměstí, tel. 585-237-186).

Moravská Restaurace (Moravian Restaurant), on the Upper Square, is the one touristy place in town. If you're feeling homesick, step in here, and you'll see happy tourists attracted by ads all over town, "authentic" Moravian folk costumes on the waiters, walls decorated with Moravian painted ceramics...and prices that will make you feel like you're back at home (essentially the same menu as Hanácká Hospoda for triple the price, daily 11:30–23:00, reservations recommended, Horní Náměstí, tel. 585-222-868).

Svatováclavský Pivovar (St. Wenceslas Brewery), just off the square (on the street behind the plague column), serves 100 percent natural, unpasteurized yeast beer. The fresh-beer list includes both the traditional barley varieties and stouts, as well as wheat beer with lemon, a rare treat in the Czech Republic. The beer is supplemented by a long dining menu. Choose between the modern interior with rustic decor or the street-side terrace (Mon–Sat 11:00–24:00, Sun 11:00–22:00, Riegrova 22, tel. 585-203-641).

Mekáč (McDonald's), on the Upper Square, is filled with teenagers and moms with kids during the week. On a weekend, you can sit here and watch folks from the countryside, dressed in their Sunday best and coming to town for a "Bikmek" taste of the world.

Centrum Česká Jídelna (Czech Eatery) is ideal if you're short on time and want some local-style fast food. They offer a world of traditional Czech dishes, ready and warmed, as well as an array of sandwiches and salads. Choose your meal by pointing at what you want (Mon–Fri 6:30–18:00, Sat 7:30–12:00, closed Sun, directly opposite the clock).

Café Caesar, filling the Gothic vaults in the Town Hall, is a popular pizza place with fine outside seating within a flea's hop of the plague monument (daily 9:00–1:00 in the morning, tel. 585-229-287). The little gallery next door, run by the café, promotes local artists.

Café Restaurant Konvikt is a modern-feeling place in the delightfully restored former Jesuit college. They cater primarily to businessmen, though some philosophy students also wander here from the classrooms upstairs. In summer, they offer seating in a peaceful courtyard above the city walls and greenbelt (daily 11:00–24:00, Univerzitní 3, tel. 585-631-190).

Cafés, Teahouses, Pubs, and Clubs

Olomouc is the Moravian university town, and every aspect of student life (except sleeping) happens right in the old center. Being a student town, Olomouc is lively and cheap during the school year but slower in July, August, and September (although foreign students coming here for summer programs in languages, music, and history are doing their best to make up for the annual vacation energy drain).

Café 87 has the longest list of espresso drinks, iced coffees, frappés, pancakes, and desserts in town. The handful of Olomouc expats converge here daily just before lunch to have the chocolate cake—heavenly but highly addictive (daily 10:00–19:00, between the art and natural-history museums on Náměstí Republiky).

Kratochvíle Teahouse offers a wide array of freshly harvested tea leaves, as well as coffee, Moravian wines, and the increasingly popular hookahs (water pipes). This contemplative, bamboo-lined space also hosts exhibitions, concerts, and author readings

(Mon–Fri 11:00–23:00, Sat–Sun 15:00–23:00, Sokolská 36, mobile 739-643-856).

Minipivovar Moritz, which brews fresh yeasty beer on site, serves Bohemian cuisine and Galician specialties. Dine in their atmospheric, circa-1900 cellar or on the park-like square, in front of the dilapidated, picturesque Maria Theresa Gate. Taking its name from a German-Jewish industrialist (Moritz Fischer), it opened near a former synagogue in 2006 (precisely one hundred years after the death of the man responsible for developing Olomouc into a modern manufacturing center). Today Moritz is one of the trendiest places in town. Head down to the basement to check out the kosher beer-making process, the unique "pivovod" (beer pipes that lead under the street to the outdoor bar on the square), and the portrait of Moritz's grandmother, who set the standard for hospitality that the owners hope to match (daily 11:00–23:00, Nešverova 2, on Palachovo Náměstí, tel. 585-205-560).

Captain Morgan's Pizza, Bar Rasputin, The Crack Irish Bar, and **Club Belmondo** fill the massive redbrick, 18th-century town wall with nightlife inspired by various corners of Europe. Fueled by the vibrant local crowd, these spots are open much of the day, but they don't really start to swing until around 21:00, when the disco and live music begin. All are free except for Club Belmondo, which charges a 100 Kč cover. Head to the corner of Mlýnská and Pavelčákova, just across the Třída Svobody from Maria Theresa Gate.

Jazz Club Tibet has nothing to do with Tibet, but it does offer good food and live jazz twice a week in a modern, pub-like setting (Mon–Fri 11:00–24:00, Sat 12:00–24:00, closed Sun, Sokolská 48, tel. 585-230-399).

Konvikt is a hip club right next to the restaurant of the same name (see above). In summer, it's a popular hangout for foreign students (Mon–Sat 14:00–24:00, closed Sun, tel. 585-631-191).

U-Klub, a 10-minute walk out of the center in the dorms, is the university's own concert hall. Bands play folk, jazz, rock, punk...you name it (Šmeralova 12, tel. 585-638-117).

TRANSPORATION CONNECTIONS

Olomouc is on several major rail lines (such as the one from Prague to Kraków).

From Olomouc by Train to: Kroměříž (hourly, 1–1.5 hrs, transfer in Hulín, see next page), **Prague** (hourly, 2–3 hrs), **Brno** (buses and trains at least hourly, 1.5 hrs), **Frenštát pod Radhoštěm** (near **Trojanovice;** 8/day, most connections require transfer in Hranice na Moravě and Valašské Meziříčí, allow 2.5 hrs total), **Břeclav** (10/day, 2 hrs, may transfer in Brno or Přerov), **Kraków**

(4/day, 4–6 hrs, transfer in Katowice, Poland and possibly Přerov, Czech Republic; one 5-hr overnight train), **Vienna** (8/day, 3–4 hrs, transfer in Brno, Břeclav, or Přerov), **Budapest** (6/day, 5.5–6 hrs, transfer in Brno or Přerov).

From Olomouc by Bus to: Rožnov (3/day, 2 hrs, transfer in Valašské Meziříčí and maybe also Hranice).

To Třeboň, Telč, and Třebíč: Take the bus or train to **Brno** (see above), then take the bus in the direction of **České Budějovice** (5/day Mon–Fri, 2/day Sat–Sun—see page 197).

Kroměříž

While Olomouc was the official seat of the Moravian archbishops, Kroměříž (KROH-myehr-eezh) was the site of their lavish summer château. In 1948, this castle and its enormous gardens were nationalized and opened to the public. Kroměříž—showing off the richness of this corner of the Czech Republic—is the most lavish and best-renovated Rococo castle in the country. The 19th-century English-style park, with lakes, woods, and Chinese pavilions, is good for a walk or picnic.

While there are no other worthwhile sights in town, the pleasant square, streets filled with little bakeries, and a chance to experience a small Moravian town offers a perfect complement to the grandeur of the archbishop's estate. The town and château of Kroměříž combine for a perfect half-day excursion from Olomouc to enjoy the genteel art and gentle life of Moravia.

ORIENTATION

Tourist Information
The humble TI on the main square hands out a useful map with brief descriptions of all major sights, as well as a list of events (Mon–Fri 8:30–17:00, Sat–Sun 9:00–13:00, open weekdays until 18:00 in July–Aug, closed Sun Nov–April, Velké Náměstí 45/50, tel. 573-331-473, www.mesto-kromeriz.cz).

Arrival in Kroměříž
Turn right out of the train station, then take the first left over the bridge. The main square (Velké Náměstí) and the entrance to the château are an easy 10-minute walk away.

Helpful Hints
Music: Throughout the summer, the city government joins forces with art schools and conservatories to enliven the historical spaces by holding weekly concerts. The quality of the

performers and the unique setting—in the château halls and gardens—make a visit worthwhile (ticket booking and purchase at the TI on Velké Náměstí, www.hudba-kromeriz.cz). The Kroměříž Music Summer Festival is held in September (tel. 573-341-400).

Internet Access: DC Internet Café, located on the main square, is right below the town museum (40 Kč/hr, Mon–Fri 10:00–19:00, Sat–Sun 13:00–19:00, Velké Náměstí 39).

SIGHTS

Archbishop's Château (Arcibiskupský Zámek)—Dominating the main square and the whole town, this château was rebuilt in Baroque style by archbishop Karel Lichtenstein (dubbed the "Moravian Richelieu") after an earlier castle was severely damaged in the Swedish siege during the Thirty Years' War. The furniture and decorations are in the Rococo style (from the second half of the 18th century). The breathtaking chandeliers are made of Czech crystal.

The château is famous for one historic event: The Austrian parliament moved here from unstable Vienna during the tumultuous year of 1848, when a wave of revolutions spread across the Hapsburg lands. The parliament drafted the first Austrian constitution in the château's main hall.

Hours: May–Sept Tue–Sun 9:00–17:00, closed Mon; April and Oct Sat–Sun only 9:00–17:00, closed Mon–Fri; closed Nov–March. Tel. 573-502-011, www.azz.cz.

Tours: You can see the art gallery (described next) and climb the tower (40 Kč) on your own, but you can tour the château interior only with a guide (90 Kč with a Czech-speaking group). Try asking for an English-language tour—you'll pay double, but you might be the only one on the tour. Tours run about every hour and last 70 minutes, with the time about evenly split between the first floor (eight rooms) and second floor (which has a beautifully painted ceiling depicting the history of the bishopric, and overlooks a stunning library interior with 80,000 books).

Art Gallery: Art-lovers should consider visiting the bishop's art gallery. Sure, it's not the Louvre—but it's the best Moravian collection of European paintings from 1400–1800, with works by Titian, Lucas Cranach, Albrecht Dürer, and Paolo Veronese (60 Kč, same hours as château).

Castle Garden (Podzámecká Zahrada)—This green space, filled with little ponds, exotic trees, and Chinese pavilions, offers a peaceful refuge. It's in the English style—wilder and more natural than the geometrically designed French gardens (July–Aug daily 5:30–20:30; May–June and Sept Tue–Sun 9:00–17:00, closed Mon; April and Oct Sat–Sun only, closed Mon–Fri; closed Nov–March).

SLEEPING

Kroměříž works best as a day trip from Olomouc, but if you want to see a concert and stay the night, try **$$ Hotel Bouček.** This well-renovated traditional townhouse on the main square rents 11 decent rooms (Sb-900 Kč, Db-1,400 Kč, extra bed-500 Kč, Velké Náměstí 108, tel. 573-342-777, hotel.boucek@seznam.cz).

EATING

All of these eateries are on or just off the main square (Velké Náměstí).

Bistro u Zámku is a popular place to sip a frappé or iced coffee (daily, on the corner of main square next to the château).

Zámecká Myslivna (Château Hunting Lodge) specializes in game. Your venison might have been shot by the archbishop, who still comes here during the summer (Sun–Thu 11:00–22:00, Fri–Sat 11:00–24:00, just off main square, Sněmovní Náměstí 41).

Radniční Kavárna is perfect if you want to eat on cushioned chairs outside—because it's a bit stuffy inside (daily 9:00–22:00, at top of main square across street from Town Hall).

Bistro Avion, a blue-collar, self-service cafeteria on the main square, is good for a basic, filling meal (Mon–Fri 6:00–18:00, Sat 8:00–15:00, Sun 7:00–14:00). The place has no menus—just point to what looks good, and wash it down with Slovakia's best beer, Zlatý Bažant (Golden Pheasant).

TRANSPORTATION CONNECTIONS

Day-trip from Olomouc to Kroměříž: From Olomouc, take one of the frequent trains in the direction of Přerov and Břeclav (hourly, 7:31 or 9:30 train is convenient). Get off at Hulín (the stop after Přerov on fast trains, 45 min), walk through the train station to the other side of the building, and hop on the small motor train to Kroměříž (departure scheduled to coincide with the arrival of Břeclav-bound trains, 8 min). On the way back, most trains from Kroměříž to Hulín connect with an Olomouc-bound train.

WALLACHIA

The mountainous region of Wallachia (vah-LAH-chee-ah)—where Slovakia and Poland meet the eastern edge of the Czech Republic—is ideal for an escape into nature, where you can enjoy both the ruggedness of the mountains and the easy tourist facilities of an accessible recreational area.

Wallachia (Valašsko) is made up of three east–west ridges separating three long valleys. The Beskydy Mountains—the westernmost part of the Carpathian mountain range—make an impressive backdrop.

Wallachia has a sparse but proud population, the Wallachians (Valaši). They were originally Romanian shepherds who, following their sheep, drifted west along the pristine meadows and rugged canyons of the hauntingly beautiful Carpathians. In exchange for guarding the border, these shepherds received many privileges—most importantly, exemption from taxes.

Today, the Wallachians have their own tongue-in-cheek, tax-free "kingdom." In local restaurants and hotels, you can buy Wallachian "passports," which come with a brochure explaining in English why you should emigrate. The 90 Kč is a small price to pay for a passport when you consider that it frees you from the far-reaching clutches of the IRS.

Getting Around Wallachia

This region is best with a car. It's a headache, though doable, by public transportation. **Olomouc** is the nearest big city. From Olomouc, direct buses take you to **Rožnov** (3/day, 2 hrs, transfer in Valašské Meziříčí and possibly Hranice). By train from Olomouc, you can get to **Frenštát pod Radhoštěm** (near **Trojanovice** and **Pustevny**, 8/day, transfer in Valašské Meziříčí, most require additional transfer in Hranice na Moravě, allow 2.5 hrs total). From

Rožnov by bus to Frenštát pod Radhoštěm is a 20-minute ride (6/day). For specifics on getting up to the mountaintop at Pustevny, see below.

Rožnov

Industrial Rožnov (ROHZH-novh), the largest town in the region, may not be worth an overnight stay, but it certainly merits a visit for its **Wallachian Open-Air Folk Museum** (Valašské Muzeum v Přírodě), rated ▲. The museum, which re-creates a traditional Wallachian vil-

lage, is divided into three parts. Touring the "Little Wooden Town" is sufficient to give you a good sense of Eastern European mountain architecture, which blends here with elements of Moravian house-building. The museum is also the resting place for the most distinguished Wallachians, among them the incredible runner Emil Zátopek, who won three gold medals at the Helsinki Olympics in 1952.

Cost, Hours, Location: 50 Kč, May–Sept daily 8:00–18:00; April Tue–Sun 9:00–17:00, closed Mon; Jan–March and Oct Tue–Sun 9:00–16:00, closed Mon; closed most of Nov and part of Dec (www.vmp.cz). On Rožnov's main square, you'll find direction markers for the museum (it's a 10-min walk).

Tours: Although you can visit the complex on your own, to fully appreciate the site, call a few days ahead to reserve an English-speaking guide (400 Kč for an hour-long tour, reserve at tel. 571-757-111 between 6:00–14:00, prohlidka@vmp.cz).

Pustevny

Pustevny (POO-stehv-nee, "Hermitage") is a small, pleasant resort atop the Beskydy (BEH-skih-dee) Mountains' most sacred ridge, in a spot where a legendary hermit once lived. The style of the mountain huts here is an imaginative combination of Art Nouveau and wooden village architecture. Peak season here is June through August for hiking, and from Christmas through Easter for skiing. Restaurants are open only on weekends during other months.

The 30-minute **hike** from Pustevny along the red-marked trail on the ridge toward the west will take you to a statue of Radegast,

the old Slavic god of sun, friendship, and harvest. (Eerily, the area around the statue is one of the few places in the Czech Republic without mobile-phone coverage.) If you hike farther along the ridge for two miles, you'll reach the top of the sacred Radhošť mountain and statues of the Slavic ninth-century missionaries, St. Cyril and St. Methodius. They hold a page of the beginning of the Gospel according to John, which they translated for the Slavic people more than 1,100 years ago. A wooden church dedicated to these two patrons of all Slavs stands behind the statue.

At the base of the mountain below Pustevny is the crossroads village of **Trojanovice** (TROH-yah-noh-veet-seh). Basically a wide spot in the road, it offers nothing of interest besides a nice hotel (Hotel u Kociána—see below) and convenient chairlift access up to Pustevny (also described below).

Getting to Pustevny

To get to Trojanovice and Pustevny by **public transportation,** take the train to the town of Frenštát pod Radhoštěm (2 miles away). Arrange a pickup with the Hotel u Kociána or take a taxi (less than 100 Kč). A 15-minute walk up the road from Trojanovice's Hotel u Kociána takes you to a chairlift that runs up to Pustevny (40 Kč, hourly, takes about 15 min, daily in summer 9:00–18:00, daily in winter 9:00–16:00, confirm hours with hotel off-season). On arriving in Pustevny, be sure to check the schedule for the last chairlift back down to Trojanovice.

If you're **driving,** follow signs from Frenštát to Trojanovice; the Hotel u Kociána is on the left. The easiest way up to Pustevny is to simply park at the hotel and walk to the chairlift (described above). If you want to drive all the way to Pustevny, you'll have to take the long (45-min), poorly marked route around the back of the mountain. The advantage of driving is that the route takes you through Rožnov, so you can stop on the way to tour the Wallachian Open-Air Folk Museum (see above).

SLEEPING AND EATING

(20 Kč = about $1, country code: 420)

At Pustevny
$ Hotel Tanečnica, large and modern, is the best option for sleeping on top of the mountain (Db-1,000 Kč, 20 percent less off-season, includes pool, tel. 556-835-341, www.tanecnica.cz).

The nearby **Koliba u Záryša** restaurant, with a shepherd's-hut setting, serves great Wallachian food: garlic soup and hearty dishes of pork, potatoes, kraut, and cabbage.

Below Pustevny, in Trojanovice
$ Hotel u Kociána, a popular local hangout run by a can-do family, is a delightful alternative to the comparatively impersonal Hotel Tanečnica (Db-800–1,200 Kč, cash preferred, tel. 556-835-206, mobile 604-858-967, www.hotelukociana.cz).

TRANSPORTATION CONNECTIONS

From Frenštát pod Radhoštěm (near Trojanovice) by Train to: Olomouc (8/day, transfer in Valašské Meziříčí, most require additional transfer in Hranice na Moravě, allow 2.5 hrs total).

MIKULOV WINE REGION

The Mikulov region produces the Czech Republic's most famous wine. The village of Pavlov, with its beautiful rural architecture and wine cellars filled with singing Moravians, is the ideal place to experience Moravia's wine culture. The surrounding Pálava Hills and water sports make days here as enjoyable as the nights. The historic town of Mikulov—the center of the region—is a pleasant lunch stop between Pavlov and Lednice. And the large Lednice–Valtice complex of castles and 19th-century English-style parks is a unique feat of environmentally friendly landscaping.

Getting Around the Mikulov Wine Region

The main railway junction of Břeclav is the gateway to the Mikulov wine region.

By Train and Bus from Břeclav to: Mikulov (10 trains/day, 30 min, goes through Valtice), **Valtice** (10 trains/day, 15 min), **Lednice** (8 buses/day Mon–Fri, 4/day Sat–Sun, 20 min; on summer weekends, a cute historical train runs between Břeclav and Lednice: 4/day, 20 min), **Prague** (9/day direct, 3 hrs, most arrive at Prague's Holešovice station), **Olomouc** (10/day, 2 hrs, may transfer in Brno or Přerov). To get to **Pavlov,** you'll first take the

train to Mikulov (see above), then a bus to Pavlov (4/day Mon–Fri, 1/day Sat–Sun, 30 min).

By Car: Although it's possible to connect all these destinations by public transportation, renting a car in Břeclav or elsewhere can save lots of time (see Mikulov's "Helpful Hints" on page 256).

Pavlov and the Pálava Hills

The traditional village of Pavlov, stretching from the banks of the Nové Mlýny dam up toward the dramatic hilltop ruin of Dívčí Hrady ("Girls' Castle"), has everything you need for a fun one- or two-day wine adventure. In deep brick cellars, you can taste local wines and spicy Hungarian salami while hearing the dreamy tunes of Moravian songs. You'll see Moravian village architecture; choose from a wealth of neat, family-run pensions; take nature walks along the wooded slopes of the white Pálava Hills; and tackle an expanse of water however you like, from swimming to windsurfing.

The only drawback is communication: While German works well, few locals speak more than broken English. But fear not—the genuine hospitality of the locals makes struggling with the language barrier both fun and rewarding. So be brave, and pull your hands and your phrase books out of those pockets.

ACTIVITIES

Wandering the Town—Česká street, stretching from Restaurace u Venuše (described below) to the parking lot above the church, is lined with traditional vintners' houses. The owners live on the first floor, wine is pressed on the ground floor, and extensive cellars run deep into the mountain. The farmsteads along the park by the church are some of the finest examples of Moravian Baroque village architecture.

Wine Cellars—Ask your host whether a dulcimer band is playing in any of the wine cellars. Locals often bring their guitars along. September is a wild month here—the whole country converges on the region, and everyone drinks the hugely popular young wine (burčák).

Floating on the River—During the day, the Yacht Club at the bottom of the village rents a variety of floatables, including paddleboats, canoes, and windsurfing boards. The shallow water is warm for most of the summer, and the beaches seem endless.

Three successive dams, planned for decades as part of an immense irrigation project intended to water most of southern Moravia, were completed in the early 1990s. By then, the collectivized fields and vineyards had been returned to individual owners. For these small producers, building channels or pumping water from the dams turned out to be too expensive. So in the end, the costly project boosted the local economy only indirectly—by drawing in thousands of fishing and sailing enthusiasts.

Hiking in the Pálava Hills—For a perfect half-day hike, follow the green-marked trail from the church past Pension a Restaurace Florián, then up through the beech woods to the ruined castle (1.5 miles, 45 min). Continue on the ridge, on the red-marked trail, to the highest point of the hills, called Děvín (60 min). Descend on the other side of the mountain to Klentnice. From here, you can return to Pavlov either along the blue-marked trail through the woods on the western slopes of the Pálava Hills, or along the educational winemaking route (marked by white signs with diagonal green stripes) through the vineyards east of the hills.

SLEEPING

During hot summer months and in September, getting a room on short notice can be difficult—book ahead.

$$ Hotel Iris, part of a Czech chain, is the only real hotel in the village. Its 22 rooms are relatively expensive, but it's a suitable fallback if the pensions (below) are full. The standardized experience comes with TV, a sauna, and a fitness center. The ease of communication in English might make up for the lack of village

Mikulov Region

Sleep Code

(20 Kč = about $1, country code: 420)
S = Single, **D** = Double/Twin, **T** = Triple, **Q** = Quad, **b** = bathroom, **s** = shower only. Unless otherwise noted, credit cards are accepted, English is spoken, and breakfast is included.

To help you sort easily through these listings, I've divided the rooms into two categories based on the price for a standard double room with bath:

$$ Higher Priced—Most rooms 1,000 Kč or more.
$ Lower Priced—Most rooms less than 1,000 Kč.

---

ambience (Sb-800 Kč, Db-1,400 Kč, tel. 519-515-310, www.hotel -iris.cz, hotel.iris@vasstav.cz).

$ Pension a Restaurace Florián, with six homey rooms, is run by an energetic woman who speaks no English. Fortunately, both her son and daughter, who worked in England and are some of the best English-speakers in the village, are usually around to help. They would like to see more Americans come to Pavlov, so even if their place is booked up, ask for help arranging a room elsewhere. They make you feel like part of the family—home-cooking is available all day. In the evenings, they run a wine cellar–restaurant behind the pension. They're also able to recommend other nearby wine cellars where English is spoken (Db-750 Kč, 5 percent discount for readers of this book, Podhradní 195, tel. 519-515-323, mobile 736-760-463, www.pensionflorian.cz, info @pensionflorian.cz).

$ Pension u Bednářů rents 23 rooms scattered through three houses—two traditional, one hotelesque. The owners, who speak only German, also run their own wine cellar–restaurant (Db-820 Kč, rooms #110–113 have no windows, tel. 519-515-110, fax 519-515-341, mobile 607-108-450, penziony@breclavske.cz).

EATING

Your host can recommend a music performance or a wine tasting in one of the many small wine cellars in the village. In addition to the Restaurace u Venuše, both of the pensions listed above run large, traditional wine cellar–restaurants (daily 17:00–23:00).

Restaurace u Venuše is perhaps the most atmospheric of the wine cellar–restaurants. The owner, Antonín Brenko, has been making and serving wine here for 40 seasons. A good host, he's keen on finding a wine to suit the tastes of each of his guests. He's a treasure trove of hospitality and wine knowledge, but speaks only

Mikulov Wines

Czech wine is more than just a drink—it's a way of life. Although the Moravians might not have captured the sweetness of the Portuguese varieties, they did manage to ferment the taste of grapes into their own authentic culture. Without experiencing the wine tradition of southern Moravia, you will have missed a good part of the country's spirit.

Wine has been made in the Mikulov region since Roman times. Because no Roman soldier would fight without his daily two-liter ration of wine, and since it was difficult to transport unpasteurized wine over long distances, the 10th legion of Marcus Aurelius planted its own vines on this region's limestone hills (which reminded them of their homes in Tuscany). The Slavs and the Germans found the vines long after the Romans were gone and continued the tradition. In the 16th century, Anabaptist refugees from Switzerland brought new energy to the winemaking process. Today, the warm climate and the soil rich in calcium (from the limestone) make the Mikulov region one of the best wine-producing areas in Eastern Europe.

The most commonly used grapes are Ryzlink, Veltlínské Zelené, Rulandské Bílé, Chardonnay, and Sauvignon for whites, and Svatovavřinecké, Frankovka, and Cabernet Sauvignon for reds. The locally bred grapes are Pálava and Aurelius. The variety of grape is only one factor that contributes to each wine's distinct taste. Vintners discern wines by the type of soil in which they grow, the orientation of the slope (which determines the amount of sun), and—most importantly—the sugar content. The best

Czech and German. Antonín can also help you arrange a home stay in some of the neighboring villages (closed Sun–Mon, tel. 519-415-742 or 519-515-230, www.sklepymoravy.cz).

Mikulov

An important border town on the amber road from the Baltic Sea to the Adriatic, Mikulov (MEE-kuh-lohv, think "Mikulov, not war") was briefly the capital of Moravia. When the Austrian kings expelled the Jews from Austria in the early 1400s, the Jews settled here on the border, making up half the town's

wines are from hand-picked late vintages, with sugar content reaching 27 percent.

The quirky local specialties are straw and ice wines. The grapes for straw wines mature in barns for months spread on dry straw. Ice wines, a Moravian and German specialty, are made by storing grapes for most of the winter, then pressing them at negative 6 degrees Celsius. As these two wines are very difficult to make—the process is practically alchemy, as even the best vintners cannot predict which grapes will turn into a good ice wine—they are also the most expensive. A tiny .3-liter bottle (about 10 oz.) costs more than 700 Kč.

The communists mismanaged wine production by using bad shoots prone to diseases. Over the last 15 years, vintners have replaced most of these old vines with young, quality ones. Moravian wines improve from year to year. Look for vintages from odd years, which have been better in the past decade than even ones. Among older vintages, 1994 was outstanding.

One of the most prominent wine companies in the country is Reisten, the exclusive supplier of Prague's luxury restaurants and the president of the Czech Republic. Reisten produces its wines in Pavlov, in the cellars next door to Restaurace u Venuše. The owner will take you down for a tasting (open most of the day; coming from the church and Florián, turn left by Restaurace u Venuše and then look on your right for a small *Reisten* sign; tel. 519-515-222, mobile 777-151-299).

Mikulov Region

population and forming the largest Czech Jewish community outside of Prague. The railway line to Vienna bypassed Mikulov, condemning it to a stagnation that mercifully protected it from Industrial Age construction. Mikulov was the seat of the leading Moravian rabbi until World War II.

Today, all that remains of Mikulov's past glory are a synagogue, a cemetery, and a few traditional houses along Husova street below the castle. Still, it's an enjoyable and historic town that comes alive during vintage festivals. Mikulov makes a fine lunch stop if you're driving to Lednice or Vienna.

ORIENTATION

Tourist Information

The TI on the main square is a wealth of information about the entire region. They give out free maps and good biking information, and can help arrange accommodations (Mon–Fri 8:00–18:00,

Sat–Sun 9:00–18:00, tel. 519-510-855 or 519-512-200, www
.mikulov.cz).

Helpful Hints

Bike Rental: A popular way to explore the surrounding wine
region is on bicycle (the TI hands out a free map describing
trails and can direct you to a rental place).

Car Rental: If you're arriving in the Czech Republic from Vienna
or Budapest and will need to return there, consider getting
off in nearby Břeclav to pick up a rental car. **Bors** in Břeclav is
handy and rents Renaults (1 day with insurance and unlimited
mileage starts at 850 Kč; Mon–Fri 8:00–17:00, Sat 8:00–11:00,
closed Sun, tel. 519-444-200, mobile 731-606-242, www.bors
.cz, safrankova@bors.cz). To get to Bors from Břeclav's train
station, either take a cab (less than 50 Kč) or walk for 10 minutes (exit into park, turn left, walk along main street past the
post office, then under railway bridge to gas station and Bors
Renault dealership).

SIGHTS

Of the scant sights in town, only the **synagogue museum,** which
chronicles the history of local Jews, is worth a visit (daily July–Aug
10:00–17:00, May–June and Sept 13:00–17:00, closed Oct–April,
on Husova street). You can skip the large castle complex in the
middle of the town; the castles in nearby Lednice and Valtice are
far more interesting (see below).

SLEEPING

$$ Hotel Tanzberg is a beguiling Baroque townhouse, formerly
the home of one of Mikulov's richest Jewish families. When you
step in the atmospheric interior, you're transported back to the
1930s (Db-900–1,300 Kč, apartment-2,000 Kč, across from syna-
gogue at Husova 8, tel. 519-510-692, fax 519-511-695, www.hotel
-tanzberg.cz, provoz@hotel-tanzberg.cz).

EATING

Restaurace Alfa, the best restaurant in town, is on the main
square in the white Renaissance house with sgraffiti decorations.
Their fresh daily specials, available from 11:00, land on your table
before the foam settles on your beer (daily 10:00–22:00, Náměstí
27, tel. 519-510-877).

At **Le Patio Café,** in a graceful Renaissance courtyard com-
plete with balconies and a gallery, you can peacefully sip a Turkish

coffee and munch sweet Moravian crêpes under the blue sky (open daily, enter from left side of same house as Restaurace Alfa and walk through the passageway).

TRANSPORTATION CONNECTIONS

From Mikulov to: Pavlov (4 buses/day Mon–Fri, 1/day Sat–Sun, 30 min), **Valtice** (10 trains/day, 15 min), **Lednice** (2 buses Mon–Fri afternoons only, 20 min), **Moravský Krumlov** (2 trains every afternoon, 1.5 hrs, transfer in Hrušovany).

Lednice and Valtice

The twin towns of Lednice and Valtice—connected by a lush, walkable greenbelt—each boast a proud castle. Located along the Austrian border southeast of Mikulov, they make up one of the Czech Republic's most visit-worthy castle regions.

Since the 1200s, Lednice and Valtice have been part of the Mikulov-based Lichtenstein family. The Lichtensteins were to South Moravia what the Rožmberks were to South Bohemia: either caring benefactors who turned marshes and beech woods into the promised land, or despotic aristocrats who mercilessly impoverished their serfs...depending on whom you ask. While the Rožmberks died out in the early 1600s, the Lichtensteins thrived during the Thirty Years' War (they wisely stayed loyal to the victorious Hapsburgs) and continued to enrich the region until the 1940s. While Valtice was their winter residence, they summered at Lednice (even though Lednice means "fridge," so named because

this stretch of the Dyje River is known for frequent frosts). Of the two castles, Lednice is more interesting to tour.

An even more compelling reason to make the short side-trip from Mikulov or Břeclav is the spectacular 19th-century English-style park, which extends for miles between the Lednice and Valtice castles. Native oaks and exotic cedars span their gnarled branches over wild meadows and green lakes, Romantic castles and Taj Mahal-style minarets rise in the middle of woods like apparitions, and rare birds silently glide through the sky.

ORIENTATION

The "Lednice–Valtice Area" (Lednicko–Valtický Areál) is made up of two small towns, about four miles apart: Lednice (LEHD-neet-seh, pop. 2,400) and Valtice (VAHLT-eet-seh, pop. 3,600).

Tourist Information

Lednice's TI, by the main parking lot in front of the entrance to the Lednice Castle, has free Internet access and sells an inexpensive info brochure and maps of the garden complex (June–Aug daily 8:00–17:00, shorter hours April–May and Sept–Oct, closed Nov–March; tel. 519-340-986, www.lednice.cz). For information on Valtice, see www.radnice-valtice.cz.

SIGHTS

In Lednice

Lednice Castle (Zámek Lednice)—This castle is the Moravian answer to England's Windsor Castle, an immense structure built in English Neo-Gothic style. Today, the castle houses the university for winemakers; anyone is welcome to sign up for a short summer course.

To tour the palace, choose between two routes: Route A (80 Kč) goes through the halls, and Route B (100 Kč) through the apartments (May–Aug Tue–Sun 9:00–12:00 & 13:00–17:15, closed Mon; Sept Tue–Sun 9:00–12:00 & 13:00–16:15, closed Mon; April and Oct Sat–Sun only 9:00–12:00 & 13:00–15:15, closed Mon–Fri; closed Nov–March; tel. 519-340-128).

Castle Parks—From Lednice Castle, parks extend both north and south. The 19th-century nobles loved everything Romantic, peppering these woods with a quirky architectural hodgepodge: a Neo-Roman aqueduct, a Neo-Gothic castle ruin, a Neo-Greek temple, a victory column, a rendezvous pavilion, and so on. Navigate between these perfect dating spots with the help of the map from the TI (see "Tourist Information," above).

Cost: Depending on how many of the recommended park attractions you visit, plan on spending about 190–230 Kč per person.

Getting There: To reach the minaret from Lednice Castle, you can walk (1 mile), hire a horse carriage (30 min), or take a boat. Boats and carriages depart from the little dam just behind the castle; prices depend on the number of riders. Although most horse-carriage rides throughout Europe are tourist traps, here it feels appropriate to ride through the alleys like the nobles once did—even the school groups do it. A good plan is to ride to the minaret and walk back.

❍ Self-Guided Tour: Here are some highlights of the parks.

The **Palm Greenhouse,** located near the castle entrance, takes you from Moravia to the tropics (50 Kč, similar hours as castle but open even during winter). Notice the construction above you: one of the oldest examples of a cast-iron roof in Europe. Created in England in the 1830s, this innovation was one of the great technical marvels of the 19th century, gradually spreading to create spacious train stations and market halls throughout Europe.

From the greenhouse, it's a five-minute walk to the predator bird show; en route, you'll see a small **archery stand.** If you've ever dreamed of being William Tell, stop here and try your skill on the medieval and modern crossbows. No need to bring an apple or a son—they provide the target discs and instruction (60 Kč for five shots, daily in summer, weekends only in spring and fall).

The 45-minute show of live **predator birds** features more than 20 kinds of birds from all over the world. The falcons, merlins, marsh harriers, buzzards, and goshawks demonstrate their hunting skills on simulated rabbits and quails. Some are breathtakingly fast, others comically slow. You can leave whenever you want (20 Kč for short visit, 60 Kč for whole show, pick up English brochure in ticket tent that describes every bird; July–Aug  daily at 11:30, 14:15, and 16:30; May–June and Sept weekends at 12:00 and 15:00, plus occasional shows during the week; call mobile 608-100-440 for details).

My favorite part of the park stretches north, from the castle to the minaret. The **minaret** is an impressive bit of Romantic-era garden planning that copies the kind of Muslim-style minarets that flank the Taj Mahal in India. Those climbing its 302 winding steps (60 Kč) are rewarded with a grand view. Locals say that Count Alois Josef I intended to build a new church for the village of Lednice, but no plan seemed quite right to the villagers. Their pickiness finally irritated the count so much that he decided to build a mosque with a minaret instead of a church. The mosque never materialized, but the minaret did (completed in 1804). Since the ground around the Dyje River is made up of moving sands, the 200-foot-tall tower had to be anchored almost as deep underground, on beech and oak pilings. The minaret's architect, Josef Hardtmuth, was a versatile genius. The most successful of his patents was the idea of mixing graphite and mud, and coating it with wood. The pencil factory he founded (and which bears his name) is still one of the largest in Europe.

One scholar dates the minaret a few centuries back. For a short period, the area was part of the vast Mogul Empire, ruled by Persian-speaking Muslims and centered in northern India. The great Mogul emperor Aurangzeb (1618–1707) subdued even the mighty Turks and expanded his empire from Sri Lanka to southern Moravia. The minaret, which marks the northernmost point of his exploits, was purportedly built by the Delhi "World Conqueror" to give thanks to Allah.

The four Arabic inscriptions on the sides of the minaret roughly translate: "There is no God except God, and Mohammed is his prophet. The world betrayed its people. Do not forsake your worldly possessions. There is no difference between wealth and renunciation. True happiness can be reached only in the world beyond. Only through industry and hard work can you reach well-being in this world. When fate stands against you, all plans lose meaning; indeed, without the help of fate, man does not reach redemption."

TRANSPORTATION CONNECTIONS

Consider taking the bus to Lednice, walking through the gardens to Valtice (a level four-mile stroll), and then taking the train from there.

From Lednice by Bus to: Mikulov (2/afternoon Mon–Fri only, 20 min).

From Valtice by Train to: Mikulov (10/day, 15 min), **Prague** (hourly, 4 hrs, one transfer), **Olomouc** (3/day, 2.5–4 hrs, several transfers).

CZECH HISTORY AND LANGUAGE

HISTORY

The Czechs have always been at a crossroads of Europe—between the Slavic and Germanic worlds, between Catholicism and Protestantism, and between Cold War East and West. As if having foreseen all of this, the mythical founder of Prague—the beautiful princess Libuše—named her city "Praha" (meaning "threshold" in Czech). Despite these strong external influences, the Czechs have retained their distinct culture...and a dark, ironic sense of humor to keep them laughing through it all.

Charles IV and the Middle Ages

Prague's castle put Bohemia on the map in the ninth century. About a century later, the region was incorporated into the German Holy Roman Empire. Within a couple hundred years, Prague was one of Europe's largest and most highly cultured cities.

The 14th century was Prague's Golden Age, when Holy Roman Emperor Charles IV (1316–1378) ruled from here. Born to a Luxemburg nobleman and a Czech princess, Charles IV was a dynamic man on the cusp of the Renaissance. He spoke five languages, counted Petrarch as a friend, imported French architects to make Prague a grand capital, founded the first university north of the Alps, and invigorated the Czech national spirit. (He popularized the legend of the good king Wenceslas to give his people a near mythical, King Arthur–type cultural standard-bearer.) Much of Prague's history and architecture (including the famous

Charles Bridge, Charles University, and St. Vitus Cathedral) can be traced to this man's rule. Under Charles IV, the Czech people gained esteem among Europeans.

Jan Hus and Religious Wars

Jan Hus (c. 1370–1415) was a local preacher and professor who got in trouble with the Vatican a hundred years before Martin Luther. Like Luther, Hus preached in the people's language rather than Latin. To add insult to injury, he complained about Church corruption. Tried for heresy and burned in 1415, Hus became both a religious and a national hero. While each age has defined Hus to its liking, the way he challenged authority while staying true to himself has long inspired and rallied the Czech people. (For more on Hus, see the sidebar on page 51.)

Inspired by the reformist ideas of Jan Hus, the Czechs rebelled against both the Roman Catholic Church and German political control. This burst of independent thought led to a period of religious wars, and ultimately the loss of autonomy to Vienna. Ruled by the Hapsburgs of Austria, Prague stagnated—except during the rule of King Rudolf II (1552–1612), a Holy Roman Emperor. With Rudolf living in Prague, the city again emerged as a cultural and intellectual center. Astronomers Johannes Kepler, Tycho Brahe, and other scientists flourished, and much of the inspiration for Prague's great art can be attributed to the king's patronage.

Not long after this period, Prague entered one of its darker spells. The Thirty Years' War (1618–1648) began in Prague when Czech Protestant nobles, wanting religious and political autonomy, tossed two Catholic Hapsburg officials out of the window of the castle. (This was one of Prague's many defenestrations—a uniquely Czech solution to political discord, in which offending politicians were thrown out the window.) The Czech Estates Uprising lasted for two years, ending in a crushing defeat of the Czech army in the Battle of White Mountain (1620), which marked the end of Czech freedom. Twenty-seven leaders of the uprising were executed (today commemorated by crosses on Prague's Old Town Square—see page 49), most of the old Czech nobility was dispossessed, and Protestants had to leave the country or convert to Catholicism. Often called "the first world war" because it engulfed so many nations, the Thirty Years' War was particularly tough on Prague. During this period, its population dropped from 60,000 to 25,000. The result of this war was 300 years of Hapsburg rule from afar, as Prague became a German-speaking backwater of Vienna.

Notable Czechs

These prominent historical figures are listed in chronological order.

St. Wenceslas (907–935): Bohemian duke who allied the Czechs with the Holy Roman Empire. He went on to become the Czech Republic's patron saint, and it is he who is memorialized as a "good king" in the Christmas carol. For more on Wenceslas, see page 74.

Jan Hus (c. 1370–1415): Proto-Protestant Reformer who was burned at the stake (see page 51).

John Amos Comenius (1592–1670): "Teacher of Nations" and Protestant exile (Jan Amos Komenský in Czech), whose ideas paved the way for modern education (see page 236).

Antonín Dvořák (1841–1904): Inspired by a trip to America, he composed his *New World Symphony*. For more on Czech composers, see page 144.

Tomáš Garrigue Masaryk (1850–1937): Sociology professor, writer, politician, and spiritual reformer. He was idolized during his lifetime as the "dearest father" of the Czechoslovak democracy (see page 102).

Jára Cimrman (c. 1853–1914): Illustrious, fictional inventor, explorer, philosopher, and all-around genius. Despite being overwhelmingly voted the "Greatest Czech of All Time" in a recent nationwide poll, he was not awarded the title; for details on the controversy, see page 88.

Alfons Mucha (1860–1939): You might recognize his turn-of-the-century Art Nouveau posters of pretty girls entwined in vines. Visit his museum in Prague (see page 79), marvel at his stained-glass window in St. Vitus Cathedral (page 105), and make a pilgrimage to see his magnum opus, the *Slav Epic,* in the town of Moravský Krumlov (see page 221).

Franz Kafka (1883–1924): While working for a Prague insurance firm, he wrote (in German) *The Metamorphosis* (man awakes as a cockroach), *The Trial, The Castle,* and other psychologically haunting stories and novels.

Milan Kundera (1929–): Wrote the novel *The Unbearable Lightness of Being* (which became a film). For more on Czech authors and filmmakers, see page 275.

Václav Havel (1936–): The country's first post-Soviet president, also known as a playwright and philosopher.

Martina Navrátilová (1956–): Tennis star of the 1980s. For more on Czech sports, see page 147.

It's Not You, It's Me: The Velvet Divorce

In the autumn of 1989, hundreds of thousands of Czechs and Slovaks streamed into Prague to demonstrate on Wenceslas Square. Their "Velvet Revolution" succeeded, and Czechoslovakia's communist regime peacefully excused itself.

This is the history behind the split. Ever since they joined with the Czechs in 1918, the Slovaks felt they were ruled from Prague (unmistakably the political, economic, and cultural center of the country), rather than from their own capital. And the Czechs, for their part, resented the financial burden of carrying their poorer neighbors to the east. In the post-communist world, the Czechs found themselves with a 10 percent unemployment rate...compared to 20 or 30 percent unemployment in the Slovak lands. In this new world of flux and freedom, long-standing tensions came to a head.

The dissolution of Czechoslovakia began over a hyphen, as the Slovaks wanted to rename the country Czecho-Slovakia. Ideally, this symbolic move would come with a redistribution of powers: two capitals and two UN reps, but one national bank and a single currency. The Slovaks were also less enthusiastic about abandoning the communist society altogether, since the Soviet regime had left them with a heavily industrialized economy that depended on a socialist element for survival.

Initially, many Czechs couldn't understand the Slovaks' demands. The first post-communist president of Czechoslovakia,

Czech Nationalist Revival

The end of Prague as a "German" city came gradually. As the Industrial Revolution attracted Czech farmers and peasants into the cities, the demographics of the Czech population centers began to shift. Between 1800 and 1900, though it remained part of the Hapsburg Empire, Prague went from being an essentially German town to a predominantly Czech one. As in the rest of Europe, the 19th century was a time of great nationalism, when the age of divine kings and ruling families came to a fitful end. The Czech spirit was stirred by the completion of Prague's St. Vitus Cathedral, the symphonies of Antonín Dvořák, and the operas of Bedřich Smetana performed in the new National Theatre.

After the Hapsburgs' Austro-Hungarian Empire suffered defeat in World War I, their vast holdings broke apart and became independent countries. Among these was a union of Bohemia, Moravia, and Slovakia, the brainchild of a clever politician named Tomáš Garrigue Masaryk (see page 102). The new nation, Czechoslovakia, was proclaimed in 1918, with Prague as its capital.

the Czech Václav Havel, made matters worse when he took a rare trip to the Slovak half of his country in 1990. In a fit of terrible judgment, Havel boldly promised he'd close the ugly, polluting Soviet factories in Slovakia...seemingly oblivious to the fact that many Slovaks still depended on these factories for survival. Havel left in disgrace and visited the Slovak lands only twice more in the next two and a half years.

In June 1992, the Slovak nationalist candidate Vladimír Mečiar fared surprisingly well in the elections—suggesting that the Slovaks were serious about secession. The politicians plowed ahead, getting serious about the split in September 1992. The transition took only three months from start to finish.

The people of Czechoslovakia never actually voted on the separation; in fact, public opinion polls in both regions were two-thirds *against* the split. This makes Slovakia quite possibly the only country in the history of the world to gain independence... even though its citizens didn't want it.

The Velvet Divorce became official on January 1, 1993, and each country ended up with its own capital, currency, and head of state. The Slovaks let loose a yelp of excitement, and the Czechs emitted a sigh of relief. The divorce dissolved the tensions, and a decade and a half later, most Czechs and Slovaks still feel closer to each other than to any other nationality.

Troubled 20th Century

Independence lasted only 20 years. In the notorious Munich Agreement of September 1938—much to the dismay of the Czechs and Slovaks—Great Britain and France peacefully ceded to Hitler the so-called "Sudetenland" (a fringe around the edge of Bohemia, populated mainly by people of German descent; see page 218). It wasn't long before Hitler seized the rest of Czechoslovakia...and the Holocaust began.

For centuries, Prague's cultural makeup consisted of a rich mix of Czech, German, and Jewish people—historically, they were about evenly divided. But only 5 percent of the Jewish population survived the Holocaust. After World War II ended, the three million people of Germanic descent who lived in Czechoslovakia were pushed into Germany. This forced resettlement—which led to the deaths of untold numbers of Germans—was the idea, among others, of Czechoslovak President Edvard Beneš, who had been ruling from exile in London throughout the war (see page 184). As a result of both of these policies (the Holocaust and the expulsion of Germans), today's Czech Republic is largely homogenous—about

The Wisdom of Babička Míla ("Granny Míla")

Co-author Honza Vihan's grandmother, Bohumila Vihanová, was born in 1907 in the Austro-Hungarian town of Prag (today's Praha), which was then ruled from Vienna. In the 101 years since, she's lived under seven different governments: Hapsburgs, interwar Czechoslovakia, Nazis, communists, post-communist Czechoslovakia, the Czech Republic, and the European Union. Wise beyond even her many years, she counsels family and visitors alike as follows:

- "I liked each change, because it always brought something new."
- "You must be able to take the best from whatever comes."
- "When the communists took over, that was bad—really bad. But then, my mother used to say, 'There's no point in crying over spilled milk. There's enough water in it already.' So, I tried to get by, and somehow we managed to live through it all."
- "The main thing is to keep your inner balance."
- "You should never take yourself too seriously."
- "Let everyone do whatever they want, as long as they believe something and behave accordingly."
- "Money will always be here. We won't."
- "Parents should never mix in their children's lives."
- "Good health and happy mind!"

95 percent Czechs.

Although Prague escaped the bombs of World War II, it went directly from the Nazi frying pan into the communist fire. A local uprising freed the city from the Nazis on May 8, 1945, but the Soviets "liberated" them on May 9.

The early communist chapter (1948–1968) was a mixture of misguided zeal, Stalinist repressions, and attempts to wed socialism with democracy. The "Prague Spring" period—initiated by a young generation of reform-minded communists in 1968—came to an abrupt halt because of Soviet tanks.

The charismatic leader, Alexander Dubček, was exiled (and made a forest ranger in the backwoods), and the years following the unsuccessful revolt were particularly disheartening. In the late 1980s, the communists began constructing Prague's huge Žižkov

TV tower (now the city's tallest structure)—not only to broadcast Czech TV transmissions, but also to jam Western signals. The Metro, built at about the same time, was intended for mass transit, but was also designed to be a giant fallout shelter for protection against capitalist bombs.

But the Soviet empire crumbled. Czechoslovakia regained its freedom in the student- and artist-powered 1989 "Velvet Revolution" (so called because there were no casualties...or even broken windows). Václav Havel, a writer who had been imprisoned by the communist regime, became Czechoslovakia's first post-communist president. In 1993, the Czech and Slovak Republics agreed on the "Velvet Divorce" and became two separate countries (see sidebar).

Havel ended his second (and, constitutionally, last) five-year term in 2003. While he's still admired by Czechs as a great thinker, writer, and fearless leader of the opposition movement during the communist days, many consider him less successful as a president. Some believe that the split of Czechoslovakia was partly caused by Havel's initial insensitivity to Slovak demands. The current president, Václav Klaus, was the pragmatic author of the economic reforms in the 1990s. Klaus' election in 2003 symbolized a change from revolutionary times, when philosophers became kings, to modern humdrum politics, when offices are gained by bargaining with the opposition (Communist votes in the Parliament were the decisive factor in Klaus' election). A major turning point occurred on May 1, 2004, when the Czech Republic joined the European Union (see page 100).

Today, while not without its problems, the Czech Republic is enjoying a growing economy and a strong democracy, and Prague has emerged as one of the most popular tourist destinations in Europe.

LANGUAGE

Hurdling the Language Barrier

The language barrier in the Czech Republic is no bigger than in Western Europe. In fact, I find that it's even easier to communicate in Český Krumlov than it is in Madrid. Immediately after the Iron Curtain fell in 1989, English-speakers were rare. But today, you'll find that most people in the tourist industry—and just about all young people—speak good English.

Of course, not everyone speaks English. You'll run into the most substantial language barriers in situations when you need to deal with a clerk or service person aged 40 or above (train station and post-office staff, maids, museum guards, bakers, and so on). Be reasonable in your expectations. Czech post-office clerks and museum ticket-sellers are every bit as friendly, cheery, and mul-tilingual as ours are in the US. Luckily, it's relatively easy to get your point across in these places. I've often bought a train ticket simply by writing out the name of my destination; the time I want to travel (using the 24-hour clock); and if necessary, the date I want to leave (day first, then month, then year). Here's an example of what I'd show a ticket-seller at a train station: "Olomouc – 17:30 – 15.7.2008."

If you speak German, it will likely come in handy—especially in the south of the country, where the economy depends in part on Austrian tourists from across the border.

Of course, the easiest way to hurdle the language barrier in any country is to learn some of the local words.

Pronunciation

Czech, a Slavic language closely related to its Polish and Slovak neighbors, bears little resemblance to Western European lan-guages. Slavic pronunciation can be tricky. In fact, when the first Christian missionaries, Cyril and Methodius, came to Eastern Europe a millennium ago, they invented a whole new alphabet to represent these strange Slavic sounds. Their Cyrillic alphabet is still used today in the eastern Slavic countries (such as Serbia and Russia).

Fortunately, the Czechs long ago converted to the same Roman alphabet we use, but they've added lots of differ-ent diacritics—little markings below and above letters—to represent a wide range of sounds. An acute accent *(á, é, í, ó, ú, ý)* means you linger on that vowel. The let-ter *c* always sounds like "ts" (as in "cats"). The little accent *(háček)* above the *č, š,* or *ž* makes it sound like "ch," "sh", or "zh" (as in "leisure"), respec-tively. A *háček* over *ě* makes it sound like "yeh."

Czech has one sound that occurs in no other language: *ř* (as in "Dvořák"), which sounds like a cross between a rolled "r" and "zh." Another unusual sound is *ň*, which is pronounced "ny" (as in "canyon"). These sounds are notoriously impossible for foreigners to duplicate; it's easiest just to replace them with simple "r" and "n" sounds (as we've done in the phonetics).

Give it your best shot. Use the phrases in this chapter. The locals will appreciate your efforts.

Czech Survival Phrases

English	Czech	Pronounced
Hello. (formal)	*Dobrý den.*	DOH-bree dehn
Hi. / Bye. (informal)	*Ahoj.*	AH-hoy
Do you speak English?	*Mluvíte anglicky?*	MLOO-vee-teh ANG-lits-kee
Yes. / No.	*Ano. / Ne.*	AH-no / neh
Please. / You're welcome. / Can I help you?	*Prosím.*	PROH-zeem
Thank you.	*Děkuji.*	DYACK-khuyi
I'm sorry. / Excuse me.	*Promiňte.*	PROH-meen-teh
Good.	*Dobře.*	DOHB-zhay
Goodbye.	*Na shledanou.*	nah SKLEH-dah-now
one / two	*jeden / dva*	YAY-dehn / dvah
three / four	*tři / čtyři*	tree / chuh-TEE-ree
five / six	*pět / šest*	pyeht / shehst
seven / eight	*sedm / osm*	SEH-dum / OH-sum
nine / ten	*devět / deset*	DEHV-yeht / DEH-seht
hundred	*sto*	stoh
thousand	*tisíc*	TYEE-seets
How much?	*Kolik?*	KOH-leek
local currency	*koruna (Kč)*	koh-ROO-nah
Where is...?	*Kde je...?*	gday yeh
...the toilet	*...vécé*	vayt-SAY
men	*muži*	MOO-zhee
women	*ženy*	ZHAY-nee
water / coffee	*voda / káva*	VOH-dah / KAH-vah
beer / wine	*pivo / víno*	PEE-voh / VEE-noh
Cheers!	*Na zdraví!*	nah zdrah-VEE
The bill, please.	*Účet, prosím.*	OO-cheht PROH-zeem

Here are some English words that all Czechs know: super, pardon, stop, menu, problem, and no problem.

Czech Place Names

Here's a rough pronunciation key for places mentioned in this book. For pronunciation help for specific sights and neighborhoods in Prague, see page 35.

Name	Pronounced
Beskydy (mountains)	BEH-skih-dee
Brno	BURR-noh
České Budějovice	CHESS-keh BOO-dyeh-yoh-vee-tseh
Český Krumlov	CHESS-key KROOM-loff
Karlštejn (castle)	KARL-shtayn
Konopiště (castle)	KOH-noh-peesh-tyeh
Křivoklát (castle)	KREE-vohk-laht
Kroměříž	KROH-myehr-eezh
Kutná Hora	KOOT-nah HO-rah
Lednice	LEHD-nee-tseh
Litoměřice	LEE-toh-myer-zhee-tseh
Mikulov	MEE-kuh-lohv
Moravský Krumlov	MOH-rahv-skee KROOM-loff
Mucha (artist)	MOO-kah
Olomouc	OH-loh-moats
Pálava (hills)	PAH-lah-vah
Pavlov	PAHV-lohv
Pustevny	POO-stehv-nee
Rožnov	ROHZH-nohv
Slavonice	SLAH-voh-neet-seh
Šumava (mountains)	SHOO-mah-vah
Telč	telch
Terezín	TEH-reh-zeen
Třebíč	TREH-beech
Třeboň	TREH-bohn
Trojanovice	TROH-yah-noh-vee-tseh
Valtice	VAHL-tee-tseh
Valašsko	vah-LAH-she-skoh

Czech History

APPENDIX

CONTENTS

RESOURCES

Tourist Information Offices

In the US

The Czech national tourist office in the US is a wealth of information. Before your trip, get the free general information packet and request any specifics you may want (such as regional and city maps and festival schedules). Basic information and a map are free; additional materials are $4 (prepaid by check). Call 212/288-0830 or visit www.czechtourism.com (info-usa@czechtourism.com).

In the Czech Republic

The tourist information office is your best first stop in any new town. Try to arrive, or at least telephone, before it closes. Have a list of questions ready, and pick up maps, brochures, and walking-tour information. In this book, I'll refer to a tourist information office as a **TI.**

In almost every town covered in this book, you'll find a TI on the main square. Most of these TIs offer English-speaking staff;

a free map of the town; a selection of hiking and biking maps; listings of events, activities, and accommodations (but usually not a room-booking service); bus and train schedules; Internet access; and an opportunity to buy concert tickets or hire a local guide. Almost all of the TIs in the Czech Republic are run by the town governments, which means their information isn't colored by a drive for profit.

Resources from Rick

Guidebooks and Online Updates

I've done my best to make sure that the information in this book is up-to-date, but things change. For the very latest, visit www .ricksteves.com/update. Also at my website, you'll find a valuable list of reports and experiences—good and bad—from fellow travelers who have used this book (www .ricksteves.com/feedback).

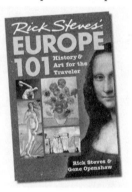

This book is one of more than 30 titles in my series on European travel, which includes country guidebooks, city and regional guidebooks, and my budget-travel skills handbook, *Rick Steves' Europe Through the Back Door*. My phrase books—for German, French, Italian, Spanish, and Portuguese—are practical and budget-oriented. My other books are *Europe 101* (a crash course on art and history, newly expanded and in full color), *European Christmas* (on traditional and modern-day celebrations), and *Postcards from Europe* (a fun memoir of my travels over 25 years). For a complete list of my books, see the inside of the last page of this book.

Public Television and Radio Shows

My TV series, *Rick Steves' Europe*, covers European destinations in 70 shows, including several episodes on Eastern Europe and one focusing on Prague. My weekly public radio show, *Travel with Rick Steves*, features interviews with travel experts from around the world. All the TV scripts and radio shows (which are easy and free to download to an MP3 player) are at www.ricksteves.com.

Free Audiotours

If your travels take you beyond the Czech Republic to France or Italy, take advantage of the free, self-guided audiotours we offer of the major sights in Paris, Florence, Rome,

Begin Your Trip at www.ricksteves.com

At our travel website, you'll find a wealth of free information on European destinations, including fresh monthly news and helpful tips from thousands of fellow travelers.

Our **online Travel Store** offers travel bags and accessories specially designed by Rick Steves to help you travel smarter and lighter. These include Rick's popular carry-on bags (wheeled and rucksack versions), money belts, totes, toiletries kits, adapters, other accessories, and a wide selection of guidebooks, planning maps, and DVDs.

Choosing the right **railpass** for your trip—amidst hundreds of options—can drive you nutty. We'll help you choose the best pass for your needs, plus give you a bunch of free extras.

Rick Steves' Europe Through the Back Door travel company offers **tours** with more than two-dozen itineraries and 450 departures reaching the best destinations in this book... and beyond. We offer several tours that visit Prague and destinations in the Czech Republic, including our seven-day in-depth Prague City Tour; our 12-day Berlin, Prague, and Vienna tour (which also includes the charming village of Český Krumlov); and our 17-day Best of Eastern Europe tour. You'll enjoy great guides, a fun bunch of travel partners (with small groups of generally around 25), and plenty of room to spread out in a big, comfy bus. You'll find European adventures to fit every vacation length. For all the details, and to get our Tour Catalog and a free Rick Steves Tour Experience DVD (filmed on location during an actual tour), visit www.ricksteves.com or call the Tour Department at 425-608-4217.

Appendix

and Venice. The audiotours, produced by Rick Steves and Gene Openshaw (the co-author of seven books in the Rick Steves series) are available through iTunes and at www.ricksteves.com. Simply download them onto your computer and transfer them to your iPod or MP3 player. (Remember to bring a Y-jack and extra set of ear buds for your travel partner.)

Maps

The black-and-white maps in this book are concise and simple. My staff, who are well-traveled in the Czech Republic, have created the maps to help you locate recommended places and get to local TIs, where you can pick up a more in-depth map of the city or region (usually free).

Many of Prague's bookstores have road, hiking, and cycling maps covering all of the country. One of the best is the Kiwi Map Store near Wenceslas Square (see page 139).

For drivers, I'd recommend a 1:100,000 atlas of the Czech Republic. If you have hiking plans (near Křivoklát, around Český Krumlov, in the Šumava and Beskydy Mountains, around Třeboň, or near Slavonice), get the excellent 1:50,000 *Edice Klub Českých Turistů* maps (based on military reconnaissance maps), or the much less detailed but sufficient 1:100,000 *Kartografie Praha* maps. Train travelers usually manage fine with the freebies they get at the local tourist offices.

Other Guidebooks

Especially if you'll be traveling beyond my recommended destinations, you may want some supplemental information. When you consider the improvements that they'll make in your $3,000 vacation, $30 for extra maps and books is money well-spent. Particularly for several people traveling by car, the extra weight and expense of a small trip library are negligible. One budget tip can save the price of an extra guidebook. Note that none of the following books are updated annually; check the publication date before you buy.

Lonely Planet's guides to the Czech and Slovak Republics and Prague are thorough, well-researched, and packed with good maps and hotel recommendations. The similar Rough Guides to these destinations are hip and insightful, written by British researchers.

Students and vagabonds will like the highly opinionated Let's Go series, which is updated by Harvard students. Let's Go is best for backpackers who travel by train or bus, stay in hostels, and seek out the youth and nightlife scene.

Older travelers enjoy guides from Frommer's, even though, like the Fodor's guide, they ignore alternatives that enable travelers to save money by dirtying their fingers in the local culture.

The popular, skinny green Michelin Guides are excellent, especially if you're driving. Michelin Guides are known for their city and sightseeing maps, dry but concise and helpful information on all major sights, and good cultural and historical background. English editions are sold in Europe at gas stations and tourist shops. The encyclopedic Blue Guides are dry but just right for scholarly types.

The Eyewitness series is popular for great, easy-to-grasp graphics and photos, 3-D cutaways of buildings, aerial-view maps of historic neighborhoods, and cultural background. But written content in Eyewitness is relatively skimpy, and the books weigh a ton. I simply borrow them for a minute from other travelers at certain sights to make sure that I'm aware of that place's highlights.

The Time Out travel guide to Prague provides good, detailed coverage, particularly on arts and entertainment.

Recommended Books and Movies

Czech children, adults, and grandparents delight in telling stories. In Czech fairy tales, there are no dwarfs and monsters. Czech writers invented the robot, the pistol, and Black Light Theater (an absurd show of illusion, puppetry, mime, and modern dance).

The most famous Czech literary figure is the title character of Jaroslav Hašek's *Good Soldier Švejk,* who frustrates the World War I Austro-Hungarian army he serves by cleverly playing dumb.

Bohumil Hrabal, writing in a stream-of-consciousness style, mixes tales he had heard in pubs from sailors, self-made philosophers, and kind-hearted prostitutes into enchanting fictions that express the Czech spirit and sense of humor better than any other work—the best are *I Served the King of England, The Town Where Time Stood Still*, and *Too Loud a Solitude*. (Jiří Menzel turned some of Hrabal's writings into films, the most famous of which is the Oscar-winning *Closely Watched Trains*—for more on Czech cinema, keep reading.)

Other well-known Czech writers include Václav Havel (playwright who went on to become Czechoslovakia's first post-communist president—he authored many essays and plays, including *The Garden Party*); Milan Kundera (author of *The Unbearable Lightness of Being,* set during the "Prague Spring" uprising); and Karel Čapek (novelist and playwright who created the robot in the play *R.U.R.*).

But the most famous Czech writer of all is the existentialist great, Franz Kafka, a Prague Jew who wrote in German about a person turning into a giant cockroach *(The Metamorphosis)* and an urbanite being pursued and persecuted for crimes he knows nothing about *(The Trial)*.

Some lesser-known Czech writers are also worth discovering. Arnošt Lustig's *Dita Saxová* covers the fate of Czech Jews during the war, while Ota Pavel's *Golden Eels* and Josef Škvorecký's *The Cowards (Zbabělci)* describe the world of a generation coming of age just after the war. Dominika Dery's *The Twelve Little Cakes* is a delightful memoir of her childhood (spent near Prague) at the end of communism in the late 1970s and early 1980s. Surprisingly, the 1990s were not a very exciting time for Czech literature. The one exception, and the definitive book of the 1989 generation, is Jáchym Topol's *Sister.* Topol captures "the years after the Time exploded" in a rich mixture of colloquial Czech that's full of German and

English loanwords and neologisms. The English translation is excellent.

The Nobel Prize–winning poet Jaroslav Seifert experienced during his long life all the diverse movements of the 20th century—Dadaism, Surrealism, communism, anti-communism—and created a medium of his own, in which everyone finds a poem to his or her own liking.

The Czech film tradition has always been strong, and the 1960s were its heyday, giving birth to Jiří Menzel's *Closely Watched Trains* and *Larks on the String*; Ivan Passer's *Intimate Lighting;* and Miloš Forman's *Firemen's Ball* and *Loves of a Blonde*. After his 1968 escape from communist Czechoslovakia, Forman made it big in the US with films such as *One Flew Over the Cuckoo's Nest* and *Amadeus.*

The 1990s saw the arrival of two more excellent Czech filmmakers, Jan Svěrák (*The Elementary School* and the Oscar-winning *Kolya*) and Jiří Hřebejk (*Divided We Fall*, nominated for an Oscar).

One of the most inspiring Czech artists is a painter, animator, director, and surrealist—Jan Švankmajer. His *Something from Alice*, *Lesson Faust*, and *Food* combine all of the author's artistic skills into a highly original style that is guaranteed to change the way you look at the world. His two most recent films—*Little Otík* and *Mad*—blend in more realism.

The Czechs have a wonderful animation tradition that successfully competes with Walt Disney in Eastern Europe and China. *Pat a Mat*, *Krteček (The Little Mole)*, or *Maxipes Fík* are intelligent gifts to bring to your little ones at home.

MONEY MATTERS

Damage Control for Lost Cards

If you lose your credit, debit, or ATM card, you can stop people from using it by reporting the loss immediately to the respective global customer-assistance centers. Call these 24-hour US numbers collect: Visa (410/581-9994), MasterCard (636/722-7111), and American Express (623/492-8427).

At a minimum, you'll need to know the name of the financial institution that issued you the card, along with the type of card (classic, platinum, or whatever). Providing the following information will allow for a quicker cancellation of your missing card: full card number, whether you are the primary or secondary cardholder, the cardholder's name exactly as printed on the card, billing address, home phone number, circumstances of the loss or theft, and identification verification (your birth date, your mother's maiden name, or your Social Security number—memorize this, don't carry a copy). If you are the secondary cardholder, you'll also need to provide the primary cardholder's identification-verification details. You can generally receive a temporary card within two or three business days in Europe.

If you promptly report your card lost or stolen, you typically won't be responsible for any unauthorized transactions on your account, although many banks charge a liability fee of $50.

Tipping

Tipping in the Czech Republic isn't as automatic and generous as it is in the US, but for special service, tips are appreciated, if not expected. As in the US, the proper amount depends on your resources, tipping philosophy, and the circumstance, but some general guidelines apply.

Restaurants: Tipping is an issue only at restaurants that have table service. If you order your food at a counter, don't tip.

At Czech restaurants that have a waitstaff, service is included, although it's common to round up the bill after a good meal (usually 5–10 percent; e.g., for a 370-Kč meal, pay 400 Kč). If you warm up the waiter with a few Czech words, such as please (*prosím;* PROH-zeem) and thank you (*děkuji;* DYACK-khuyi), you'll get better service and won't be expected to tip more than a local. But if you greet your waiter in English, he'll want a 15 percent tip. Believe me: The slightest attempt at speaking Czech (see phrases on page 269) will turn you from a targeted tourist into a special guest, even in the most touristy restaurants.

Taxis: To tip the cabbie, round up about 5 percent. If the cabbie hauls your bags and zips you to the airport to help you catch your flight, you might want to toss in a little more. But if you feel like you're being driven in circles or otherwise ripped off, skip the tip. Again, if you use some Czech words, your cabbie will be less likely to try to scam you.

Special Services: It's thoughtful to tip someone who shows you a special sight and who is paid in no other way. Tour guides at public sights sometimes hold out their hands for tips after they give their spiels; if I've already paid for the tour, I don't tip extra, though some tourists do (about 20–30 Kč), particularly for a job well done. I don't tip at hotels, but if you do, give the porter about 30 Kč for carrying bags and leave about the same amount in your room at the end of your stay for the maid if the room was kept clean. In general, if someone in the service industry does a super job for you, a tip (of up to about 50 Kč) is appropriate...but not required.

When in doubt, ask: If you're not sure whether (or how much) to tip for a service, ask your hotelier or the TI; they'll fill you in on how it's done on their turf.

Getting a VAT Refund

As is the case throughout the European Union, wrapped into the purchase price of your souvenirs is a Value Added Tax (VAT); in the Czech Republic it's set at 19 percent. If you make a purchase of more than 2,000 Kč (about $100) at a store that participates in the VAT-refund scheme, you're entitled to get most of that tax back. Getting your refund is usually straightforward and, if you buy a substantial amount of souvenirs, well worth the hassle.

If you're lucky, the merchant will subtract the tax when you make your purchase. (This is more likely to occur if the store ships the goods to your home.) Otherwise, you'll need to:

Get the paperwork. Have the merchant completely fill out the necessary refund document, called a "cheque" (not to be confused with a "Czech"). You'll have to present your passport at the store.

Get your stamp at the border or airport. Process your cheque(s) at your last stop in the EU (e.g., at the airport) with the customs agent who deals with VAT refunds. It's best to keep your purchases in your carry-on for viewing, but if they're too large or dangerous (such as knives) to carry on, track down the proper customs agent to inspect them before you check your bag. You're not supposed to use your purchased goods before you leave. If you show up at customs wearing your new chic Czech outfit, officials might look the other way—or deny you a refund.

Collect your refund. You'll need to return your stamped document to the retailer or its representative. Many merchants work with a service, such as Global Refund (www.globalrefund.com) or Premier Tax Free (www.premiertaxfree.com), which have offices at major airports, ports, or border crossings. These services, which extract a 4 percent fee, can refund your money immediately in your currency of choice or credit your card (within two billing cycles). If the retailer handles VAT refunds directly, it's up to you to contact the merchant for your refund. You can mail the documents from home, or quicker, from your point of departure (using a stamped, addressed envelope you've prepared or one that's been provided by the merchant)—and then wait. It could take months.

Customs for American Shoppers

You are allowed to take home $800 worth of items per person duty-free, once every 30 days. The next $1,000 is taxed at a flat 3 percent. After that, you pay the individual item's duty rate. You can also bring in duty-free a liter of alcohol (slightly more than a standard-size bottle of wine; you must be at least 21), 200 cigarettes, and up to 100 non-Cuban cigars. Food in cans or sealed jars is permissible as long as no meat is included. Some, but not all, types of cheese are allowed. Fresh fruits and vegetables are prohibited. Note that you'll need to carefully pack any bottles of wine and other liquid-containing items in your checked luggage due to the three-ounce limit on liquids in carry-on baggage. To check customs rules and duty rates before you go, visit www.cbp .gov, and click on "Travel," then "Know Before You Go."

TELEPHONES, EMAIL, AND MAIL

Telephones

Smart travelers learn the phone system and use it daily to reserve or reconfirm rooms, get tourist information, reserve restaurants, confirm tour times, or phone home.

Types of Phones

You'll encounter various kinds of phones on your trip:

Card-operated phones, in which you insert a locally bought phone card into a public pay phone, are common in the Czech Republic.

Coin-operated phones, the original kind of pay phone (but now increasingly rare), require you to have enough change to complete your call.

Hotel room phones are sometimes cheap for local calls (confirm at the front desk first), but can be a rip-off for long-distance calls unless you use an international phone card (described below). But incoming calls are free, making this a cheap way for friends and family to stay in touch, provided they have a good long-distance plan for calls to Europe.

American mobile phones work in Europe if they're GSM-enabled, tri-band, or quad-band, and on a calling plan that includes international calls. They're convenient, but pricey. For example, with a T-Mobile phone, you'll pay $1 per minute for calls.

European mobile phones run about $75 (for the most basic models) and come without contracts. These phones are loaded with prepaid calling time that you can recharge as you use up the minutes. As long as you're not "roaming" outside the phone's home

country, incoming calls are free. If you're traveling to multiple countries within Europe, make sure the phone is electronically "unlocked," so that you can swap out its SIM card (a fingernail-sized chip that holds the phone's information) for a new one in other countries. For more information on mobile phones, see www.ricksteves.com/plan/tips/mobilephones.htm.

Using Phone Cards

Get a phone card for your calls. Prepaid cards come in two types: international phone cards (usable from any phone) and insertable phone cards (usable only in pay phones). Both are described below.

Prepaid **international phone cards** are the cheapest way to make international calls from Europe—calls to the US generally cost 10–40 cents per minute—and they also work for domestic calls.

Currently the only brand widely available in the Czech Republic is **Smartcall** (look for a black-and-orange advertisement), which you can buy at newsstands, exchange bureaus, Internet cafés, hostels, souvenir shops, and mini-marts in tourist towns such as Prague or Český Krumlov (they're not available in less touristy towns like Olomouc). The cards come in denominations of 150 Kč, 300 Kč, 500 Kč, and 1,000 Kč. Because they're occasionally duds, avoid the high denominations. Cards purchased in the Czech Republic will work only within the country, not elsewhere in Europe.

You can use international phone cards from any type of phone, even your hotel-room phone (if the phone is set on "pulse," switch it to "tone"), avoiding pricey hotel rates; make sure, however, that your hotel isn't overcharging you to dial the access number.

To use a card, scratch off the back to reveal your code. After you dial the access phone number, the message tells you to enter your code and then dial the phone number you want to call. A voice may announce how much is left in your account before you dial. Usually you can select English, but if the prompts are in Czech, experiment: Dial your code, followed by the pound sign (#), then the number, then pound again, and so on, until it works.

To call the US, see "Dialing Internationally," below. To make calls within the Czech Republic, dial the area code plus the local number; when using an international phone card, the area code must be dialed even if you're calling across the street.

To make numerous, successive calls with an international phone card without having to redial the long access number each time, press the keys (see instructions on card) that allow you to launch directly into your next call. Remember that you don't need the actual card to use a card account, so it's sharable. You can write down the access number and PIN (Personal Identification Number) in your notebook and share it with friends. Give the number of a still lively card to another traveler when you're leaving the country.

Insertable phone cards are a convenient way to pay for calls from public pay phones and can be purchased at any post office. Simply take the phone off the hook, insert the prepaid card, wait for a dial tone, and dial away. The price of the call (local or international) is automatically deducted while you talk. These are a good deal for calling within Europe, but calling the US can be more expensive (at least 50 cents/min) than using an international phone card. Be aware that with the prevalence of mobile phones, public phones are getting harder to find.

Using Hotel-Room Phones, VoIP, or US Calling Cards

The phone in your **hotel room** is convenient...but expensive. While incoming calls (made by folks back home) can be the cheapest way to keep in touch, charges for *outgoing* calls can be a very unpleasant surprise. Make sure you understand all the charges and fees associated with outgoing calls before you pick up that receiver. I find hotel room phones handy for making local calls.

Dialing direct from your hotel room—without using an international phone card (described above)—is usually quite pricey for international calls. If your family has an inexpensive way to call Europe, either through a long-distance plan or prepaid calling card, have them call you in your hotel room. Give them a list of your hotels' phone numbers before you go. Then, as you travel, send them an email or make a quick pay-phone call to set up a time for them to give you a ring.

If you're traveling with a laptop, consider trying **VoIP (Voice over Internet Protocol).** With VoIP, two computers act as the phones, allowing for a free Internet-based call. The major providers are Skype (www.skype.com) and Google Talk (www.google.com/talk).

US Calling Cards (such as the ones offered by AT&T, MCI, and Sprint) are the worst option. You'll nearly always save a lot of money by paying with a phone card (see above).

How to Dial

Calling from the US to Europe, or vice versa, is simple—once you break the code. The European calling chart on page 282 will walk you through it.

Dialing Domestic Calls

The Czech Republic has a direct-dial phone system (no area codes). To call anywhere within the Czech Republic, just dial the number. For example, one of my recommended Prague hotels is 224-812-041. To call it from a Prague train station, just dial 224-812-041. If you call it from Český Krumlov, it's the same: 224-812-041. All phone numbers in the Czech Republic are nine digits. If a number starting with 0800 doesn't work, replace the 0800 with 822.

Dialing Internationally

If you want to make an international call, follow these three steps:
   1) Dial the international access code (00 if you're calling from

Appendix

European Calling Chart

Just smile and dial, using this key:
AC = Area Code, LN = Local Number.

European Country	Calling long distance within ...	Calling from the US or Canada to ...	Calling from a European country to ...
Austria	AC + LN	011 + 43 + AC (without the initial zero) + LN	00 + 43 + AC (without the initial zero) + LN
Belgium	LN	011 + 32 + LN (without initial zero)	00 + 32 + LN (without initial zero)
Bosnia-Herzegovina	AC + LN	011 + 387 + AC (without initial zero) + LN	00 + 387 + AC (without initial zero) + LN
Britain	AC + LN	011 + 44 + AC (without initial zero) + LN	00 + 44 + AC (without initial zero) + LN
Croatia	AC + LN	011 + 385 + AC (without initial zero) + LN	00 + 385 + AC (without initial zero) + LN
Czech Republic	LN	011 + 420 + LN	00 + 420 + LN
Denmark	LN	011 + 45 + LN	00 + 45 + LN
Estonia	LN	011 + 372 + LN	00 + 372 + LN
Finland	AC + LN	011 + 358 + AC (without initial zero) + LN	999 + 358 + AC (without initial zero) + LN
France	LN	011 + 33 + LN (without initial zero)	00 + 33 + LN (without initial zero)
Germany	AC + LN	011 + 49 + AC (without initial zero) + LN	00 + 49 + AC (without initial zero) + LN
Greece	LN	011 + 30 + LN	00 + 30 + LN
Hungary	06 + AC + LN	011 + 36 + AC + LN	00 + 36 + AC + LN
Ireland	AC + LN	011 + 353 + AC (without initial zero) + LN	00 + 353 + AC (without initial zero) + LN

Appendix

European Country	Calling long distance within ...	Calling from the US or Canada to ...	Calling from a European country to ...
Italy	LN	011 + 39 + LN	00 + 39 + LN
Montenegro	AC + LN	011 + 382 + AC (without initial zero) + LN	00 + 382 + AC (without initial zero) + LN
Netherlands	AC + LN	011 + 31 + AC (without initial zero) + LN	00 + 31 + AC (without initial zero) + LN
Norway	LN	011 + 47 + LN	00 + 47 + LN
Poland	LN	011 + 48 + LN (without initial zero)	00 + 48 + LN (without initial zero)
Portugal	LN	011 + 351 + LN	00 + 351 + LN
Slovakia	AC + LN	011 + 421 + AC (without initial zero) + LN	00 + 421 + AC (without initial zero) + LN
Slovenia	AC + LN	011 + 386 + AC (without initial zero) + LN	00 + 386 + AC (without initial zero) + LN
Spain	LN	011 + 34 + LN	00 + 34 + LN
Sweden	AC + LN	011 + 46 + AC (without initial zero) + LN	00 + 46 + AC (without initial zero) + LN
Switzerland	LN	011 + 41 + LN (without initial zero)	00 + 41 + LN (without initial zero)
Turkey	AC (if no initial zero is included, add one) + LN	011 + 90 + AC (without initial zero) + LN	00 + 90 + AC (without initial zero) + LN

- The instructions above apply whether you're calling a land line or mobile phone.
- The international access codes (the first numbers you dial when making an international call) are 011 if you're calling from the US or Canada, or 00 if you're calling from virtually anywhere in Europe (except Finland, where it's 999).
- To call the US or Canada from Europe, dial 00, then 1 (the country code for the US and Canada), then the area code and number. In short, 00 + 1 + AC + LN = Hi, Mom!

Europe, 011 from the US or Canada).

2) Dial the country code of the country you're calling (420 for the Czech Republic).

3) Dial the local number. For example, to call the recommended Prague hotel from the US, dial 011 (the US international access code), 420 (the Czech Republic's country code), and 224-812-041.

To call my office in Edmonds, Washington, from the Czech Republic, I dial 00 (Europe's international access code), 1 (the US country code), 425 (Edmonds' area code), and 771-8303.

Useful Phone Numbers

Emergencies: Dial 112 for medical or other emergencies.
Police: Dial 158.
Directory Assistance: Dial 1188.
US Embassy: Call 257-022-000. It's in Prague's Little Quarter below the castle (passport services Mon–Fri 9:00–11:30, Tržiště 15, www.usembassy.cz, ACSPrg@state.gov).

Email and Mail

Email: Many travelers set up a free email account with Yahoo, Microsoft (Hotmail), or Google (Gmail). Internet cafés are easy to find in big cities. Most of the towns where I've listed accommodations in this book also have Internet cafés. Many libraries offer free access, but they also tend to have limited opening hours, restrict your online time to 30 minutes, and may require reservations. Look for the places listed in this book, or ask the local TI, computer store, or your hotelier. Some hotels have a dedicated computer for guests' email needs. Small places are accustomed to letting clients (who've asked politely) sit at their desk for a few minutes just to check their email.

Wireless Internet access (Wi-Fi) is available to laptop users for a minimal fee at Internet cafés, some post offices, and an increasing number of hotels.

Mail: Get stamps at the neighborhood post office, newsstands within fancy hotels, and some mini-marts and card shops. To arrange for mail delivery, reserve a few hotels along your route in advance and give their addresses to friends. Allow 10 days for a letter to arrive. Phoning and emailing are so easy that I've dispensed with mail stops altogether.

TRANSPORTATION

By Car or Train?

Within Prague, a car is a worthless headache. If you're staying mostly in Prague and tackling a few convenient side-trips (such

as Kutná Hora and Český Krumlov), public transportation works
well. If you'll be venturing farther into the countryside, trains and
buses will get you where you need to go—but renting a car gives
you greater flexibility. For connecting Prague to international destinations (like Budapest or Kraków), stick with the train.

Trains

Trains are fairly punctual (running about 10 min late) and cover
cities well, but frustrating schedules make a few out-of-the-way
destinations I recommend not worth the time and trouble for the
less determined (try buses instead; see upcoming section).

Schedules: For Czech train and bus timetables, visit www
.vlak-bus.cz or Germany's excellent all-Europe timetable for
trains: http://bahn.hafas.de/bin/query.exe/en. Consider buying
the *Traťové Jízdní Řády*, a comprehensive, easy-to-use schedule
of all trains in the country (includes English instructions, sold at
major station ticket windows for 30 Kč). Although it's easy to look
up a connection on the Internet, having the schedule and a map of
railway lines with you gives you freedom to easily change or make
new plans as you travel.

Tickets and Tips: Tickets within the Czech Republic are
valid for two days, and international tickets are good from three
days to two months (the shorter-term ones are often cheaper). Your
ticket is valid for travel along the entire stretch from Prague to
your destination, not just for one trip on a specific train—so take
advantage of the freedom it gives you and hop on and hop off along
the way. You'll rarely need a reservation, except for international
night trains.

If you have one or more companions traveling with you by
train, ask for a group ticket. This gets you a 50 percent discount for
every extra ticket (i.e., only the first person pays full price).

If you're heading to a city near the Czech border (such as
Vienna, Bratislava, Dresden, or Nürnberg), it sometimes pays to
buy two separate tickets: one to the Czech border, and another
from the border to your destination. This also allows you to take
advantage of particular discounts in that country, such as the group
discount.

Railpasses: The Czech Republic has its own railpass, but since
point-to-point tickets are so inexpensive, it's rarely worthwhile.
Find my free Railpass Guide online at www.ricksteves.com/rail.
The Czech Republic is not a Eurail country, so Eurailpasses and
Eurail Selectpasses are not valid here (but you can buy point-to-
point tickets to fill in the Czech gaps in your coverage).

Buses

To reach many of the destinations in this book, buses are faster and cheaper than trains. Buses are also generally more punctual. No reservations are needed for buses—simply buy tickets directly from the driver (who appreciates exact change and might have difficulty breaking big bills). You'll be required to put big bags in the luggage compartment under the bus (12–24 Kč extra, depending on the distance), so have a small day bag ready to take on the bus with you. Buses don't have bathrooms, nor do they stop for bathroom breaks.

Always let the bus driver know where you want to get off. Some stops are by request only (for example, the Small Fortress at Terezín Concentration Camp), and most bus drivers are happy to let you know when your stop is coming up.

Car Rental and Leasing

To rent a car in the Czech Republic, you must be at least 21 years old with a valid license. Drivers 24 and younger may incur a young-driver surcharge and some companies may not rent to those

CZECH PUBLIC TRANSPORTATION

POLAND

To Wrocław

To Wrocław

To Katowice & Kraków

Hradec Králové

Lichkov

Pardubice

Kutná Hora

Opava

Ostrava

Bohumín

Petrovice

Zábřeh

Český Těšín

Hranice

Olomouc

Frenštát

Rožnov pod Radhoštěm

Havlíčkův Brod

REPUBLIC

Přerov

To Žilina

Jihlava

Kroměříž

Třebíč

Brno

Telč

Moravský Krumlov

Slavonice

Mikulov

Břeclav

SLOVAKIA

To Vienna

To Bratislava

AUSTRIA

Rail
Bus

over age 70. If you're considered too young or old, look into leasing, which has less-stringent age restrictions (see "Leasing," below).

Research car rentals before you go. Especially during the summer, the best deals at Czech car-rental companies need to be arranged 2–3 weeks ahead. Renting from a local Czech company (see page 39) is as convenient as using Budget or Avis; most will bring the car to your hotel. There are about a hundred car-rental companies in Prague. Alimex is a good bet (see page 39). Or do a Google search from home, take your pick, and reserve by email.

Czechs are once again proud of their locally built Škoda cars (since the 1920s, the Ford of Eastern Europe). Now owned by Volkswagen, Škoda is the biggest post-communist success story in the country. By renting one, you'll learn why most Eastern Europeans stay loyal to the brand, even as cheap Japanese cars inundate the market. (In an ironic twist, the word "Škoda"—which is the family name of an early owner of the company—also means "damage" in Czech.)

When renting, I usually get a Škoda Fabia; for more luggage space and more oomph, step up to the Škoda Octavia. On average,

you should be able to get a Škoda with full insurance and unlimited mileage for $40–50 per day. Škodas usually have manual transmission and come with alarms; you might want to supplement the alarm with a lock for the steering wheel or stick shift.

If you want an automatic, reserve the car at least a month in advance and specifically request an automatic. You'll pay about 40 percent more to rent a car with an automatic instead of a manual transmission.

When you pick up the car, check it thoroughly and make sure any damage is noted on your rental agreement. Find out how your car's lights, turn signals, wipers, and gas cap function.

If you drop your car off early or keep it longer, you'll be credited or charged at a fair, prorated price. But always keep your receipts in case any questions arise about your billing.

Returning a car at a big-city train station can be tricky; get precise details on the car drop-off location and hours. When you return the car, make sure the agent verifies its condition with you.

Car Insurance Options

When you rent a car, you are liable for a very high deductible, sometimes equal to the entire value of the car. There are various ways you can limit your financial risk in case of an accident. You

To Wrocław & Kraków

DRIVING IN THE CZECH REPUBLIC: DISTANCE AND TIME

POLAND

CZECH REPUBLIC

To Kraków

Kutná Hora

Olomouc 50m · 1.5h

Rožnov pod Radhoštěm

130m · 2.25h

105m · 2.5h

225m · 5.5h

95m · 2h

50m · 1h

30m · 1h

Kroměříž

40m · 1h Telč Třebíč Brno

15m · .5h 20m 40m 25m 30m
35m · 1h .5h 1h .75h .75h

80m · 1.25h

SLOVAKIA

35m 30m Moravský
1h 1h Krumlov Mikulov

Slavonice 25m · .75h

45m · 1h

125m · 3h

Bratislava

Vienna

have three options: buy Collision Damage Waiver (CDW) coverage from the car-rental company, get coverage through your credit card (free, if your card automatically includes zero-deductible coverage), or buy coverage through Travel Guard.

CDW includes a very high deductible (typically $1,000–1,500). When you pick up the car, you'll be offered the chance to "buy down" the deductible to zero (for $10–30/day; this is often called "super CDW").

If you opt instead for credit-card coverage, there's a catch. You'll technically have to decline all coverage offered by the car-rental company, which means they can place a hold on your card for the full deductible amount. In case of damage, it can be time-consuming to resolve the charges with your credit-card company. Before you decide on this option, quiz your credit-card company about how it works and ask them to explain the worst-case scenario.

Buying CDW insurance (plus "super CDW") is the easier but pricier option. Using the coverage that comes with your credit card saves money, but can involve more hassle.

Finally, you can buy CDW insurance from Travel Guard ($9/day plus a one-time $3 service fee covers you up to $35,000, $250 deductible, tel. 800-826-4919, www.travelguard.com). It's valid throughout Europe, but some car-rental companies refuse to honor it (especially in the Republic of Ireland and in Italy). Oddly, residents of Washington State aren't allowed to buy this coverage.

For more fine print about car-rental insurance, see www.ricksteves.com/cdw.

Leasing

For trips of two and a half weeks or more, leasing (which automatically includes CDW-type insurance with no deductible) is the best way to go. By technically buying and then selling back the car, you save lots of money on tax and insurance. Leasing provides you a new car with unlimited mileage and a 24-hour emergency assistance program. You can lease for as little as 17 days to as long as six months. Car leases must be arranged from the US. A reliable company offering 17-day lease packages for about $850 is Europe by Car (US tel. 800-223-1516, www.europebycar.com).

Driving

To drive in the Czech Republic, you must have an International Driving Permit (get through your local AAA office before you go; $15 plus two passport photos; www.aaa.com). Also be sure to bring along your valid US driver's license.

During the communist era, Eastern Europe's infrastructure lagged far behind the West's. Now that the Iron Curtain is long gone, superhighways are popping up like crazy all over the Czech Republic. You'll sometimes discover that a much faster freeway option has been built between major destinations since your three-year-old map was published (a good reason to travel with the most up-to-date maps available). As soon as a long-enough section is completed, the roads are opened to the public. Only rarely are backcountry roads the only option (as with part of the trip between Prague and Český Krumlov). These can be bumpy and slow, but they're almost always paved (or, at least, they once were).

Learn the universal road signs. Seat belts are required, and two beers under those belts are enough to land you in jail. Children under age 12 must ride in the back, and children under 80 pounds must have a child safety seat. You're required to have your headlights on anytime the engine is running, even in broad daylight. (The lights of many newer cars automatically turn on and off with the engine—ask when you pick up your car.)

Gas: At about $1.50 per liter ($6 per gallon) for unleaded ("Natural 95"), gas in the Czech Republic is still considerably cheaper than in Western Europe.

Tolls: If you're driving on highways in the Czech Republic, you're required to buy a toll sticker *(dálniční známka)* at the border, a post office, or a gas station (200 Kč/15 days, 300 Kč/2 months). Your rental car may come with the necessary sticker—ask.

Parking: You'll pay about $10–15 a day to park safely in Prague. Formerly notorious for its Russian car-theft gangs, Prague is safer now—but it's still wise to be careful. Ask at your hotel for advice. In small towns such as Třeboň or Slavonice it's better to stay on the safe side when parking overnight. Again, ask at your hotel for advice. I keep a pile of coins in my ashtray for parking meters, public phones, launderettes, and wishing wells.

Cheap Flights

While trains are usually the best way to connect places that are close together, a flight can save both time and money on longer journeys.

One of the best websites for comparing inexpensive flights is www.skyscanner.net. Other comparison search engines include www.kayak.com, www.mobissimo.com, www.sidestep.com, and www.wegolo.com.

Well-known cheapo airlines in Europe include easyJet (www .easyjet.com) and RyanAir (www.ryanair.com). Smart Wings (www.smartwings.com) is based in the Czech Republic.

Be aware of the potential drawbacks of flying on the cheap: nonrefundable and nonchangeable tickets, rigid baggage restrictions (and fees if you have more than what's officially allowed), use of airports far outside town, tight schedules that can mean more delays, little in the way of customer assistance if problems arise, and, of course, no frills. To avoid unpleasant surprises, read the small print—especially baggage policies—before you book.

HOLIDAYS AND FESTIVALS

This is a partial list of holidays and festivals. For more information, contact the Czech national tourist information office in the US (tel. 212/288-0830, www.czechtourism.com, info-usa @czechtourism.com).

Jan 1	New Year's Day
Jan 21	Anniversary of Jan Palach's Death (flowers in Wenceslas Square)
Mid-March	One World International Human Rights Film Festival, Prague (www.oneworld.cz)
Easter Sunday and Monday	March 23–24 in 2008, April 12–13 in 2009
April 30	Witches' Night (similar to Halloween, with bonfires)
May 1	Labor Day and Day of Love
May 8	Liberation Day
May (last 3 weeks)	"Prague Spring" Music Festival, Prague (May 12–June 3 in 2008, www.festival.cz)
Mid-May	Prague International Marathon (May 11 in 2008, www.pim.cz)
Early June	Festival of Song, Olomouc (June 4–8 in 2008)
Mid-June	Celebration of the Rose, Český Krumlov (June 20–22 in 2008, medieval festival, music, theater, dance, knights' tournament)
July 5	Sts. Cyril and Methodius Day
July 6	Jan Hus Day
Mid-July–Mid-Aug	International Music Festival, Český Krumlov (July 18–Aug 23 in 2008, www.czechmusicfestival.com)
July–Aug	Summer of Culture, Olomouc (www.okl.info)
July–Aug	Prague Proms (music festival, www.pragueproms.cz)
Early Aug	Šamajim festival, Třebíč (Jewish music and film)
Aug (first 2 weeks)	Telč Vacations Festival (folk music, open-air theater, exhibitions), Telč
Mid-Aug	Jazz at Summer's End Festival, Český Krumlov

Appendix

Sept (last half)	Prague Autumn Music Festival (Sept 12–Oct 1 in 2008, www.pragueautumn.cz)
Sept 28	St. Wenceslas Day (celebrates national patron saint and Czech statehood)
Oct	International Jazz Festival, Prague
Oct 28	Independence Day
Nov 17	Velvet Revolution Anniversary
Throughout Dec	Christmas markets, Prague
Dec 5	St. Nicholas Eve, Prague (St. Nicholas, devils, and angels walk the streets in search of nice—and naughty—children)
Dec 24–25	Christmas Eve and Christmas Day
Dec 26	Feast of St. Stephen
Dec 31	St. Sylvester's Day, Prague (fireworks)

CONVERSIONS AND CLIMATE

Numbers and Stumblers

- Europeans write a few of their numbers differently than we do. 1 = 1, 4 = 4, 7 = 7.
- In Europe, dates appear as day/month/year, so Christmas is 25/12/08.
- Commas are decimal points and decimals commas. A dollar and a half is 1,50, and there are 5.280 feet in a mile.
- When counting with fingers, start with your thumb. If you hold up your first finger to request one item, you'll probably get two.
- What Americans call the second floor of a building is the first floor in Europe.
- On escalators and moving sidewalks, Europeans keep the left "lane" open for passing. Keep to the right.

Metric Conversions (approximate)

1 foot = 0.3 meter
1 yard = 0.9 meter
1 mile = 1.6 kilometers
1 centimeter = 0.4 inch
1 meter = 39.4 inches
1 kilometer = 0.62 mile

1 square yard = 0.8 square meter
1 square mile = 2.6 square kilometers
1 ounce = 28 grams
1 quart = 0.95 liter
1 kilogram = 2.2 pounds
32°F = 0°C

Climate

The first line is the average daily high; the second line, the average daily low. The third line shows the average number of days without rain. For more detailed weather statistics for destinations throughout the Czech Republic (as well as the rest of the world), check www.worldclimate.com.

J	F	M	A	M	J	J	A	S	O	N	D
31°	34°	44°	54°	64°	70°	73°	72°	65°	53°	42°	34°
23°	24°	30°	38°	46°	52°	55°	55°	49°	41°	33°	27°
13	11	10	11	13	12	13	12	10	13	12	13

Temperature Conversion: Fahrenheit and Celsius

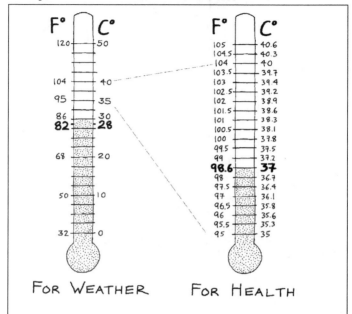

Europe takes its temperature using the Celsius scale, while we opt for Fahrenheit. For a rough conversion from Celsius to Fahrenheit, double the number and add 30. For weather, remember that 28°C is 82°F— perfect. For health, 37°C is just right.

Essential Packing Checklist

Whether you're traveling for five days or five weeks, here's what you'll need to bring. Remember to pack light to enjoy the sweet freedom of true mobility. Happy travels!

- ❑ 5 shirts
- ❑ 1 sweater or lightweight fleece jacket
- ❑ 2 pairs pants
- ❑ 1 pair shorts
- ❑ 1 swimsuit (women only—men can use shorts)
- ❑ 5 pairs underwear and socks
- ❑ 1 pair shoes
- ❑ 1 rainproof jacket
- ❑ Tie or scarf
- ❑ Money belt
- ❑ Money—your mix of:
  - ❑ Debit card for ATM withdrawals
  - ❑ Credit card
  - ❑ Hard cash in US dollars
- ❑ Documents (and backup photocopies)
- ❑ Passport
- ❑ Airplane ticket
- ❑ Driver's license
- ❑ Student ID and hostel card
- ❑ Railpass/car-rental voucher
- ❑ Insurance details
- ❑ Daypack
- ❑ Sealable plastic baggies
- ❑ Camera and related gear
- ❑ Empty water bottle
- ❑ Wristwatch and alarm clock
- ❑ Earplugs
- ❑ First-aid kit
- ❑ Medicine (labeled)
- ❑ Extra glasses/contacts and prescriptions
- ❑ Sunscreen and sunglasses
- ❑ Toiletries kit
- ❑ Soap
- ❑ Laundry soap (if liquid and carry-on, limit to 3 oz.)
- ❑ Clothesline
- ❑ Small towel
- ❑ Sewing kit
- ❑ Travel information
- ❑ Necessary map(s)
- ❑ Address list (email and mailing addresses)
- ❑ Postcards and photos from home
- ❑ Notepad and pen
- ❑ Journal

Appendix

Hotel Reservation

To: _____   _____
                hotel   *email or fax*

From:_____   _____
                name   *email or fax*

Today's date: _____ /_____ /_____
                    day   *month*   *year*

Dear Hotel _____ , ·

Please make this reservation for me:

Name: _____

Total # of people: _____   # of rooms: _____   # of nights: _____

Arriving: _____ /_____/_____   My time of arrival (24-hr clock): _____
              day   month   year   (I will telephone if I will be late)

Departing: ____ /____ /____
              day   month   year

Room(s): Single____   Double ____   Twin ____   Triple ____   Quad____

With: Toilet _____   Shower _____   Bath _____   Sink only ____

Special needs: View____ Quiet____ Cheapest ____ Ground Floor____

Please email or fax confirmation of my reservation, along with the type of room reserved and the price. Please also inform me of your cancellation policy. After I hear from you, I will quickly send my credit-card information as a deposit to hold the room. Thank you.

_____
Name

_____
Address

_____
City   *State*   *Zip Code*   *Country*

Appendix

Before hoteliers can make your reservation, they want to know the information listed above. You can use this form as the basis for your email, or you can photocopy this page, fill in the information, and send it as a fax (also available online at www.ricksteves.com/reservation).

INDEX

Travel smart...carry on!

The latest generation of Rick Steves' carry-on travel bags is easily the best—benefiting from two decades of on-the-road attention to what really matters: maximum quality and strength; practical, flexible features; and no unnecessary frills. You won't find a better value anywhere!

Rick Steves' Convertible Carry-On $99.⁹⁵

Our roomy, versatile 9" x 21" x 14" carry-on has a large 2600 cubic-inch main compartment, plus four outside pockets (small, medium and huge) that are perfect for often-used items. Wish you had even more room to bring home souvenirs? Pull open the full-perimeter expando-zipper and its capacity jumps from 2600 to 3000 cubic inches. When you want to use it as a suitcase or check it as luggage (required when "expanded"), the straps and belt hide away in a zippered compartment in the back. It weighs just 3 lbs.

Rick Steves' Classic Back Door Bag $79.⁹⁵

This ultra-light (1½ lbs.) version of our Convertible Carry-On features the same 9" x 21" x 14" dimensions and hideaway straps, but does not include a waistbelt or expandability. This is the bag that Rick lives out of for three months a year!

Rick Steves' 21" Roll-Aboard $139.⁹⁵

Our sturdy 21" Roll-Aboard is rucksack-soft in front, but the rest is lined with a hard ABS-lexan shell to give maximum protection to your belongings. We've spared no expense on moving parts, splurging on an extra-long button-release handle and big, tough inline skate wheels for easy rolling on rough surfaces. It features the same 9" x 21" x 14" carry-on dimensions, pocket configuration and expandability as our Convertible Carry-On—and at 7 lbs. it's the lightest roll-aboard in its class.

Prices and features are subject to change.

Start your trip at
www.ricksteves.com

Rick Steves' website is packed with over 3,000 pages of timely travel information. It's also your gateway to getting FREE monthly travel news from Rick—and more!

Free Monthly Travel News

Fresh articles on Europe's most interesting destinations and happenings. Rick will even send you an email every month (often direct from Europe) with his latest discoveries!

Timely Travel Tips

Rick Steves' best money-and-stress-saving tips on trip planning, packing, transportation, hotels, health, safety, finances, hurdling the language barrier...and more.

Travelers' Graffiti Wall

Candid advice and opinions from thousands of travelers on everything listed above, plus whatever topics are hot at the moment (discount flights, politics, nude beaches, scams...you name it).

Rick's Guide to Eurail Passes

The clearest, most comprehensive guide to the confusing array of railpass options out there, and how to choo-choose the railpass that best fits your itinerary and budget.

Great Gear at Our Travel Store

In the past year alone, more than 50,000 travelers have enjoyed great online deals on Rick's guidebooks, maps, DVDs—and his custom-designed carry-on bags, day packs, and light-packing accessories.

Rick Steves Tours

This year, 12,000 lucky travelers will explore Europe on a Rick Steves tour. Learn about our 28 different one- to three-week itineraries, read uncensored feedback from our tour alums, and get our free Tour Experience DVD.

Rick on TV, Radio and Podcasts

Read the scripts from the popular Rick Steves' Europe TV series, and listen to or download your choice of over 100 hours of our Travel with Rick Steves radio show.

Respect for Your Privacy

Whether you buy something from us or subscribe to Rick's monthly Travel News emails, we'll never share your name or email address with anyone else. You won't be spammed!

Have fun raising your Travel I.Q. at
www.ricksteves.com

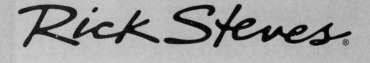

More *Savvy*. More *Surprising*. More *Fun*.

COUNTRY GUIDES

Croatia & Slovenia
England
France
Germany & Austria
Great Britain
Ireland
Italy
Portugal
Scandinavia
Spain
Switzerland

CITY GUIDES

Amsterdam, Bruges & Brussels
Florence & Tuscany
Istanbul
London
Paris
Prague & The Czech Republic
Provence & The French Riviera
Rome
Venice

BEST OF GUIDES

Eastern Europe
Best of Europe

As the #1 authority on European travel, Rick gives you inside information on what to visit, where to stay, and how to get there—economically and hassle-free.

www.ricksteves.com

PHRASE BOOKS & DICTIONARIES

French
French, Italian & German
German
Italian
Portuguese
Spanish

MORE EUROPE FROM RICK STEVES

Europe 101
Europe Through the Back Door
Postcards from Europe

RICK STEVES' EUROPE DVDs

All 70 Shows 2000–2007
Britain
Eastern Europe
France & Benelux
Germany, The Swiss Alps & Travel Skills
Ireland
Italy
Spain & Portugal

PLANNING MAPS

Britain & Ireland
Europe
France
Germany, Austria & Switzerland
Italy
Spain & Portugal

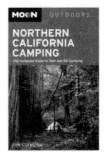
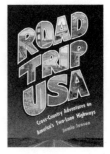

Rick Steves' Guidebook Series

Country Guides

Rick Steves' Best of Europe
Rick Steves' Croatia & Slovenia
Rick Steves' Eastern Europe
Rick Steves' England
Rick Steves' France
Rick Steves' Germany & Austria
Rick Steves' Great Britain
Rick Steves' Ireland
Rick Steves' Italy
Rick Steves' Portugal
Rick Steves' Scandinavia
Rick Steves' Spain
Rick Steves' Switzerland

City and Regional Guides

Rick Steves' Amsterdam, Bruges & Brussels
Rick Steves' Florence & Tuscany
Rick Steves' Istanbul
Rick Steves' London
Rick Steves' Paris
Rick Steves' Prague & the Czech Republic
Rick Steves' Provence & the French Riviera
Rick Steves' Rome
Rick Steves' Venice

Rick Steves' Phrase Books

French
German
Italian
Spanish
Portuguese
French/Italian/German

Other Books

Rick Steves' Europe Through the Back Door
Rick Steves' Europe 101: History and Art for the Traveler
Rick Steves' Postcards from Europe
Rick Steves' European Christmas

(Avalon Travel Publishing)

Honza Vihan would like to offer special thanks to Victor Chen, Cimrmanologist par excellence.

Avalon Travel
a member of the Perseus Books Group
1700 Fourth Street
Berkeley, CA 94710, USA

Printed in the United States of America by Worzalla. First printing February 2008.

Portions of this book were originally published in *Rick Steves' Best of Eastern Europe* © 2004, by Rick Steves and Cameron Hewitt; and in *Rick Steves' Germany, Austria & Switzerland* © 2003, 2002, 2001, 2000, 1999, by Rick Steves.

For the latest on Rick Steves' lectures, guidebooks, tours, public radio show, and public television series, contact Europe Through the Back Door, P.O. Box 2009, Edmonds, WA 98020, tel. 425/771-8303, fax 425/771-0833, www.ricksteves.com, rick@ricksteves.com.

ISBN (10): 1-56691-864-2
ISBN (13): 978-1-56691-864-0
ISSN: 1554-3870

Europe Through the Back Door Managing Editor: Risa Laib
ETBD Editors: Jennifer Hauseman (Senior Editor), Jennifer Madison Davis
Avalon Travel Senior Editor & Series Manager: Madhu Prasher
Avalon Travel Project Editor: Kelly Lydick
Copy Editor: Ellie Behrstock
Proofreader: Patrick Collins
Indexer: Carl Wikander
Production & Typesetting: McGuire Barber Design
Cover Design: Kari Gim, Laura Mazer
Cover Art Manager: Laura VanDeventer
Maps & Graphics: David C. Hoerlein, Laura VanDeventer, Lauren Mills, Barb Geisler, Mike Morgenfeld, Chris Markiewicz, Brice Ticen, Kat Bennett
Photography: Cameron Hewitt, Rick Steves, Honza Vihan, Mike Potter
Cover Photos: Front image, Old Town Square, Prague © Cameron Hewitt; back image, Český Krumlov © Cameron Hewitt
Front Matter Color Photo: Charles Bridge, Prague © Cameron Hewitt
Distributed to the book trade by Publishers Group West, Berkeley, California